The Genus
ECHINOCEREUS

A KEW MAGAZINE MONOGRAPH

The Genus
ECHINOCEREUS

Nigel P Taylor B.Sc.(Hons. Bot.)

Illustrated by

Christabel King B.Sc.(Hons. Bot.)

Series Editor

Christopher Grey-Wilson B.Sc.(Hort.), Ph.D.

The Royal Botanic Gardens, Kew
in association with

TIMBER PRESS

ACKNOWLEDGEMENTS

By far the greatest contribution to the present study has been that of Mr David Parker, without whose help the past two years' work would have been much harder and the results less complete. His comprehensive, documented collection of *Echinocereus* at Birmingham has been the source of much material for study and illustration, including valuable liquid-preserved flowers, seeds and many excellent photographs. In addition, much useful information has been obtained through correspondence he has initiated with other enthusiasts, of whom Mr A. J. Ward (Scarborough) deserves special thanks for preserving flowers and supplying photographs of less common species, such as *E. nivosus* and *E. delaetii*. The following have also assisted by way of advice, plant material, photographs or copies of original publications: Mr G. E. Cheetham, Mr D. Minnion, Mr T. Hewitt (Holly Gate Nurseries, Sussex), Mr R. Simpson, Mr A. Forno, Dr D. R. Hunt (Kew), Mr R. Mottram, Mr G. Rowley, Mr B. Lamb, Dr H. Heine (Paris), Mr S. Brack (USA), Herr Dr B. E. Leuenberger (Berlin), Herr Dr W. Glaetzle (Reutte, Austria), Herr J. D. Supthut (Zurich) and Herr Prof. Dr W. Barthlott (Bonn). Mr H. K. Airy Shaw kindly supplied the Latin diagnoses validating four new taxa, while Joan Curtis of the R.B.G. Kew Typing Pool carefully deciphered the author's untidy manuscript. However, even with so much help from those named above, this book would be quite incomplete without Christabel King's fine botanical paintings, which seem to be unrivalled in the extant literature. Last, but not least, I must thank Ruth for tolerating so much 'cactus talk'! N.P.T.

Title page figure.
Echinocereus viridiflorus var. *davisii,* × 1½.

First published in 1985 in the United Kingdom by
Collingridge Books

First published in the USA in 1985 by:

TIMBER PRESS
9999 S.W.Wilshire,
Portland, Oregon 97225

ISBN 0-88192-052-5

Printed in Great Britain

CONTENTS

LIST OF COLOUR PLATES

INTRODUCTION

The name *Echinocereus* represents a rather distinct group of low-growing, mostly large-flowered cacti from the warmer parts of North America, long prized by that unusual breed of horticulturist, the cactophile. With 44 species the genus is one of medium size within the Cactus Family (Cactaceae), being considerably smaller than *Mammillaria*, its North American competitor for horticultural popularity, but much more diverse, both in stem and flower form. This diversity is reflected in the wide variety of native habitats in which members of the genus can be found. These range from the classic hot, low altitude desert or semi-desert types, whether open and rocky or covered in thorny trees and shrubs, to elevated montane forest and high grassy meadows. Some of the plants from the latter type of environment have become highly specialized, their weakly-spined, inconspicuous stems having retracted into the ground in the manner of many bulbous plants, leaving only the apex visible, and then only during the growing season.

Most people who grow cacti as a hobby have one or more species of *Echinocereus* in their collection–often one of the many forms of the attractive and easily flowered *E. reichenbachii* or the easily grown and very hardy *E. viridiflorus*. But the genus is also an ideal one in which to specialize, having enough species to make building up a comprehensive collection a challenge, and sufficient variety *en masse* to prevent it from seeming too uniform. There is also a range in terms of difficulty of cultivation and availability, but most of all, there is the interest in unravelling the correct identity of each plant from among the plethora of synonyms and misidentifications which characterize so many cactus species in cultivation. Hopefully, the account presented here will make a sometimes almost impossible task a little easier, and perhaps stimulate further interest in the genus at the same time.

Nigel P. Taylor

HISTORY OF THE GENUS

The First Species Discovered

Credit for the discovery and introduction to cultivation of the first-described species of *Echinocereus* goes to two Europeans, the Irishman Thomas Coulter and the Hungarian Baron von Karwinsky, both of whom were primarily interested in the Mexican mining industry. They discovered plants of the genus around 1827-28, almost certainly in the state of Hidalgo, and sent them back to Europe, where De Candolle studied Coulter's collections and Martius those of Karwinsky. In 1828 De Candolle published *Cereus cinerascens* and *C. pentalophus*, which were followed in 1832, by the unusual *Echinocactus pulchellus* of Martius. Next to be discovered was *Echinocereus berlandieri*, from S Texas in 1834, but this did not receive a botanical name until 1856, when Engelmann called it *Cereus berlandieri*. Two more species were collected and named before 1848, the year Engelmann recognized the genus as we know it today. The first of these was discovered at the close of 1837 by the French collector Galeotti, in the Mexican state of San Luis Potosi, and was sent to Belgium and described as *Echinocactus pectinatus* by Scheidweiler the following year. Some time before 1843 a similar-looking plant was introduced to living collections in Germany from Mexico and named *Echinocactus reichenbachii* by Walpers (1843). Here began one of the first serious confusions in the genus, *E. reichenbachii* being mistaken for *E. pectinatus*, which had died out soon after its introduction to cultivation a few years earlier.

Then, in 1848, the species of *Echinocereus* saw a sudden increase, when Dr George Engelmann described various plants collected by his friend Dr Wislizenus on an expedition through the SW United States and northern Mexico during 1846-47. In the Botanical Appendix to the report of the expedition Engelmann decided to erect the genus *Echinocereus* for a number of low growing cerei with short-tubed diurnal flowers and tuberculate seeds (Engelmann, 1848). Of the species he included, seven are still recognized today, and five of these he described for the first time: *E. viridiflorus*, *E. triglochidiatus*, *E. polyacanthus*, *E. adustus* and *E. enneacanthus*. Subsequent exploration in this same region yielded additional species, so that by the end of 1856 Engelmann and others, such as Salm-Dyck and Scheer, had named nine more (*E. rigidissimus*, which is counted here, was recognized only as a variety), giving the genus a total of twenty species.

Since 1856, a further 24 distinct species have been described, and all but four of these are endemic to Mexico. New species are still turning up from this fascinating country, with no less than five having received valid names for the first time in the last decade. Field collectors, such as Alfred Lau, are as active as ever in Mexico today, and we can doubtless expect more novelties to be christened in future years.

Echinocereus as a Genus

In a family where generic limits are often vague or much debated, *Echinocereus* Engelm. (1848) is remarkably well-defined. However, no sooner had Engelmann described the genus when, in 1849, he submerged it back into *Cereus*, where half of its known species had previously resided. This move was prompted by correspondence with the great cactologist Salm-Dyck, who conservatively advocated the treatment of *Echinocereus* as an infrageneric division of *Cereus* in his famous *Cacteae in Horto Dyckensi*, published in 1850. This down-ranking of *Echinocereus* in botanical circles continued for nearly half a century, Engelmann describing various new species after 1849 as members of the all-embracing *Cereus* Miller.

However, in horticultural circles *Echinocereus* suffered no such demise, and has been accepted as a genus since the 1850s. In 1868 the horticultural writer and botanist Charles Lemaire employed the name in a broader sense than Engelmann, including species now referred to the South American genus *Echinopsis*, and to *Nyctocereus*, both of which have nocturnally pollinated flowers. In a similar publication Ruempler (1885) continued this trend, expanding the genus to include other South American cacti now classified in *Haageocereus* and *Erdisia*. He also referred *Cereus emoryi* Engelm. here, a North American species with strong similarities to *Echinocereus*, but arguably referable to its own genus, *Bergerocactus* Britton & Rose (1920). With the emergence, soon after, of Karl Schumann as the nineteenth century's great monographer of the Cactus Family, *Echinocereus* at first looked like becoming a 'dustbin' genus, with the inclusion of any South American species possessing superficially similar stems and flowers. Fortunately, Schumann took a different view in his eventual monograph, *Gesamtbeschreibung der Kakteen* (1897-99), in which *Echinocereus* Engelm. takes on its present form.

Since Schumann's day a certain amount of 'pruning' has affected *Echinocereus*. Britton & Rose (1909, 1920) removed *E. poselgeri* as the type of their genus *Wilcoxia* and, more recently, Rowley (1974) has excised *E. pensilis* as the monotypic *Morangaya*. Both of these segregates are resubmerged into *Echinocereus* here.

Apart from accounts of the genus in the monographs of the Cactaceae by Britton & Rose (1922) and Backeberg (1960), which are now very out-of-date and quite inadequate, there have been no comprehensive treatments of *Echinocereus* before the present. Due to the limitations of time and resources the revision offered here has had to be based primarily on a study of the literature, which is extensive, and of documented, preserved and living specimens available in the United Kingdom. As in other cactus genera, our knowledge of the plants in the field is severely restricted, and for this reason it is likely that reassessments of the limits of certain species and varieties will be necessary in the not too distant future. However, it is the author's hope that the framework in which they are now classified will largely stand the test of time.

Besides fieldwork, there is also the need for further investigation into other areas where our knowledge is incomplete. In particular the study of pollen and seed morphology, of which there is already a good nucleus of data, should greatly enhance our understanding of relationships. Most of all, however, there is a requirement for more preserved, documented plant material (especially alcohol-preserved flowers) to facilitate the study of the less well known Mexican species, some of which include varieties awaiting formal description. Amateur and professional growers could do much in this regard by thoroughly describing or preserving the flowers of these plants as they become available.

NOTES ON CULTIVATION

by David Parker and Nigel Taylor

GENERAL REQUIREMENTS

Although a number of *Echinocereus* species can be grown with some success indoors on a sunny windowsill, here it is assumed that the serious collector will have either a heated greenhouse or frame in which to grow his or her plants. This accommodation should ideally be in a situation fully exposed to the sun, for although not all *Echinocereus* species need this much light, it is possible to provide shading but not extra sunlight if a house or tree is in the way. Whether greenhouse or frame is employed, adequate ventilation is essential, and becomes increasingly critical as the structure gets smaller. Ventilation is needed whenever the temperature rises above 20°C, but its regulation in early spring and late autumn can be a problem if plants are to be kept out of cold draughts and changeable weather allowed for. Automatic vent opening gadgets can be very useful if there is no one on hand to open and close greenhouse windows during the day. In good summer weather the door of the greenhouse can be left open, but a wire net should be put in its place to keep out birds and cats. During very warm spells plants can be placed outdoors while the greenhouse or frame is thoroughly spring-cleaned with a strong disinfectant (e.g. Jeyes Fluid) to eliminate pests hiding in its nooks and crannies, on greenhouse staging, etc. Some growers will even leave some plants outside for the summer, but good weather cannot be guaranteed, at least in Britain.

LIGHT

For many cacti, and especially the densely spiny species of *Echinocereus*, abundant sunlight is essential for healthy growth and flowering. However, in relatively dull climates, such as in Britain, care must be taken that the sudden appearance of the sun in spring does not cause scorching or discoloration of the epidermis. If the greenhouse is in a very sunny spot It may be desirable to thinly apply some proprietary greenhouse shading or dilute white emulsion to the glass in spring, which will gradually wash off during summer as the plants become acclimatized. Scorching should not occur if the house is properly ventilated, but at least one grower believes that it is aggravated by nutrient deficiency (possibly caused by use of hard tap water). The light requirements of individual species can be judged by the density of their spines; weakly spined plants, such as *E. subinermis* and *E. scheeri* var. *gentryi*, needing less sun than *E. engelmannii* for example. Light in autumn and winter is especially important as it increases the plants' resistance to cold and disease, and so any shading should be removed in late summer.

WATERING

There are few exact rules about watering echinocerei or cacti in general, except that the water should ideally be clean rainwater (not tap water) and is normally completely withheld, at least in Britain, for much of the period from October to March. The time for breaking this dry winter rest depends on the minimum temperature maintained in the greenhouse and on the weather. If the spring is a bad one then watering should be delayed until conditions improve. At first a light spray over the plants on a fine day is sufficient, but once warm sunny weather occurs, a thorough soaking should be given. Some growers water their plants from below, relying on the capillary action of the compost to draw up the moisture. However, care is needed to ensure that excess water is not allowed to remain in the receptacle beneath the plant container. Watering from above with clean rainwater helps wash dust off the plant surface, but care should be taken that large water droplets are not allowed to rest on the plant during cool weather. Furthermore, spraying over the plants with water helps discourage red spider mites, which can be a problem in greenhouses with very dry air. Water should be allowed to reach the ambient temperature in the greenhouse before use. In general the slower-growing, pectinate-spined species, such as *E. pectinatus*, *E. rigidissimus* and *E. primolanatus*, should be watered more sparingly and never until the compost has almost completely dried from previous applications. They tend to start into growth later than the other species and water can be withheld until well into April in most cases. The rule with watering is "if in doubt, don't."

POTTING COMPOSTS AND CONTAINERS

Most *Echinocereus* specialists grow their plants in pots, but if a shortage of greenhouse space is not a serious problem the caespitose species, and in particular those from sections *Triglochidiatus* and *Echinocereus*, do well planted out in a sunny greenhouse bed. This must be constructed from very porous material, and watering carefully controlled, since evaporation from the wet soil may be too slow, except during the height of summer. A good example of how successful this mode of culture is for certain species can be seen at the Holly Gate Reference Collection (see p.17), but not all species benefit from a free root run.

Cultivation of echinocerei in pots is easy, but the caespitose species need wide pans after a while and can eventually become quite a handful when repotting becomes necessary. Those with tuberous roots may need deeper than usual pots. Most growers use plastic containers, sometimes with enlarged drainage holes, though the more porous clay pot may be desirable for species subject to losing their roots through rot, such as *E. pulchellus*. In general such problems can be countered by making the potting compost more open and porous.

Potting composts for cacti have long been a cause for some debate, but so long as the chosen medium cannot become waterlogged and is well aerated, all will be well. However, unless the compost is well supplied with the major and minor plant nutrients a balanced liquid feed should be given regularly during spring and summer. A good brand is 'Cactigrow' supplied by Holly Gate Nurseries (see p.17), Sussex. A satisfactory compost can be made up using the loam based John Innes formula as a basis (7 parts by volume sterilized loam, 3 parts peat, 2 parts washed coarse sand) but, if this is purchased already made up, care should be taken that the ingredients used are of good quality, and it may be necessary to shop around until a reliable supplier is found. To this compost it is desirable to add up to an equal amount of washed, coarse sharp sand mixed with fine (6 mm) grit and a smaller amount, say one quarter by volume, of peat. These additives will ensure that the compost remains well aerated and quick draining, but as they contain no nutrient some bone meal and superphosphate should be included. Echinocerei seem to enjoy nutrient rich composts, high in mineral matter but low in organic materials. The use of peat-based composts, other than with copious additions of sand and grit, is not recommended, and if these are watered with tap water they tend to shrink away from the side of the pot as they dry leaving the rootball exposed. Re-wetting such composts in spring can be very difficult and since the peat contains little nutrient more regular watering with liquid fertilizers will be necessary. Plants grown in good loam based composts do not need repotting so frequently, although young, rapidly growing specimens may require a move each spring to allow them enough root room.

Species with tuberous rootstocks need more careful treatment. The upper part of the tuberous taproot should be surrounded by very coarse grit and only the finer feeding roots placed in the compost. The same applies to the stem bases of the choicer, slow-growing species, which should be kept free of damp compost by a thick layer of gravel. This can be the same gravel as is used by many growers to topdress the compost in their pots, but some prefer not to cover the compost in order that its water content can be more easily assessed.

HEATING

Many species of *Echinocereus* are remarkably hardy once the stem tissues have become slightly flaccid after water has been withheld for two months or more. Most will withstand one or two degrees of frost in this condition and those from altitudes in the wild of more than 2000 metres will usually survive quite severe frosts for short periods when absolutely dry. However, if a comprehensive collection of the genus is contemplated, then winter heating will be required for the open-spined types from lower altitudes, e.g. *E. papillosus*, *E. berlandieri*, *E. pentalophus*, *E. scheeri* etc., which appreciate a minimum of 5°C. The more hardy members of the genus will not mind these warmer conditions and can be grown with a wider margin for error—if, for example, there should be a leak in the greenhouse roof during winter. Also some species which undoubtedly withstand considerable cold in the field, do so in conditions of very low humidity, which is seldom true of conditions in winter in more temperate climates. These include species like *E. chisoensis* and *E. primolanatus*, whose rarity demands that they be cosseted a bit anyway. Some lowland species (see taxonomic text for details of altitudes), such as *E. papillosus*, may need winter conditions even warmer than the

5°C minimum already suggested if they are to flower, but the majority of echinocerei will, at least, survive if only 0°C minimum can be provided, so long as they are kept dry from early autumn onwards. However, warmer conditions permit a longer growing season and maintain a greater level of health.

The choice of heater for the greenhouse or frame depends on circumstances and cost. In a small greenhouse a thermostatically controlled electric fan heater is probably the best type to use and has the advantage that it can be employed in summer with the thermostat turned down to increase air circulation in small greenhouses. Of course electricity is quite expensive, but insulation in the form of bubble-plastic attached to the inside of the greenhouse can help cut down costs, as can the use of "offpeak" electricity. In a frame, electric soil warming cables run along between the pots is a satisfactory form of heating. Paraffin and gas heaters are not so good as they produce much moisture, which may prevent the plants from properly going to rest and affect their ability to resist cold.

PESTS AND OTHER PROBLEMS

Species of *Echinocereus* are no more prone to pests and diseases than other cacti, and the same controls or preventive measures apply. Probably the commonest pest is the mealy bug, of which there are different species, some attacking the stems, others the roots. They are best controlled by using a systemic insecticide and a contact insecticide at different times during the growing season (e.g. in spring and at the onset of autumn). This regime should prevent the build-up of resistance to these poisons. Red spider mite, which is encouraged by dry conditions and will also attack during winter, is a difficult pest to control, but only affects certain unlucky collections. Regular spraying with clean rainwater during warm weather is the best preventive measure, insecticides being only partially effective but worth trying nonetheless. A relatively minor pest is the common garden aphid, which will sometimes take a liking to the slow-developing flower-buds of *Echinocereus* species, but will not attack the tough epidermis of their stems. Their control with any one of various garden insecticides is straightforward.

Of the microscopic infections that can affect cacti, the reddish-brown bacterial rot, which can spread up the stems through the vascular tissue, is the most serious. More often than not it indicates bad conditions at the roots, especially those of inadequate drainage and poor aeration. Once discovered, all affected parts of the plant must be removed and destroyed, and any remaining parts that can be salvaged treated as cuttings or scions.

Discolorations of the epidermis and other unsightly marks may occur from time to time, apparently without obvious cause. There is an increasing suspicion that these may be due to nutrient deficiency or the effects of using tapwater highly charged with harmful salts. It is always worth repotting any plants affected in this way and experimenting with fertilizers containing trace elements, or with a different water supply. A few of the less-hardy species will be marked if winter heating is insufficient, but this is unlikely if a minimum of 5°C is maintained.

Propagation

All species of *Echinocereus* can be raised from seed in the manner of other cacti, and adequate instructions on this process can be found in nearly all popular cactus texts (a detailed account worth consulting is that by Brian Fearn in *Cactus & Succulent Journal of Great Britain*, 43: 13-17. 1981). The necessity of obtaining reliably identified seed is obvious; home-produced seed will be of doubtful purity unless the plants used in its production were isolated from other species while in flower. Seeds and seedlings of this genus are quite small, and the former must not be buried in more than their own diameter (i.e. c. 1-2mm) of fine grit in the seed tray. Pricking out of seedlings is probably best left until the start of their second year, by which time they will be large enough to handle without fear of damage. One pest that can seriously affect success at this stage is the sciara (sciarid) fly, or rather its grubs. These insects are encouraged by the presence of moist organic material so that the sooner seedlings are removed to a more mineral compost the better. Systemic insecticides (or Jeyes Fluid) will control the sciara grubs (which eat the roots and insides out of small seedlings), but great care is needed in their use as some seedlings are sensitive to these treatments. An experiment conducted on a few non-essential seedlings is wise before a general application of insecticide is given.

Vegetative propagation of *Echinocereus* is commonplace with the caespitose or branching species, especially those from sections I-IV & VI of the genus. Apical sections of the stems or whole branches can be severed by means of a very sharp, clean knife or new razor blade and must then be left for their wounds to heal over in a warm, dry place out of the full sun. Once a thick skin (callus) has formed over the cut end (1 week in hot weather, otherwise 2-3 or more weeks) they can be placed *on* very slightly moist normal potting compost that has had 50 per cent more sharp sand added to it. In summer cuttings may root if placed in a position in slight shade among other plants, but rooting will be quicker if a propagator with a source of gentle bottom heat is available. This is especially desirable in winter.

Grafting as a means of speeding up propagation of slow growing or solitary-stemmed species is very useful, often encouraging the rapid formation of offsets. It also enables pieces of rare plants to be saved when some problem has caused much of the plant to die. For seedlings and very small pieces of stem, slender *Pereskiopsis* stock is used, but larger scions require something stouter, such as *Echinopsis (Trichocereus) spachiana*. The techniques employed do not differ from those described for other cacti in the popular horticultural literature on the Family. One thing to remember about grafted echinocerei is that their hardiness will be greatly impaired, and they may no longer be able to withstand temperatures near freezing. A winter minimum of about 5°C is probably best for such plants.

The preceding notes represent a summary of cultivation requirements for *Echinocereus*. Further details are given under individual species in the systematic account which follows.

Requirements According to the Seasons

During the period October to March most growers rest adult *Echinocereus* plants, giving them no water and perhaps only spraying them with insecticide if a pest outbreak has been detected. The collection can be virtually forgotten about during these months, but this is not usual, as certain jobs that were not accommodated during the busy spring and summer periods can be done at this slack time of year, such as repotting, labelling and bringing records up-to-date. Also, heating systems need to be checked regularly unless only very hardy species are being grown, and any leaks in the greenhouse roof or condensation drips must be spotted and rectified. This time of year is a good one for planning what should be propagated later on, and as spring comes nearer some seed sowing can begin in a propagator. Any fruits that have been allowed to develop on plants from flowers of the previous year should be watched in case they should ripen unexpectedly and go mouldy, causing rot to infect the stem to which they are attached.

Towards the end of March and during April the appearance of the sun for a few days will signal the first general spray over the collection with water or the first proper watering of the compost if conditions are really favourable. Soon after a careful watch must be kept for plants that have not overwintered well. These may suddenly collapse or fail to show signs of growth, and should be removed from their pots and examined for pests or rot if they continue to refuse to recognize the presence of spring. A general application of insecticide can be given now, so long as the plants have begun to grow. Shading may be applied to the greenhouse glass during April if the weather dictates. In May flower-buds will be well developed or opening on some plants and care when moving these within the greenhouse will be required. Waterings and feeding with liquid fertilizer should be stepped up, and plants not showing signs of flower production can be repotted if necessary.

June to August is the time of greatest flowering and also the best season for taking cuttings, grafting and pricking out second year seedlings. Some plants can be stood outdoors during good spells of weather to allow the easy movement of plants within the greenhouse, facilitating careful inspection for flower-buds, offsets or pests. This is especially important in large or very crowded collections.

September is a very important time. Plants should be given as much sun and air as possible to ripen the spring growth and encourage flower production in the following year. The presence of pests should be investigated and their depredations controlled before the onset of the resting period. Watering should decrease, even though continuing good weather may suggest otherwise, and by the middle of October slight signs of shrinkage should be detectable in plants that are going to have to withstand rather cold conditions later in the winter. Plants known to be tender should be moved into warmer positions, near the heat source, or at least away from the glass, and every opportunity to ventilate the greenhouse and remove excess moisture should be taken.

Sources of Plants

Probably the best means of obtaining *Echinocereus* species, all of which are now in cultivation, is via other enthusiasts. The British Cactus & Succulent Society and national societies abroad have branch meetings and publish journals, wherein nurserymen advertise plants and seeds. These organizations are the key to obtaining plants and exchanging ideas or advice, and some also have correspondence 'round robins' for this purpose. Just recently Mr David Parker, P.O. Box 251, Bordesley Green, Birmingham, U.K. has established the first 'Echinocereus Reference Collection', a non-profit organization set-up to facilitate the exchange of documented plants between enthusiasts, and to promote the conservation of species in cultivation, thereby relieving pressures on wild populations. This worthy cause deserves support, since it should help in the dissemination of accurately named plants to other enthusiasts.

SOME USEFUL ADDRESSES

Cactus Societies
British Cactus & Succulent Society, 19 Crabtree Road, Botley, Oxford OX2 9DU, U.K.
Cactus & Succulent Society of America, 3599 Via Zara, Fallbrook, CA 92028, U.S.A.

Nurserymen
Holly Gate Cactus Nursery, Billingshurst Lane, Ashington, W. Sussex RH20 3BA, U.K.
Whitestone Gardens Ltd, Sutton-under-Whitestonecliffe, Thirsk, N. Yorkshire YO7 2PZ, U.K.
Rod & Ken Preston Mafham, 2 Willoughby Close, Kings Coughton, Alcester, Warwickshire B49 5QJ, U.K.
Mesa Garden, P.O. Box 72, Belen, New Mexico 87002, U.S.A.

TAXONOMY

The Position of Echinocereus within the Family Cactaceae

Although systems of classification for the Cactaceae have undergone continuous development since Linnaean times, it seems sufficient to begin a discussion of the systematic position of *Echinocereus* with Britton & Rose (1922). The American monographers divided the Family into three tribes, with the largest, the 'Cereeae' (properly Cacteae), further divided into eight subtribes, one being 'Echinocereanae'. Besides *Echinocereus* this included five low-growing, but only superficially similar, South American genera (e.g. *Echinopsis*, *Lobivia*, etc.) and thus represented a highly artificial arrangement, especially since the related segregate genus *Wilcoxia* Britton & Rose, typified by *Echinocereus poselgeri*, was classified in the subtribe 'Cereanae'. Berger (1926) soon dispensed with this unsatisfactory system and associated *Echinocereus* and its ally *Wilcoxia* with a primarily North American group of cereoid genera in his 'Sippe Nyctocerei' of subtribe 'Cereae'. These included *Nyctocereus* and *Bergerocactus*, which share a number of stem and floral features in common with *Echinocereus*, and also genera with more superficial similarities, i.e. *Harrisia*, *Heliocereus*, *Machaerocereus* and *Rathbunia*. Buxbaum (1958) removed *Nyctocereus*, *Harrisia* and *Heliocereus* from Berger's 'Nyctocerei', and placed them in his tribe Hylocereeae, while the remainder, including *Echinocereus* etc., he called Echinocereeae. Backeberg (1960) treated *Echinocereus* and *Wilcoxia* as 'Sippe Echinocerei' of his subtribe Boreocereinae. This small bigeneric group, while natural in itself, was placed in sequence after the South American *Zehntnerella*, and the ill-assorted genera which make up the subtribe as a whole preclude this arrangement from serious consideration.

In modernizing and reshaping the Britton & Rose system, Hunt (1967) employed *Echinocereus* as a broad concept, including *Wilcoxia* (but not *Neoevansia* and *Cullmannia)* and *Bergerocactus* in its synonymy. The genus was referred to a diverse cereoid group, but separated from the unrelated South American genera of Britton & Rose's 'Echinocereanae'.

The most recent and most satisfactory, comprehensive system for the Cactaceae is that presented by Buxbaum (1974). This represents a considerable revision of his earlier classification of 1958. Tribe Echinocereeae is reduced to two genera, *Echinocereus* and *Bergerocactus*, with *Wilcoxia* removed to the Hylocereeae subtribe Nyctocereinae. However, this latter genus was of uncertain position and later Buxbaum (1975) considered its affinities to be equivocal between the two tribes. Indeed the difference between the Echinocereeae and subtribe Nyctocereinae seems rather unclear and Barthlott (1979) has associated *Echinocereus* and its segregates, *Wilcoxia* and *Morangaya*, with the genus *Peniocereus* from Buxbaum's latter group. The writer agrees with this, but would also bring in *Nyctocereus* and *Bergerocactus* here. These six genera have many points in common, provided that the highly specialized habit of some species of *Echinocereus* is allowed for. A characteristic of the group is the frequent occurrence of tuberous roots, which help to distinguish them from similar but probably unrelated taxa, such as *Aporocactus* and *Heliocereus*. In their flowers, fruits and seeds *Wilcoxia* and *Morangaya* are much more closely related to *Echinocereus* and are here included in it despite differences in habit, which seem of lesser importance. Circumscribed in this way, *Echinocereus* can be distinguished from the remaining genera of the group by the combination of small tuberculate seeds and flowers adapted for diurnal pollination. The characters of green stigma-lobes and flower-buds which burst through the stem epidermis also set the genus apart, but are not reliable as a means of recognizing all its species, since some of those included in it *sensu stricto* have white stigmas and/or buds which develop normally at the stem areoles. The following key aims to summarize the differences between *Echinocereus sensu lato* and its proposed allies:

1. Flowers brightly coloured, adapted for diurnal pollination, though sometimes opening in the afternoon and remaining open at night 2
   Flowers white, nocturnal 4

2. Fruit dehiscent from apex, the seeds and juicy pulp escaping via a pore and drying upon the spiny fruit surface ....**Bergerocactus**
   Fruit dehiscent by one or more splits in the pericarp wall or indehiscent, the seeds and pulp not escaping as above 3

3. Stem epidermis conspicuously papillose-pubescent; seeds 2-5 mm long, not strongly tuberculate; stigmas never green ....**Peniocereus** (incl. *Cullmannia* & *Neoevansia*)
   Stem epidermis glabrous; seeds 0.8-2 mm long, strongly tuberculate; stigmas often green ....**Echinocereus** (incl. *Wilcoxia* & *Morangaya*)

4. Stem epidermis papillose-pubescent, dark green or brownish, or mottled; stem ribs 3-8; spines mostly inconspicuous, those on the fruit short ....**Peniocereus**
   Stem epidermis glabrous, light green; stem ribs 5-17; spines conspicuous, sometimes very well developed on the fruit ....**Nyctocereus**

Relationships Within Echinocereus

Determining the number of species in a genus such as *Echinocereus* is not simply a matter of looking for discontinuities in variation but must include detailed consideration of interrelationships. As in other cactus genera of large or medium size, the species of *Echinocereus* fall into relatively few infrageneric taxa (here ranked as sections) some of which can be further divided into two or more, less well-defined species groups. Until these sections and groups are recognized, detailed comparison of species is an uncertain procedure, since the repeated occurrence of convergent evolution means that what might at first seem related may in fact be only superficially similar. Previous classifications of *Echinocereus* illustrate this point very well.

The earliest infrageneric division of the species belonging here was by Engelmann (1849), who distinguished two sections comprising those with few-ribbed stems (the *Costati*) and those with more than 10 ribs (the *Sulcati*). Salm-Dyck (1850) employed a similar arrangement using the names *Lophogoni* and *Proliferi*, respectively. However, he further subdivided each of these primary divisions using rib number and spine characters, but ignoring floral details, which for many species were quite unknown. These early and highly artificial arrangements, based on few vegetative characters, were probably intended mainly as aids to identification, and this applies equally to Engelmann's later publications, in which flower colour alone was employed to delimit smaller units within the larger, vegetatively defined groups (Engelmann, 1856, 1859).

A more elaborate system of 'Reihen' and 'Unterreihen' was developed by Schumann (1897), and formed the basis for subsequent classifications employed by Backeberg (1960) and Buxbaum (1974). Unfortunately, Schumann's divisions are based entirely on vegetative features and associate convergent species with fundamentally different flower morphologies. The reason for this reliance on stem morphology is easy to explain, since the stems of these plants can be compared at any time of year, but their flowers, when or if produced, last but a few days and can only be studied properly if preserved in alcohol. The present study has, for the first time, investigated floral morphology in some detail. Accordingly, flowers have been preserved in spirit and their examination has led to the conclusion that the primary divisions within the genus must be founded on a combination of floral and vegetative features. When this is done the resulting classification suggests that certain adaptive or specialized syndromes, such as a many-ribbed stem densely covered in numerous short spines, may have evolved independently in as many as four different lines. The accompanying table aims to show how artificial Schumann's arrangement of the species is, since only his monotypic Reihe *Graciles* corresponds to a section in the system presented here. His fourth Reihe, *Erecti*, is particularly heterogeneous, containing elements found in each of the two preceding Reihen in addition to species for which section *Erecti* is used here.

A Comparison Of The Classification Of Species Known To
Schumann (1897) With That Adopted Here
(GP = species group)

Schumann 1897	Taylor 1985
Reihe *Graciles*	
1. *E. tuberosus* (= *E. poselgeri*)	section 6. *Wilcoxia*
Reihe *Subinermes*	
2. *E. subinermis*	section 5. *Reichenbachii*, GP.1
3. *E. knippelianus*	section 7. *Pulchellus*, GP.2
4. *E. pulchellus*	section 7. *Pulchellus*, GP.2

Reihe *Prostrati*
    Unterreihe *Melanochlori:*
5. *E. scheeri*
6. *E. salm-dyckianus* } (= *E. scheeri*)   section 3. *Triglochidiatus*

    Unterreihe *Nigricantes:*
7. *E. berlandieri*
8. *E. blanckii* (hort.) } (= *E. berlandieri*)   section 4. *Echinocereus*, GP.2
9. *E. poselgerianus*
10. *E. papillosus*   section 4. *Echinocereus*, GP.2

    Unterreihe *Pentalophi:*
11. *E. procumbens*
12. *E. leptacanthus* } (= *E. pentalophus*)   section 4. *Echinocereus*, GP.1
    Unterreihe *Oleosi:*
13. *E. glycimorphus* (= *E. cinerascens*)   section 4. *Echinocereus*, GP.2

    Unterreihe *Leucacanthi:*
14. *E. ehrenbergii*
15. *E. cinerascens* } (= *E. cinerascens*)   section 4. *Echinocereus*, GP.2
16. *E. leonensis* (= *E. pentalophus*)   section 4. *Echinocereus*, GP.1
17. *E. enneacanthus*   section 4. *Echinocereus*, GP.2

Reihe *Erecti:*
    Unterreihe *Pectinati:*
18. *E. longisetus*   section 4. *Echinocereus*, GP.3
19. *E. chloranthus*   section 4. *Echinocereus*, GP.3
20. *E. viridiflorus*   section 4. *Echinocereus*, GP.3
21. *E. dasyacanthus*
22. *E. ctenoides* } (= *E. pectinatus*)   section 2. *Erecti*, GP.2
23. *E. pectinatus*
Included under no. 23:
    E. rigidissimus   section 5. *Reichenbachii*, GP.2
    E. reichenbachii   section 5. *Reichenbachii*, GP.3
    E. adustus   section 7. *Pulchellus*, GP.1
24. *E. roetteri*   suspected hybrid (sect. 2x3?)

    Unterreihe *Decalophi:*
25. *E. maritimus*   section 2. *Erecti*, GP.1
26. *E. fendleri*   section 2. *Erecti*, GP.2
27. *E. engelmannii*   section 2. *Erecti*, GP.1
28. *E. dubius*
29. *E. merkeri* } (= *E. enneacanthus*)   section 4. *Echinocereus*, GP.2
30. *E. conglomeratus*
31. *E. stramineus* } (= *E. stramineus*)   section 4. *Echinocereus*, GP.2
32. *E. mojavensis*
33. *E. paucispinus*
34. *E. phoeniceus* } (= *E. triglochidiatus*)   section 3. *Triglochidiatus*
35. *E. roemeri*
36. *E. polyacanthus*
37. *E. acifer* } (= *E. polyacanthus*)   section 3. *Triglochidiatus*
38. *E. leeanus*

As noted already, the classifications adopted by more modern authors, e.g. Backeberg, follow Schumann's system closely and are equally artificial. Backeberg (1960) merely removes Unterreihe *Melanochlori* of Schumann from Reihe *Prostrati* and gives it separate status. However, he then adds *E. brandegeei* and *E. pensilis* to the *Prostrati*, making it more of a mixture than before. Reihe *Erecti* remains totally heterogeneous, the only modifications being the addition of two more Unterreihen, '*Longiseti*' and '*Baileyani*', neither of which present any improvement, since their closest allies are to be found amongst a great mixture of species in the Unterreihen *Pectinati* and *Decalophi*.

Characters Considered Important or Deserving Further Study

The reliance on vegetative characters by previous students of *Echinocereus* resulted in a very one-sided view of diversity within the genus. In fact the vegetative features that can be employed are rather few. Here they are used mainly in support of flower, fruit and seed characters, which are far more numerous and seem significant at a higher rank. Indeed many aspects of the stems and roots are so obviously adaptive that the risk of comparing features that are convergent is considerable. Although convergence in flower, fruit and seed characters is just as likely, there are so many more of them to be observed that the chances of misinterpretation are greatly reduced.

The following floral characteristics seem to be important: shape and thickness of the receptacle-tube (the usually green part of the flower beneath the perianth-segments, which is hollow above but encloses the ovary towards its base); presence or absence of loose to dense wool on the receptacle-tube, and the type of spines present; size and shape of the nectar chamber (the hollow part of the receptacle-tube beneath the lowest point of insertion of the stamens); perianth-segment arrangement, shape and thickness (can be densely inserted and not fleshy, or loosely inserted with thick fleshy bases); colour-patterning of flower (whether dark in the throat or lighter); position of flower on the stem; stamen length; shape and size of ovary locule at anthesis.

Three types of fruit can be recognized, each of which may or may not dehisce when ripe. The two commonest types are the very juicy, sweet-smelling and often large, edible fruit, and the small to large, drier, white-pulped fruit. The third type has very little pulp, is rather small and usually few-seeded.

Seed characters have not been used extensively, as they are inadequately known for a number of key taxa. However, seed size and testa morphology appear to be significant below sectional level. A comprehensive study of *Echinocereus* seeds, utilizing the Scanning Electron Microscope (SEM), would certainly be of value. In fact many SEM pictures have already been published, although not all of these have represented satisfactorily documented seeds. Another fruitful source of data may come from the study of pollen morphology. Leuenberger

(1976) has already examined a number of species and his results suggest some support for the classification presented here. Unfortunately, as in the case of seed morphology, various key taxa are yet to be studied.

Perhaps the most interesting avenue for further investigation is that involving the chemistry of flower pigments. This has been started by J.M. Miller and co-workers (see Bibliography), but to date the published results encompass only five species, from the sections *Triglochidiatus* and *Echinocereus* (including the E. CINERASCENS and E.VIRIDIFLORUS GROUPS). At this stage its value is difficult to assess, but in view of the differences observed between the few taxa so far investigated its potential for supplementing morphological characters would seem to be considerable.

Unspecialized and Derived Characters

The species of *Echinocereus* exhibit a remarkable range in their degree of relative specialization for conservation of water and other resources. Unspecialized vegetative characters include exposed, branched stems with few, high ribs and few, not very dense spines (e.g. *E. enneacanthus*). In contrast, solitary stems with many low ribs completely covered in fine short spines, or those which are retracted underground by a tuberous root, are much better adapted for water conservation and seem more derived (e.g. *E. primolanatus* and *E. knippelianus*). Floral characters can also be interpreted in this way, some plants producing very extravagant, large fleshy flowers (e.g. *E. engelmannii*), which are relatively wasteful of the plant's resources (and thus unspecialized) when compared to the smaller, more delicate perianths of species like *E. viridiflorus* and *E. pulchellus*. Although it can clearly be argued that a large flower may be more effective in attracting pollinators, this can be compensated for in smaller flowers by having numerous narrow petals, for it is believed that insects are particularly good at seeing structures with edges. The range of fruit types in the genus is also an indication of specialization towards economy. The large juicy fruits of most species in sections *Erecti* and *Echinocereus* can be compared with the small, almost dry fruits in section *Pulchellus*.

Geography of the Sections and Species Groups

The distribution of *Echinocereus* species in relation to their infrageneric classification is of considerable interest, and offers some clues as to the origin of the genus. All but one of the 44 species are believed to occur in Mexico, of which 27 are endemic. With a few exceptions, the species in Mexico can be divided almost equally into those found west of the Sierra Madre Occidental watershed, and those found to the east. On the west side the monotypic section *Morangaya* and three species groups are endemic, while on the east side section *Echinocereus*, including three species groups, and one other group are endemic. In other words, this mountain barrier has isolated species and species groups, but appears less significant at sectional rank, five out of the seven sections being common to both western and eastern parts of Mexico. However, examination of the species, which make up these five sections, suggests that in each case those with the most unspecialized characters are found in the west, where *E. pensilis*, the least derived species in the genus, is also found. Besides *E. pensilis* (sect. *Morangaya*), these unspecialized species comprise the E. ENGELMANNII GROUP and *E. ferreirianus* (sect. *Erecti*), *E. scheeri* (sect. *Triglochidiatus*), *E. spinigemmatus* and *E. subinermis* (sect. *Reichenbachii*), *E. leucanthus* (sect. *Wilcoxia*), and *E. pamanesiorum* (sect. *Pulchellus*). They are all found in the region including S Baja California, Sinaloa, W Durango, W Zacatecas and NW Jalisco, in which the genus, it is now suggested, may have originated and initially diversified. The more derived taxa in each of the large sections appear to have evolved as the genus radiated outwards into the Sonoran and Chihuahuan Deserts, or to the high mountains or plains of eastern and central Mexico. Examples of these are *E. pectinatus* (sect. *Erecti*, Chihuahuan Desert), *E. grandis* (sect. *Reichenbachii*, Sonoran Desert) and *E. pulchellus* (sect. *Pulchellus*, central Mexican plateau). Section *Echinocereus* does not conform to this pattern since none of its species ranges west of the Sierra Madre Occidental. However, its least specialized representatives are mostly from lowland habitats in E Mexico, while its derived species are found in highlands within the Chihuahuan Desert and further north in the cooler regions of the United States. Therefore, to generalize for the genus as a whole, the species found near the periphery of its range, at higher altitudes where conditions are more extreme, are mostly highly specialized and unrelated to one another, their closest but less derived relatives being found nearer the proposed centre of radiation in W Mexico.

Notes on the Systematic Treatment

The systematic account of the genus, its sections, species groups and species, which follows, needs clarification on a few points. References cited in the notes preceding the species descriptions can mostly be found among the bibliographic details accompanying the name and its synonymy (which follow the description). If not, they will appear in the general Bibliography on p.155. In the descriptions, numbers given for radial and central spines are those per areole; measurements of the receptacle-tube always include the ovary, which it encloses at its base; the nectar chamber is the hollow part of the receptacle-tube below the bases of the lowest stamens and above the ovary, and contains the base of the style. In the formal documentation of the accepted name and its type etc., the bibliographic references have been selected either because of their historic importance or (and more especially) because they relate to good illustrations of the plant, facilitating its identification. The same applies to any synonyms cited, which are sometimes given solely to draw attention to good illustrations. Other synonyms, not mentioned in the preceding text or elsewhere, are given in the index, which includes all relevant *Echinocereus* binomials and most infraspecific epithets employed by authors since the monograph of Britton & Rose (1922).

It will soon become obvious that species are frequently divided into two or more infraspecific taxa, for which the rank of variety (*varietas*) has been used throughout. In most cases these varieties would probably be treated as subspecies by authors not familiar with the quirks of cactus taxonomy, although a few, i.e. those not known to be geographically separate from their infraspecific sister taxa, might rank as genuine varieties. However, use of the term subspecies in a family with such an overwhelming interest among amateur horticulturists is likely to weaken the chances of the classification being accepted, the word variety being much more familiar to the majority of those being catered for.

ECHINOCEREUS

Echinocereus Engelm. in Wislizenus, Mem. Tour. North. Mex. 91, in adnot. (1848); Schumann, Gesamtb. Kakt. 245 (1897); Britton & Rose, Cact. 3: 3 (1922); Backeberg, Die Cact. 4: 1970 (1960); F. Buxb. in Krainz, Die Kakteen, Lfg 60 (1975). Lectotype (Britton & Rose, loc. cit.): *E. viridiflorus* Engelm. (cf. ICBN, 1983, Art. 8, line 5; this choice subsequently confirmed by all authors).
Cereus subgenus *Echinocereus* (Engelm.) A. Berger in Rep. Mo. Bot. Gard. 16: 79 (1905).
Wilcoxia Britton & Rose in Contrib. US. Nat. Herb. 12: 434 (1909).
Morangaya G. Rowley in Ashingtonia (GB) 1: 44 (1974).

DESCRIPTION. *Stems* branched or solitary, prostrate or erect, to 1-60 cm high without support or clambering through other vegetation, rarely to 2(-4) metres long, < 1-15 cm in diameter, globose to cylindric, sometimes arising from a tuberous rootstock and/or ± retracted into the ground, mostly rather spiny, apical scale leaves absent except in sect. *Morangaya*. *Ribs* 4-26, sometimes ± dissolved into tubercles, high and acute to very low and obtuse. *Flower-buds* developing at the upper edge of the stem areoles or bursting through the epidermis above them. *Flowers* small to large, often brightly coloured, adapted for diurnal entomophily or (sect. *Triglochidiatus*) ornithophily. *Receptacle-tube* (incl. ovary) short to long, bearing spiny to bristly and sometimes very woolly areoles subtended by small ± triangular scales (the latter not usually noted in the species descriptions). *Nectar chamber* simple, not protected, often rather small or almost filled by base of style (well developed in sect. *Triglochidiatus*). *Stigmas* white to pale or dark green. *Fruit* globose to ovoid, green to red, spiny or spines deciduous, sometimes dehiscent by one or more longitudinal splits in the pericarp, sometimes sweet-scented, interior juicy or with whitish pulp, rarely almost dry. *Seeds* ovoid to ± globose, 0.8-2 mm long, testa tuberculate, mostly black.

DISTRIBUTION. 44 species, ranging from S Central Mexico (N Oaxaca), north to SW South Dakota (U.S.A.), west to Cent. S California, and east to SE Texas; semi-desert, scrub, dry woodlands and grassy highlands, from sea-level to c. 3100 metres altitude.

Key to Species

The artificial key presented below relies heavily on floral characters, without which the identification of *Echinocereus* species is either impossible or very unreliable, especially with regard to cultivated specimens. A number of species key out in more than one place and in some cases a particularly distinct variety of a species is keyed as such. This does not necessarily mean that the variety in question will not also key out with the species as a whole. Once or twice knowledge of the plant in habitat is required, but in general it should be possible to key most members of the genus from cultivated material without field data. However, distributional information is included to enhance its usefulness in the field and when identifying documented material. Hybrids, whether natural or man-made, are omitted, and in view of their increasing frequency in cultivation, it is important to check the plant once keyed against the full description for the taxon concerned.

1. Inner perianth-segments bright yellow, sometimes contrasted with red or green at base, at least some > 5 mm wide...2
   Inner perianth-segments primarily orange, red, pinkish, purplish or brownish, sometimes with a zone of bright yellow or white towards base, or very pale yellow to white, *or* flowers greenish-yellow *and* perianth-segments to only c. 4 mm wide...6

2. Inner perianth-segments orange-red/purplish at base (S Texas & perhaps adjacent Mexico) ....15. **E. papillosus**
   Inner perianth-segments yellow or green at base 3

3. Base of inner perianth-segments green, rather fleshy...
   ....8c. **E. pectinatus** var. **dasyacanthus**
   Base of inner perianth-segments yellow, not particularly fleshy 4

4. Central spines and the similar upper radial spines 7-10, strongly flattened or angular towards base, at least 3 cm long (Pacific coast of Baja California) 5. **E. maritimus**
   Central spines 1-4, terete (rounded), or minute or absent......................................5

5. Stems with 5-11 ribs, solitary or with branches arising above ground; nectar chamber to 6 mm long (Sinaloa, S Sonora & adjacent parts of SW Chihuahua) ....
   ....25. **E. subinermis**
   Stems with 11-16 ribs, solitary or adjacent stems connected by underground rhizomes (but sometimes branching above ground in cultivation); nectar chamber to c. 2 mm long (S & E Sonora & W Chihuahua) ....26. **E. stoloniferus**

6. Stems long and slender, only 0.3-2 cm thick, arising from tuberous roots of much greater diameter and relying on surrounding vegetation for support, 8-10-ribbed (cultivated specimens of *E. palmeri* may key here, see lead 23)............................7
   Stems and habit not as above (but roots sometimes tuberous)..............................9

7. Spines of stem hairlike, rootstock napiform (Queretaro) ....39. **E. schmollii**
   Spines of stem rigid, short; rootstock dahlia-like 8

8. Flowers pink to magenta, receptacle-tube with conspicuous wool, perianth-segments to 12mm wide (NE Mexico & S Texas) ....38. **E. poselgeri**

Flowers white, receptacle-tube ± glabrous, perianth-segments c. 4mm wide (SW Sonora & NW Sinaloa) ....37. **E. leucanthus**

9. Perianth-segments bright orange or slightly pinkish red to deep pure red with no admixture of blue, lighter towards base, > 4 mm wide, *or* pink to salmon-pink (often zoned orange in the throat) *and* the receptacle-tube elongate, only gradually flared, the part above the ovary 3.5-6 cm long, its nectar chamber 7-19 mm long, 4-7 mm wide..10
   Perianth-segments shades of pink or purplish-magenta, yellowish-green or whitish, lighter to darker towards base, *or* none > 4 mm wide; receptacle-tube and nectar chamber not as above...13

10. Stigmas white to cream-coloured, never greenish; stems to 1-4 m long, additional spines developing at old areoles (S Baja California)......................1. **E. pensilis**
    Stigmas light to dark green; stems rarely > 60 cm long, spines newly developing only at young areoles near stem apex (widespread, but absent from S Baja California).11

11. Stems ± elongate-cylindric, 10-60 cm or more long, 1.5-4 cm in diameter, the areoles 2-6(-7) mm apart on the ribs; flower-buds pointed (NW Mexico: Pacific drainage of Sierra Madre Occidental, 800-2000 m altitude) ....9. **E. scheeri**
    Stems ovoid to cylindric, mostly 5-30 cm long, 2-15 cm in diameter, the areoles 6-12 mm apart; flower-buds rounded at apex..12

12. Areoles on receptacle-tube bearing diffuse cobwebby wool; inner perianth-segments acute to bluntly rounded (N-Cent. & NW Mexico, SW New Mexico & SE Arizona, mostly above 1700 m altitude) ....10. **E. polyacanthus**
    Areoles on receptacle-tube bearing only very short areolar felt (besides the usual spines); inner perianth-segments bluntly rounded to emarginate (widespread in SW USA and adjacent N Mexico, 150-3000 m altitude) ....11. **E. triglochidiatus**

13. Receptacle-tube* short but broad, c. 0.5-2.5 cm long 14
    Receptacle-tube > 2.5 cm long *or* very slender and conspicuous 18

14. Flowers green to yellowish-green, lemon-scented; perianth-segments rounded to acute at apex; stem globose to ovoid or cylindric (Cent.-S USA: South Dakota to W Texas, 900-2700 m altitude) ....23. **E. viridiflorus**
    Flowers various shades of pink, magenta, red, brown or white, *or* if yellowish-green then not lemon-scented, the perianth-segments sharply acute and the stems cylindric..15

15. Stems cylindric, 7.5-30 cm high, conspicuous..16
    Stems depressed-globose or only the apex visible above ground, inconspicuous..17

16. Central spines 0-12, to 2.5(-3) cm long (Chihuahua, W Texas & S New Mexico, 900-1830 m altitude) ....22. **E. chloranthus**
    Central spines 4-7, at least one 3-5.5 cm long (NE Mexico)........21. **E. longisetus**

17. Ribs 9-15, spines 3-11 per areole, adpressed (N Oaxaca to Zacatecas & S Nuevo Leon) ....43. **E. pulchellus**
    Ribs 5-7, spines (0-)1-4, ± porrect (SE Coahuila & S Nuevo Leon) ....
    ....44. **E. knippelianus**

18. Receptacle-tube slender, 4-10 mm in overall diameter immediately above ovary, bearing few, widely spaced, very woolly areoles; nectar chamber 6-12 mm long, 2

---

* This always includes the ovary.

mm wide; fruit nearly dry with scant pulp (Sierra Madre Occidental: W Zacatecas to E Sonora) 19

Receptacle-tube stout or receptacular areoles, nectar chamber or fruit not as above.21

19. Stigmas white or very pale green; stems 5-8(-12) cm in diameter (E flanks of S.M. Occidental in Chihuahua & Durango) ....41. **E. adustus**

Stigmas deep green, *or* rather pale green *and* stems < 5 cm in diameter (Pacific drainage of S.M. Occidental) 20

20. Areoles 10-20 mm apart on the ribs (W Zacatecas) ....40. **E. pamanesiorum**

Areoles c. 4-5 mm apart on the ribs (E Sonora) ....42. **E. laui**

21. Areoles on receptacle-tube bearing conspicuous cobwebby wool, *or* stems with > 11 ribs *and* covered in numerous short spines not exceeding 15 mm in length.......22

Areoles on receptacle-tube not as above *and* stems with either < 12 ribs or with spines > 15 mm long or < 10 per areole 35

22. Ribs 4-10 23

Ribs (10-)11-26 24

23. Areoles at least 10 mm apart on the ribs; roots fibrous; flowers with a conspicuous white to yellow throat (E.-Cent. & NE Mexico to S Texas)..12. **E. pentalophus**

Areoles c. 3-4 mm apart on the ribs; roots tuberous; flowers slightly paler to greenish in the throat (Chihuahua) ....33. **E. palmeri**

24. Perianth-segments loosely inserted and very fleshy at base, the dark outermost segments long, narrow and fleshy; flower-buds bursting through stem epidermis, not woolly; perianth-limb broadly bowl-shaped; receptacle-tube lacking cobwebby wool...25

Perianth-segments densely inserted, not fleshy; flower-buds developing at the areoles, often woolly; perianth-limb funnel-shaped; receptacle-tube with or without sparse to dense cobwebby wool..26

· 25. Ribs 13-16; spines 12-15 per areole; plants caespitose (Arizona) ....
....7c. **E. fendleri** var. **bonkerae**

Ribs 13-23; spines 15-35 per areole; stems solitary, more rarely sparsely branched (Chihuahuan Desert) ....8. **E. pectinatus**

26. Receptacle-tube clothed in cobwebby wool and long slender, hair-like bristles; at least some perianth-segments > 6 mm wide (Chihuahuan Desert, NE Mexico, E New Mexico, Texas, Oklahoma & Colorado) 27

Receptacle-tube clothed with wool and dense spines, or spines only, *or* perianth-segments only c. 6 mm wide (Sonoran Desert and regions W of Sierra Madre Occidental watershed, SE Arizona & SW New Mexico) 29

27. Radial spines 11-16 per areole, not arranged like the teeth of a comb; flower with a conspicuous white throat (S Big Bend of Texas to SW Coahuila & adjacent Durango)..34. **E. chisoensis**

Radial spines 12-36, comb-like on each side of areole, *or* flowers lacking a white throat 28

28. Ribs (21-)25-26 (S Coahuila)...35. **E. primolanatus**

Ribs 10-19 (NE Mexico, Texas except in W, E New Mexico, W Oklahoma & S Colorado)..36. **E. reichenbachii**

29. Central spines 0; inner perianth-segments pinkish-magenta above, white in lower half, not green at base (W Chihuahua, N & E Sonora & adjacent corners of Arizona & New Mexico) ....32. **E. rigidissimus**
Central spines 1-12; inner perianth-segments not as above or green at base 30

30. Ribs 10-17 (mainland localities & Isla Tiburon) 31
Ribs 18-25 (islands in Gulf of California) 34

31. Inner perianth-segments pink near apex, fading to pure white in lower half, then green at base; stem solitary (W Sonora & Isla Tiburon) ....28. **E. scopulorum**
Inner perianth-segments pinkish or purplish, only becoming paler, whitish or greenish at base; plants mostly caespitose..32

32. Rootstock somewhat tuberous; receptacle-tube at anthesis densely clothed in spines only (Cape region of S Baja California & NW Sinaloa) ....27. **E. sciurus**
Rootstock entirely fibrous; receptacle-tube with spines and conspicuous wool at anthesis 33

33. Ribs 10-14 (NW Jalisco & W Zacatecas) ....24. **E. spinigemmatus**
Ribs 15-16 (Cent. E Sonora to SE Arizona) ....31. **E. bristolii**

34. Inner perianth-segments bright pink near apex, white in the throat, green at base; stems to 8 cm in diameter (Isla San Pedro Nolasco) ....29. **E. websterianus**
Inner perianth-segments either white, very pale pink or very pale yellow, changing to green at the base; stems to 12 cm in diameter (Islas San Esteban, San Lorenzo & de las Animas) ....30. **E. grandis**

35. Inner perianth-segments darkening (to deep magenta, orange or crimson) towards base, giving the flower a dark throat *and* stem ribs 5-10....................................36
Inner perianth-segments paler or white to whitish green in lower half or near base, giving the flower a lighter throat, or uniformly coloured, *or* stems with > 10 ribs.41

36. Stigmas rather pale green to whitish; perianth-segments to c. 11 mm wide; ribs 8-10 (Baja California S of 29° N) 37
Stigmas deep green; perianth-segments to 15-25 mm wide *or* ribs 5-7 38

37. Central spines 4, distinct from radials, cruciform, strongly flattened and angled; stems 20-100 cm or more long (Baja California S of 29° N)................2. **E. brandegeei**
Central spines up to 9, not well distinguished from radials, neither conspicuously cruciform, nor markedly flattened or angled; stems 10-20(-30) cm long (S Baja California: Islas Magdalena & perhaps Santa Margarita)..3. **E. barthelowanus**

38. Stems mostly prostrate, only the apex weakly ascending, 5-7-ribbed (NE Mexico & S Texas) ....14. **E. berlandieri**
Stems ± erect; ribs 7-10 or more..39

39. Central spines 4-7, mostly cruciform, strongly flattened or angled at least near base; stem ribs 10 or more (USA & NW Mexico W of 110° W) .....4. **E. engelmannii**
Central spines 0-4, not obviously cruciform, perfectly terete, *or* stem ribs 7-10 ...40

40. Nectar chamber c. 2 mm long, 3 mm in diameter; ovary locule ± spherical at anthesis; central spines terete; areoles to 2.5 cm apart on the ribs (Sonora, N Chihuahua, Arizona, S Colorado, New Mexico & W Texas, in the Sonoran Desert, grasslands & woodlands)..7. **E. fendleri**
Nectar chamber c. 5 mm long, 2 mm in diameter; ovary locule oblong at anthesis; central spines mostly somewhat flattened or angled at least near base; areoles to 4.5

cm apart (Cent.-N & NE Mexico, S New Mexico & W & S Texas, Chihuahuan Desert and lowland brushlands) ....13. **E. enneacanthus**

41. Plants highly caespitose forming white to straw-coloured hemispherical mounds of numerous closely packed, very spiny, 10-17-ribbed stems; flowers paler in the throat 42
Stems solitary or branched but not forming mounds as above, *or* ribs < 10, *or* flowers darker in the throat 43

42. Perianth-segments 15-25 mm or more wide; spines 9-18 per stem areole (widespread in the Chihuahuan Desert, c. 600-1600 m altitude)................17. **E. stramineus**
Perianth-segments to c. 8.5 mm wide; spines up to 50 per stem areole (SE Coahuila in the Sierra Madre Oriental, c. 2000 m altitude) ....19. **E. nivosus**

43. Central spines strongly flattened or angular near base; stems erect, 10-13-ribbed (USA & NW Mexico W of 110° W).....................................4. **E. engelmannii**
Central spines terete near base, *or* stems ± procumbent *or* with > 13 ribs..........44

44. Flower darker in the throat and/or bases of perianth-segments widely spaced and rather fleshy, to c. 16 mm wide near apex...45
Flower paler in the throat; perianth-segments densely inserted, not particularly fleshy at base, *or* to 20-25 mm wide near apex 47

45. Spines 2-20 per stem areole, to 10 cm long..46
Spines 14-30 or more, to 2.5 cm long ....8. **E. pectinatus**

46. Central spines 1-3(-5); stigmas never whitish (Sonora & N Chihuahua northwards) ....7. **E. fendleri**
Central spines 4-7; stigmas whitish to pale or dark green (Cent.-E Baja California) ....6. **E. ferreirianus**

47. Flowers arising very near stem apex; seeds c. 1 mm long (NW Jalisco & W Zacatecas) ....24. **E. spinigemmatus**
Flowers mostly arising well away from stem apex; seeds 1-2 mm long (Cent.-E & NE Mexico) 48

48. Ribs (14-)17-24 (S Coahuila) ....20. **E. delaetii**
Ribs 5-15..49

49. Perianth-segments to 4-12 mm wide; central spines long, downwardly directed; stem ribs (8-)10-15 (Cent.-N Coahuila to Cent.-W Nuevo Leon) .....21. **E. longisetus**
Perianth-segments to 15-25 mm wide, central spines not as above, *or* stem ribs < 8 50

50. Stems 5-6-ribbed, 1.5-6 cm in diameter, clothed in ± glassy white spines to 4.5 cm long (Hidalgo, 1600-2000 m altitude)...............16b. **E. cinerascens** var. **ehrenbergii**
Stems 7-12-ribbed, 6-12 cm in diameter, *or* if 6-ribbed and < 6 cm in diameter then spines minute to absent or some brownish 51

51. Stems 4-12 cm in diameter; areoles 8-15 mm or more apart on the ribs; central spines yellow to brownish; seeds c. 1.2 mm long (E.-cent. Mexico: states of Mexico, Distrito Federal, Hidalgo, Querétaro, Guanajuato & San Luis Potosí, at or above 2000 m altitude)...16. **E. cinerascens**
Stems 2-7.5cm in diameter; areoles 5-10 mm apart on the ribs; central spines yellow to whitish, or spines ± absent; seeds 1.5-2 mm long (NE Mexico: SW Tamaulipas to Cent.-W Nuevo Leon, 350-2000 m altitude) ....18. **E. viereckii**

Section I. Morangaya

Echinocereus sect. **Morangaya** (G. Rowley) N.P. Taylor, stat. nov.
Morangaya G. Rowley in Ashingtonia 1: 44 (1974). Type: *E. pensilis* (K. Brandegee) J. Purpus. (For map see p.34)
The characteristics of this monotypic section from S Baja California are as described below.

1. ECHINOCEREUS PENSILIS

Many cactophiles are already more familiar with this Baja species under the name *Morangaya*, the genus erected for it by Gordon Rowley (1974). Its stems and habit are certainly quite unusual for an *Echinocereus* and at first suggest a closer relationship with *Aporocactus* Lemaire, where its slender red flowers would not be out of place. Reid Moran (1977) has studied the plant in some detail and concludes that it should definitely be excluded from *Echinocereus*, its closest relative being *Aporocactus*. However, the characters he identifies as separating it from the former are mostly indicative of its unspecialized nature and may not be significant, *viz.* the elongate (cereoid) stems, presence of minute leaves at the apex of the young shoots, and the ability of the older stem areoles to grow new spines. The development of flower buds at the stem areoles, rather than their bursting through the adjacent epidermis, is also unspecialized, but it is not a disinguishing feature in respect of *Echinocereus*, where every intermediate between the two types of bud origination can be found. Nor is too much significance to be attached to the cream-coloured stigmas of *E. pensilis* since, once again, every intermediate between white and very pale to dark green can be found among the remainder of *Echinocereus* (indeed such a range is actually found within another Baja species, *E. ferreirianus*, as well as within groups of very closely allied taxa, e.g. the E. ADUSTUS GROUP).

Of greater importance are its seeds, which are extremely like those seen elsewhere in *Echinocereus*, with characteristic tuberculate testa sculpturing. They are also within the size range for the genus (i.e. 0.8-2 mm long). On the basis of seed morphology *E. pensilis* does not appear to be related to *Aporocactus* (or at least to the type species, *A. flagelliformis*, which has smooth seeds) and, as Moran has noted, there are not insignificant differences in their stem epidermal morphologies. In the absence of any derived characters in common, convergence between *E. pensilis* and *Aporocactus* cannot be ruled out and their similarities may be misleading.

Looking at the likely relatives of *Echinocereus*, which comprise the genera *Peniocereus*, *Nyctocereus* and *Bergerocactus*, it is not difficult to accommodate *E. pensilis* in *Echinocereus*. Both *Peniocereus* and *Bergerocactus* have specialized features adequately distinguishing them, but *Nyctocereus* seems relatively unspecialized and at least one species, *N. chontalensis* Alexander, is very similar to *E. pensilis* in habit (cf. Backeberg, 1960: 2088; Lau quoted in Rowley, 1974). The principal differences between *Nyctocereus* and *E. pensilis* are their seeds (smooth and larger in *Nyctocereus*) and floral adaptation to nocturnal or (*E. pensilis*) diurnal pollinators. *Nyctocereus* is restricted in the wild state to the subtropical parts of S Mexico, an area where various seemingly old and less specialized cactus species are found. The cactus flora of S Baja California has clear connexions with this region–witness, for example, the remarkable relationship between the unspecialized *Ferocactus robustus* of Puebla and the more derived *F. peninsulae* of S Baja (cf. N.P. Taylor in Bradleya 1: 3-8. 1983; ibid. 2: 27-30. 1984). The majority of *Echinocereus* species in mainland Baja California are also of an unspecialized type (section *Erecti*) and this area is part of the W Mexican region, W of the Sierra Madre Occidental crestline, from which the genus, as we know it today, seems to have radiated. In view of these considerations it appears just as likely that *Echinocereus pensilis* may represent the 'missing link' between the generally more derived remainder of *Echinocereus* and its putative, less specialized ancestor, i.e. a genus like the extant S Mexican *Nyctocereus*. All this, of course, is speculation, but until a full investigation of all the possible relatives of *E. pensilis* has been made it seems premature to shift it into any other genus. Its retention in *Echinocereus* does not weaken the boundaries of the genus unduly, for the principal distinctions of small, tuberculate seeds combined with flowers adapted for diurnal pollination remain.

Echinocereus pensilis is easy to grow and to propagate from cuttings. It does well in a hanging basket or where its long stems can trail without risk of damage. It will not withstand temperatures much below freezing, despite its mountain origin.

DESCRIPTION. *Stems* cylindric, but tapered near apex, erect then arching or hanging from rocks, branched and becoming tangled, 1-4 m long, 2-5 cm in diameter, bright yellowish-green, producing aerial roots. *Ribs* 8-10, rounded, strongly tuberculate near stem apex, later well-defined and the tubercles less conspicuous. *Areoles* circular, 2-3 mm in diameter, with persistent white wool, 1.4-2.2 cm apart, retaining the capacity to produce new spines and wool when old. *Spines* pale yellow, acicular, to 2.5 cm long, at first 6-10, including 1 central, later increasing to 70 or more, variously radiating or porrect. *Flowers* narrowly tubular-funnelform, to 6.5 cm long and 4.5 cm in diameter, arising from near stem apex or from much older parts of stem; buds developing at the areoles not bursting through epidermis. *Receptacle-tube* 3-4 cm long, ovary occupying basal 5-10 mm, 6-8 mm in diameter, tube contracted to 5-7 mm above ovary then flared to 10 mm in diameter at apex, exterior green below, brown to red above, bearing white-woolly areoles with 0-13, 5-25 mm long, acicular, whitish spines. *Nectar chamber* 1.5-2 mm in diameter, length (?). *Perianth-segments* oblong-lanceolate, 1.8-2.5 cm long, 4-6 mm wide, acuminate to apiculate, orange-red, with darker midstripes, the outermost segments often slightly recurved. *Stamen-filaments* 8-26 mm long; *anthers* narrowly oblong, to 3 mm long, cream-coloured. *Style* 3-4 cm long, 1 mm in diameter, pink; stigmas 9, 5-6 mm long, cream. *Fruit* c. 4-5 cm long, 2-3 cm in diameter, spiny, red, pulp red, many-seeded. *Seeds* ovoid, 1.7-2 mm long, tuberculate, black.

DISTRIBUTION. NW Mexico: SW Baja California Sur (Cape region); on rocks and cliffs in pine/oak forest in the Sierra Victoria and Sierra de la Laguna, 950-1900 m altitude.*

Echinocereus pensilis (K. Brandegee) J. Purpus in Monatsschr. Kakteenk. 18: 5, with pl. (1908); H. Gates in Cact. Succ. J. (US) 6: 153-154, with figs. (1935); Werderm. in Kakteenk. 1937: 180-182, with pl. (1937); G. Lindsay in Cact. Suc. Mex. 12: 83-84, 88, figs. 34, 45 & 46 (1967); E. & B. Gay in Cact. Succ. J. (US) 41: 191, fig. 23 (1969).

Cereus pensilis K. Brandegee in Zoe 5: 192 (1904). Type: Mexico, Baja California Sur, Cape region, Sierra de la Laguna, Jan./Feb. 1890 and subsequently, *T.S. Brandegee* 246 (UC).

Morangaya pensilis (K. Brandegee) G. Rowley in Ashingtonia 1(4): 44-45, 43 (excellent colour illustrations) (1974); Moran in Cact. Suc. Mex. 22: 27-35, figs. 16 & 17 (1977).

* Although it must rank as one of the most distinct endemic species in Baja California, it is completely omitted from the *Flora* of the peninsula by I.L. Wiggins (1980).

Section II. Erecti

Echinocereus sect. **Erecti** (Schumann) H. Bravo-H. ('Erecta') in Cact. Suc. Mex. 27: 16 (1982).

Echinocereus Reihe *Erecti* Schumann, Gesamtb. Kakt. 247 (1897). Lectotype (F. Buxbaum, 1974): *E. engelmannii* (Parry ex Engelm.) Lemaire.

Cereus subsect. *Erecti* (Schumann) A. Berger in Rep. Mo. Bot. Gard. 16: 80 (1905).

Among the species originally included by Schumann was *E. viridiflorus* Engelm., which Britton & Rose (1922) and others subsequently chose as lectotype of the generic name *Echinocereus* Engelm. If this section (based on Schumann's Reihe) were to include *E. viridiflorus* today, it would have to be renamed sect. *Echinocereus* according to ICBN Art. 22.1. It could be argued that Art. 32.1(b) of the Code makes Schumann's series name invalid although *at the time of its publication* no lectotype for *Echinocereus* had been chosen. However, while Principle VI of the Code states that 'the Rules of nomenclature are retroactive . . .' the writer does not believe this should be interpreted to include the effect of lectotypifications which might retroactively invalidate names perfectly valid under the present rules *when* originally published (cf. wording re legitimacy of names in Art. 63).

This section of seven species represents the western-based counterpart of sect. *Echinocereus* and similarly contains species whose vegetative characters range from particularly unspecialized to moderately derived. No single character defines sect. *Erecti*, but the presence of one or more of the following enable its species to be distinguished from their look-alikes: (1) very fleshy-based and loosely inserted perianth-segments, the outermost rather long, narrow and stout; (2) flower-buds developing at the areoles, not bursting through the adjacent epidermis; (3) erect, 8-13-ribbed stems armed with strongly flattened and angular central spines, combined with either (1) or (2) above (cf. *E. enneacanthus* in sect. *Echinocereus*). Two species groups are clearly definable:

The E. ENGELMANNII GROUP (species 2-5) is endemic to Baja California, Mexico, except for the widespread *E. engelmannii*, which ranges much further north and a little to the east. They have flattened and, at least near the base, strongly angled central spines. This is probably an old group, as is suggested by the clear-cut differences between its four member species, and their vegetative habit, mode of flower-bud development and flowers show no specialized features.

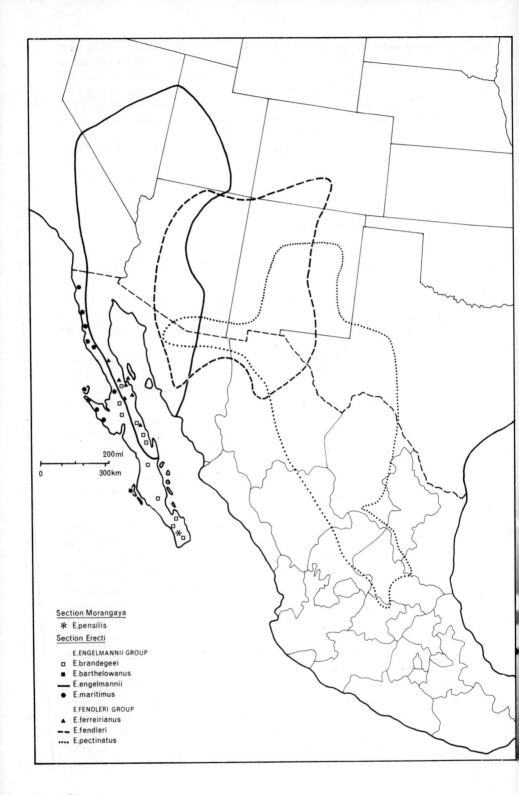

Section Morangaya
* E.pensilis
Section Erecti

E.ENGELMANNII GROUP
□ E.brandegeei
■ E.barthelowanus
— E.engelmannii
● E.maritimus

E.FENDLERI GROUP
▲ E.ferreirianus
-- E.fendleri
.... E.pectinatus

In the E.FENDLERI GROUP (species 6-8), *E. ferreirianus*, from Baja, has relatively unspecialized stems, as in the above group, but can be distinguished by its prefectly terete central spines. This also applies to the closely related complex of *E. fendleri*, which ranges further north and east, far into the U.S.A., and includes some varieties of more specialized habit. These in turn provide a connexion with *E. pectinatus*, a widespread species with a more derived, many-ribbed, solitary or little-branched stem and dense, short spines. Its large flowers develop from buds which burst through the stem epidermis and are typical of this section with very fleshy perianth-segments and therefore not very economical for the plant to produce (i.e. relatively not as specialized as its stem morphology).

2. ECHINOCEREUS BRANDEGEEI

No collection of echinocerei is complete without a specimen of this unusual species, from Mexico's desert peninsula of Baja California. It is remarkable for its stem ribs composed of large angular tubercles, whose areoles are among the most fiercely armed in the genus. The striking bicoloured flowers are exceptionally beautiful, but rarely produced in cultivation.

From the botanical standpoint *E. brandegeei* is of interest as it replaces the closely related *E. engelmannii* in S Baja and there exhibits a very similar pattern of wide infraspecific variation. Although the actual number of distinct variants is not known it is possible that there exist as many worthy of varietal rank as have been recognized for its better studied ally from further north. Surprisingly, only two additional names have been published for forms of the species and both appeared in the same paper in which Coulter (1896) described *E. brandegeei* (*Cereus brandegeei* J. Coulter), viz. *Cereus sanborgianus* J. Coulter and *C. mamillatus* Engelm. The former represents the northernmost variant from the vicinity of Misión San Borja in central Baja, while the latter, from south of Mulege, is a plant of somewhat uncertain status, Engelmann's description calling for stems with 20-25 ribs—an improbable number even for the variable *E. brandegeei*. However, the illustration in Britton & Rose (Cact. 3: fig. 54. 1922) of a plant from the Missouri Botanical Gardens, which inherited Engelmann's collections, undoubtedly shows a form of *E. brandegeei*, but with only about the normal 10 ribs. Lindsay (1967) suggests that *Cereus mamillatus* may apply to a very distinct large form widespread north and south of Mulege, but this conspicuous plant has very long yellow central spines, which do not agree with Engelmann's description. There are a number of equally distinct forms elsewhere in Baja and, if the recognition of numerous varieties as in *E. engelmannii* is meaningful, considerable study of *E. brandegeei* awaits someone in the field.

Echinocereus brandegeei inhabits the driest region of Mexico and often grows in fully exposed situations in poor, rocky soil. In cultivation it needs all available sunlight and in the UK seems to flower only in exceptionally good summers (a number of plants did so in 1984). The clumps can reach a considerable size, even under pot culture, and are also worth trying bedded-out if greenhouse space permits. Even without flowers the plant's spination is quite attractive, though some skill is required when repotting a large specimen if personal injury is to be avoided!

DESCRIPTION. *Plant* caespitose, forming groups of loosely arranged stems to 2 m in diameter. *Stems* cylindric, erect at least towards apex, base often procumbent, to 1 m or more long and 6 cm or more in diameter, but immensely variable in size and form, light green, very spiny. *Ribs* 8-10, formed from discrete, strongly angled tubercles, sometimes spiralled. *Areoles* orbicular, c. 4-5 mm in diameter, 1-3 cm apart. *Spines* dirty white, bright yellow, reddish or brownish, eventually blackish; radials 10-18, to 2 cm long, acicular, stiff, adpressed; centrals 4, 3-10(-13) cm long, cruciform, divergent-porrect, flattened and strongly angled, very stiff, sword-like. *Flowers* broadly funnelform, to 6.5 cm long and 7 cm in diameter, arising from just below stem apex to near its base. *Receptacle-tube* to 3.2 cm long, very thick, ovary occupying basal 1.5 cm, 1.5 cm in diameter, tube contracted above to 1.2 cm then flared to 2 cm in diameter at apex, exterior green, bearing large areoles with up to 10, to 9 mm long, often stout, yellowish-white spines and some long white wool. *Nectar chamber* 3 mm long, 2.5 mm diameter, almost filled by style base. *Perianth-segments* in c. 2 rows, cuneate-oblanceolate, to 3.5 cm long and 1.1 cm. wide, the innermost narrower, acuminate, pale purplish-lavender to pale pink, bright crimson in the throat. *Stamen filaments* to 1 cm long, bright red to purple; anthers oval, 1 mm long. *Style* to 2 cm long, 2.5 mm in diameter; stigmas 11-12, to 8 mm long, pale green to nearly white. *Ovary locule* nearly spherical, to 8 mm long, ovules very numerous. *Fruit* globular, 3 cm in diameter, spiny, red. *Seeds* broadly ovoid, c. 1 mm long, tuberculate.

DISTRIBUTION. NW Mexico: Baja California, from vicinity of San Borja to Cape region and adjacent islands; Sonoran Desert and arid subtropical zone, sea level to 1200 m altitude.

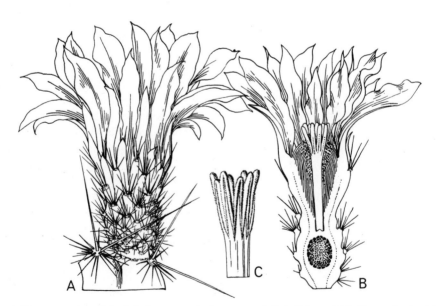

Echinocereus brandegeei. A, flower attached to stem, × 1; B, half-flower, × 1; C, top of style with stigmas, × 3 (ex Hort. D. Parker).

Echinocereus brandegeei (J. Coulter) Schumann, Gesamtb. Kakt. 290 (1897); Werderm. & Socnik, Meine Kakteen, 49 (fig.) (1938); G. Lindsay in F. Shreve & I.L. Wiggins, Veg. & Fl. Sonoran Des. 2: 999-1000 (1964) et in Cact. Suc. Mex. 12: 80-82, 87, figs. 34, 41 & 42 (1967); J. Coyle & N. Roberts, Field Guide Pl. Baja Calif. 132, with colour pl. (1975); G. Rowley in Ashingtonia 2: 148, with fig. (1976); W. Cullmann *et al.*, Kakteen, ed. 5, 153 (1984) (excellent colour pl.).

Cereus brandegeei J. Coulter ('brandegei') in Contrib. US. Nat. Herb. 3: 389 (1896). Type: Mexico, Baja California, between El Campo Alemand and San Gregorio, 1889, *T.S. Brandegee* (UC).

3. ECHINOCEREUS BARTHELOWANUS

The poorly known *Echinocereus barthelowanus* is endemic to one or perhaps two islands off the west coast of S Baja California, Mexico, and may be related to the wide-ranging *E. brandegeei*. It occurs within the floristic division known as the Magdalena Region, a seemingly uninteresting sandy plain where, however, a number of widespread Baja cactus species are supplemented by remarkably distinct and rare sister species. Examples of this phenomenon besides the *E. barthelowanus* and *E. brandegeei* species-pair are *Stenocereus eruca* (the famous 'Creeping Devil') and *S. gummosus*, *Lophocereus gatesii* and *L. schottii*, and *Mammillaria halei* and *M. poselgeri*.

Unlike its suggested ally, the ribs of *E. barthelowanus* are not conspicuously tuberculate, although its smaller stems are so densely spined that this is hard to confirm. It has far more central spines than the cruciform four that characterize the areoles of *E. brandegeei*, and these are not conspicuously angled. The close affinity of this pair is more obvious when they flower–this, however, being a very rarely observed event in the case of *E. barthelowanus*. In view of this, the author is particularly grateful to Mr Terry Hewitt of Holly Gate Nurseries Ltd (Sussex, UK) for allowing him to examine a colour transparency of a plant at the 'Reference Collection' flowering shortly after its importation from the wild (probably ex *Lau* 41). This photo indicates that the flowers of *E. barthelowanus* are of average size (i.e. c. 5-7 cm in diameter) and not minute (1-1.2 cm long) as described by Britton & Rose (1922) in their original description, which appears to have been copied by all subsequent authors. The bicoloured perianth-segments and pale-coloured stigmas also match those of *E. ferreirianus*.

DESCRIPTION. *Plant* caespitose, forming clumps of many stems to 80 cm in diameter. *Stems* eventually cylindric, erect, to 20(-30) cm long, 3.5-5 cm in diameter, obscured by dense spination. *Ribs* 8-10, somewhat tuberculate. *Areoles* large, 2-5 mm apart, with white felt at first. *Spines* brown, yellowish or grey, bright pink to red when young, black in age; radials up to 18, to 1 cm or more long, acicular; centrals to 9, to 7 cm long, porrect, stout, somewhat intergrading with radials. *Flowers* very like those of preceding species or slightly smaller. *Fruit* and seed not described.

DISTRIBUTION. NW Mexico: Baja California Sur (Pacific coast) on Isla Magdalena and (?) Isla Santa Margarita; Sonoran Desert (Magdalena region), at low elevations.

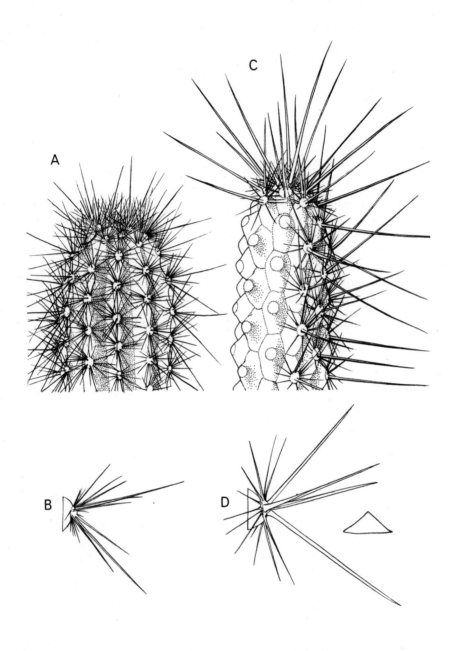

Echinocereus barthelowanus. A, stem, × 1; B, stem areole, × 1 (ex Hort. D. Parker). **E. brandegeei**. C, stem, × ⅔ (*Hunt* 8746); D, stem areole, × ⅔, cross section of central spine, × 8 (*N. P. Taylor* 52).

Echinocereus barthelowanus Britton & Rose, Cact. 3: 41 (1922); G. Lindsay in F. Shreve & I.L. Wiggins, Veg. & Fl. Sonoran Des. 2: 1000 (1964) et in Cact. Suc. Mex. 12: 79-80, 87, figs. 34 & 40 (1967); G.E. Cheetham in Nat. Cact. Succ. J. (GB) 30: 96, with fig. (1975). Type: Mexico, Baja California, Isla Magdalena, on the mesa nr Santa Maria Bay, 18 March 1911, *J.N. Rose* 16278 (US).

4. ECHINOCEREUS ENGELMANNII

The name of this fine species honours Dr George Engelmann (1809-1884), historically the most important figure in the study of North American cacti and founder, in 1848, of the genus *Echinocereus*. Engelmann, a German by birth, practised medicine at St. Louis, Missouri, indulging in botany during his spare time. His botanical work spanned an important period of exploration in the American southwest and adjacent Mexico, and led to the publication of some beautifully illustrated books on the newly discovered cacti, most notably the 'Cactaceae of the Boundary' (1859). His great talent was for detailed observation and sound interpretation of often incomplete or very limited plant material, and while he recognized the value of the herbarium, he was also a true gardener-botanist, who cultivated sterile field collected specimens at St. Louis until they flowered and fruited, to enable the completion of his plant descriptions. One of his greatest contributions was to draw attention to the importance of cactus seed morphology, the study of which has remained an essential aspect of systematic research within the Family.

Echinocereus engelmannii was discovered about 1849-50 by Dr C.C. Parry (1823-1890), an English-born American botanist and explorer. At the time he was employed by the United States authorities on the Mexican Boundary Survey and came upon this conspicuous plant in the deserts of southern California. The stems of *E. engelmannii* are usually erect, often quite large, and fiercely spiny. The spectacular magenta flowers are followed by edible, strawberry-flavoured fruits, rich in sugar and much prized by certain Indian tribes, which inhabit parts of the extensive range of the species.

Like its closest ally, the tuberculate-stemmed *E. brandegeei*, this species is extremely variable, as the list of varieties elaborated below clearly shows. How useful this system of infraspecific taxa really is remains uncertain, since the variation within var. *engelmannii* itself in Baja California is quite considerable and raises the question of how many more varieties need be recognized for the sake of consistency. The treatment followed here is that of Benson (1982), who has studied this species in considerable detail where it occurs in the United States. There it is said (*fide* Benson) to intergrade with certain members of the *E. fendleri* complex and, indeed, the superficial similarity between the two appears to be quite strong. However, the writer believes that although both are clearly referable to the same section (*Erecti* (Schumann) H. Bravo-H.) on floral and habit details, their resemblance is due to recent evolutionary convergence, as a study of all the taxa involved seems to confirm.

The only problem encountered with the cultivation of *E. engelmannii* is persuading it to flower in relatively dull climates. It is a desert species, more or less exposed to day-long sunshine in the wild, and therefore needs all available light in more temperate situations. Care must be taken, however, in spring when the sudden appearance of the sun after dull winter weather can cause scorching in poorly ventilated glass-houses. Also, it should not be forgotten that this is a large-growing plant which will probably not flower until the stems have reached at least 12-15 cm in length. It will withstand winter cold if kept in a bright, dry situation, water being withheld from the beginning of autumn. Propagation is generally by means of field-collected seed.

DESCRIPTION. *Stems* branching near base 3-60 in number, in open or compact clumps to 90 cm in diameter, mostly erect, 5-60 cm long, 3.8-8.7 cm in diameter, cylindric or tapering slightly towards apex, green, very spiny. *Ribs* c. 10-13, not obviously tuberculate. *Areoles* circular, c. 6mm in diameter, 2-3 cm apart, woolly only in the first year. *Spines* highly variable in size and colour; radials 6-14, ± adpressed, lowermost longest, to 2 cm, uppermost often minute; centrals (2-)4-7, angular, usually much stouter, the lowermost 4 longest, in some forms to over 7 cm long, straight or curved to twisted, rigid or flexible, gradually tapering to a fine, sharp point, divergent-porrect. *Flowers* shortly funnelform, to 9 cm long and in diameter, mostly arising from upper half of stem and sometimes near apex. *Receptacle-tube* only 2.5-3 cm long, the globose ovary occupying more than half, in ovary region c. 1.8 cm in diameter, contracting above to 1.5 cm before re-expanding to 2.6 cm at apex, walls very thick, green, bearing large areoles with 12-17, to 1.6 cm long, stout, whitish spines, uppermost areoles only 3-4-spined, but spines to 2.3 cm long. *Nectar chamber* very broad, 2 mm long, 5-6 mm wide, not filled by base of style. *Perianth-segments* widely separated at base; outer segments 1-3.5 cm long, grading from linear to oblanceolate, magenta to purple with green margins; inner segments in 1-2 rows, to 5 cm long and 2.5 cm wide, cuneate-oblanceolate, purplish-red to magenta or lavender, very fleshy near the deep crimson base, apex acuminate to rounded and mucronulate, margins finely serrate. *Stamen filaments* 5-12 mm long, pink to purplish; anthers oblong, 1-1.3 mm long, yellow. *Style* very stout, 19-30 mm long, to 3-4 mm in diameter, pinkish; *stigmas* 8-18, 3-5 mm long, very stout, deep green. *Ovary locule* nearly spherical, c. 9 mm long at anthesis. *Fruit* to 3 cm long and 2.5 cm in diameter, red, juicy and edible when ripe, areoles deciduous. *Seeds* broadly ovoid to 1.5 mm long, tuberculate, black.

DISTRIBUTION. NW Mexico, in N & E Baja California (N of 26°N) and NW Sonora (Guaymas northwards); SW U.S.A., in S & E California, S & E Nevada, W & S Utah and Arizona (except in the E); Sonoran & Mojavean Deserts, montane forest, chaparral, Great Plains grassland and Juniper-Pinyon woodland; near sea-level to 2400 m altitude.

Echinocereus engelmannii (Parry ex Engelm.) Lemaire, Cactées, 56 (1868); G. Lindsay in F. Shreve & I.L. Wiggins, Veg. & Fl. Sonoran Des. 2: 1000-1001 (1964) and in Cact. Suc. Mex. 12: 73 (map), 76-78, fig. 39 (1967); L. Benson, Cacti US & Can. 640-649, 943-944, 642 (map), figs. 680-687, colour pl. 98-103 (1982).

Cereus engelmannii Parry ex Engelm. in Amer. Journ. Sci. ser. 2, 14: 328 (1852). Type: U.S.A., California, 'Mountains about San Felipe, on the eastern declivity of the Cordilleras', 1849/1850, *Parry* (not found). Neotype (Benson, tom. cit.): U.S.A., 'Hill 1 mile W of Scissors Crossing, San Felipe Valley, below the Laguna Mts, San Diego Co., California, 2400 feet, granite soil', *Lyman Benson* 16386 (POM 311501/2).

The treatment of the varieties which follows is based on Benson (tom. cit.), wherein references and illustrations additional to those cited below can be found.

4a. var. **engelmannii** (PLATE 1 PRO PARTE)

Stems 5-15, to 20(-25) cm long, 5 cm in diameter. *Spines* yellow, pink or grey; centrals stout, rigid, almost straight, lowermost equalled by some of the others, paler. *Flowers* magenta.

DISTRIBUTION. Mexico, Baja California (S to 26°N, E Coast) and NW Sonora (S to Guaymas); U.S.A., S & E California, S Nevada and S & W Arizona (rare); near sea-level to 1600 m altitude.

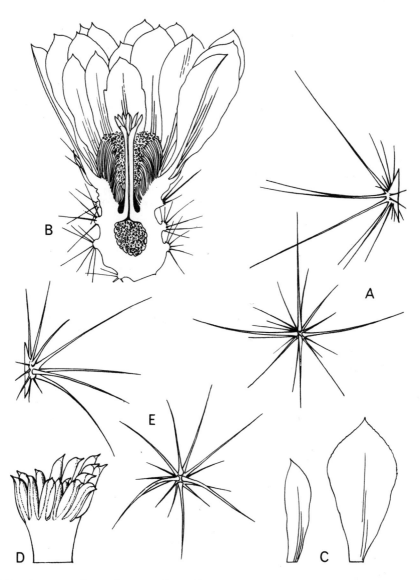

Echinocereus engelmannii var. **engelmannii**. A, stem areole, two views, × 1; B, half-flower, × 1; C, outer (left) and inner (right) perianth-segments, × 1; D, top of style with stigmas, × 3 (ex Hort. G. E. Cheetham). **E. maritimus** var. **maritimus**. E, stem areole, two views, × 1 (*N. P. Taylor* 110).

4b. var. **acicularis** L. Benson, Cacti of Arizona, ed. 3, 22, 138-139, fig. 3.19 (1969). Type: Arizona, Maricopa Co., crossing of New River, S side of Black Canyon Refuge, 1300 feet, 20 April 1966, *Lyman Benson* 16616 (POM 311313).

Stems 5-15, rarely (Palm Canyon, Yuma Co., Ariz.) aggregated in clumps of 50, 3.8-5 cm in diameter. *Central spines* weak, flexible, lowermost longest, not paler. Otherwise like var. *engelmannii*.

DISTRIBUTION. Mexico, NE Baja California and NW Sonora; U.S.A., SE California (E Riverside Co.) and S & W Arizona; 300-900 m altitude.

4c. var. **munzii** (Parish) Pierce & Fosberg in Bull. S. Calif. Acad. Sci. 32: 123 (1933). *Cereus munzii* Parish in ibid. 25: 48 (1926). Type: California, '2 miles below Kenworthy, Thomas Valley, Riverside County, alt. 1400 m, 21 May 1922', *Munz & Johnston* 5570 (UC).

Stems 5-60, aggregated into mounds or clumps. *Central spines* somewhat flexible, curving and twisting, lowermost twice length of others. Otherwise like var. *engelmannii*.

DISTRIBUTION. Mexico, Baja California (E slopes of Sierra Juarez); U.S.A., S California (San Bernardino, San Jacinto & Laguna Mts.); pine woods and chaparral, 1950-2400 m altitude.

4d. var. **nicholii** L. Benson in Proc. Calif. Acad. Sci. ser. 4, 25: 258, t. 25 (1944). Type: Arizona, Pima Co., Silver Bell Mts, 28 March 1941, *L. Benson* 10720 (ARIZ 24989).

Stems mostly 20-30, to 60 cm long and 7.5 cm in diameter. *Spines* clear yellow (to nearly white); centrals stout, rigid and straight, lowermost longest. *Flowers* lavender, paler than in the other varieties.

DISTRIBUTION. Mexico, NW Sonora; U.S.A., central S Arizona; Sonoran Desert at 300-900 m altitude.

4e. var. **armatus** L. Benson in Cact. Succ. J. (US) 41: 33 (1969). Type: U.S.A., California, San Bernardino Co., E of Victorville, Dead Man Point, 3000 feet, 1 April 1951, *L & R.L. Benson* 14767 (POM 284927).

Stems 5-25, to 20(-30) cm long, c. 5 cm in diameter. *Central spines* stout, rigid and curving or twisting, lowermost equalled by some of the others. *Flowers* reddish-purple, large.

DISTRIBUTION. California in Inyo Co. (Argus Mts) & San Bernardino Co. (E of Victorville), S Nevada in Nye Co. (S of Ribbon Cliffs & NW of Pahute Mesa); Mojavean Desert at c. 900 m altitude.

4f. var. **chrysocentrus** (Engelm. & Bigelow) Ruempler in Foerster, Handb. Cacteenk. ed. 2, 806 (1885). *Cereus engelmannii* var. *chrysocentrus* Engelm. & Bigelow in Engelm., Syn. Cact. US. 27 (1856) and Descr. Cact. 35, t. 5, figs. 8-10 (1856). Lectotype (Benson, tom. cit.): U.S.A., Arizona, 'Bill Williams [River]', 13 Feb. 1854, *J.M. Bigelow* (MO).

Stems 3-10, to 20(-32.5) cm long and 6.2 cm in diameter. *Spines* red to yellow or reddish-brown; centrals rigid, straight or slightly curving-twisting, the lowermost longest, white or pale grey. *Flowers* purplish to magenta, large.

DISTRIBUTION. S & SE California, S & E Nevada, N & W Arizona and W Utah; mostly in Mojavean Desert at 900-1500 (-2160) m altitude.

4g. var. **howei** L. Benson in Cact. Succ. J. (US) 46: 80 (1974). Type: U.S.A., California, San Bernardino Co., E of Goffs, *D.F. Howe* 4570 (POM 317886).

Stems c. 45 cm long and 8.7 cm in diameter. *Spines* all straw-yellow; centrals very stout, rigid and straight. *Flowers* purplish-lavender, large.

DISTRIBUTION. California, near the southern tip of Nevada; Mojavean Desert at c. 340 m altitude.

4h. var. **variegatus** (Engelm. & Bigelow) Ruempler in Foerster, Handb. Cacteenk. ed. 2, 806 (1885).
Cereus engelmannii var. *variegatus* Engelm. & Bigelow in Engelm., Syn. Cact. US. 27 (1856); Descr. Cact. 35, t. 5, figs. 4-7 (1856). Lectotype (Benson, tom. cit.): Arizona, 'Head of Bill Williams Fork', 1 Feb. 1854, *J.M. Bigelow* (MO).
Stems 3-6, to 15 cm long and 5 cm in diameter. *Radial spines* nearly white; centrals rigid, nearly straight, dark red to almost black, lowermost longest, white or pale grey. *Flowers* purplish to magenta, rather dark, small.
DISTRIBUTION. NW Arizona and SE Utah; 1150-1710 m altitude.

4i. var. **purpureus** L. Benson in Cact. Succ. J. (US) 41: 126 (1969). Type: Utah, Washington Co., N of St. George, 2900 feet, 5 May 1949, *L. Benson* 13637 (POM 285578).
Stems 4-10, to 20 cm long, c. 5 cm in diameter. *Spines* dark purplish-red; centrals rigid, straight to slightly curving, slender, lowermost longest. *Flowers* purple, very dark.
DISTRIBUTION. SW Utah (near St. George); Mojavean Desert at 860 m altitude.

5. ECHINOCEREUS MARITIMUS

The yellow flowers of *Echinocereus maritimus* immediately set it apart from its Baja California allies and have no doubt contributed to the view expressed by Lindsay (1967), that its relationships with other members of the genus are obscure. However, this is not the case, and flower colour by itself is not a character of much importance in *Echinocereus*, although the deepening of colour in the perianth throat of *E. maritimus* is significant in that it is matched in the flowers of most species here referred to section *Erecti*, where this species clearly belongs. Its closest relative is probably *E. engelmannii*, which it replaces along the coastal strip of NW Baja California. In common with other members of the relatively unspecialized E. ENGELMANNII GROUP the flower buds do not burst through the stem epidermis but develop right at the areoles, and the central and large upper spines are obviously flattened and angled, not terete. In its compact growth habit and small, more economical flowers it is the most specialized member of the group.

The typical form, which is itself very variable, makes broad but low mounds of hundreds of closely packed stems, especially when growing in littoral sand flats. Its habitat near the coast is probably less drought-stricken than that of its inland and southern allies, and may explain its habit of flowering intermittently over long periods. Less well known is a giant form, here treated as var. *hancockii* (cf. Lindsay, loc. cit.), from near the southern limits of the species' range on the coast southwest of the Sierra Vizcaíno. It forms clumps of relatively few large stems and is more fiercely armed.

In cultivation *E. maritimus* grows easily and needs plenty of room to branch and spread. It does well planted out in a greenhouse bed or when grown in a wide pan rather than a large pot. It may need protection from excessive winter cold as it comes from a milder seaside environment. Flower production is unpredictable, both as to timing and as to the size of plant required before they can be expected. Vegetative propagation with such a caespitose plant is simple, though it may also be raised from seed without difficulty.

DESCRIPTION. *Plant* caespitose, branching to form groups or mounds to 40 cm high and 1-2 m or more in diameter composed of 300 or more heads. *Stems* to 5-7 cm in diameter, 5-30 cm long, light to dark green. *Ribs* 8-10, acute, to 1 cm high. *Areoles* circular, at least 4 mm in diameter, 1-1.5 cm or more apart, retaining their wool for some time. *Spines* dirty yellow to grey, bright red at first; radials (lower) spines 7-10, to 1.5(-2.5) cm long; central and upper spines 7-10, to 3-6 cm long, strongly flattened and angled, porrect to ascending. *Flowers* funnelform, to 6 cm long and opening nearly as wide when allowed by the surrounding spines, arising below stem apex from very woolly areoles; buds brownish, not bursting through the stem epidermis. *Receptacle-tube* to 3 cm long, quite slender, ovary occupying most of basal half, to 1.2 cm in diameter, tube flared above ovary to 2 cm in diameter at apex, exterior green, bearing few woolly areoles with small inconspicuous spines. *Nectar chamber* not described. *Perianth-segments* obovate-oblanceolate, to 3 cm long and 8(-10) mm wide, rounded to acuminate and somewhat lacerate at apex, outer segments abaxially brown to reddish, inner bright yellow deepening in the throat, fading to salmon in age. *Stamen filaments* short, pale green; anthers pale yellow. *Stigmas* 6-8, slender, light green. *Fruit* globular, c. 3 cm in diameter, green to red, spiny, very juicy, many-seeded. *Seeds* ovoid, to 1.25 mm long, tuberculate, dark brown to black.

DISTRIBUTION. NW Mexico: W coast of Baja California and adjacent islands, from nr Ensenada to S of Bahia San Hipolito; littoral sand dunes and on rocks a few kilometers inland, mostly at low elevations.

Echinocereus maritimus (M.E. Jones) Schumann, Gesamtb. Kakt. 273-274 (1897); Britton & Rose, Cact. 3: 15, fig. 14, t. 2.5 (1922); Backeb., Die Cact. 4: 2056-2058, Abb. 1952 (1960); E. & B. Lamb., Ill. Ref. Cact. Succ. 4: t. 207 (1966); G. Lindsay in Cact. Suc. Mex. 12: 84, 87-88, figs. 34 & 44 (1967); J. Coyle & N. Roberts, Field Guide Pl. Baja, 134, with fig. (1975).

Cereus maritimus M.E. Jones in Amer. Nat. 17: 973 (1883). Type: Mexico, Baja California
  Norte, Ensenada, April, 1882, *M.E. Jones* (POM).

5a. var. **maritimus**
  Stems 3-5 cm in diameter, forming compact mounds of c. 10-300 branches. *Spines* 14-17 per areole, to c. 4 cm long.
  DISTRIBUTION. As for species.

5b. var. **hancockii** (E. Dawson) N.P. Taylor, stat.nov.
E. hancockii E. Dawson in Desert. Pl. Life 21: 89, 91, figs. 2-4 (1949). Type: Baja California
  Sur, SW coast, N side of Bahia San Hipolito, 4 April 1949, *E.Y. Dawson* 6443 (LAM).
  Stems 5.5-7 cm in diameter, in loose or compact clumps of 10-30 branches. *Spines* 17-20 per areole, to 6 cm long.
  DISTRIBUTION. Known only from the type locality, on nearly bare hills of dark, saline shale to 75 m altitude. However, giant forms, which may be referable here, are also recorded from Isla Cedros.

6. ECHINOCEREUS FERREIRIANUS

This species, described in 1953 from central E Baja California, is clearly allied to the next species dealt with here, *E. fendleri*. They share many vegetative features in common, but *E. ferreirianus* has more numerous central spines and appears to differ in floral morphology. In particular, its receptacular areoles bear much finer, bristly spines than in *E. fendleri*, and its stigma-lobes are mostly whitish or very pale green, rather than deep green. It is not well-known in cultivation at present, but deserves to be in view of its very beautiful, bicoloured, pink and orange-red flowers.

Unlike many Mexican species of cacti, *E. ferreirianus* has been studied botanically in some detail, both in the field and in cultivation, by Reid Moran (1972). Little can be added to his thorough and well illustrated account, which should be consulted by anyone especially interested in this species. However, since his study was published a new and remarkable discovery in Baja California has required that its circumscription be broadened here. This is to accommodate the very interesting *E. lindsayi* Meyran, described in 1975.

Despite its almost globose, solitary stem and much stronger spines, *E. lindsayi* is not a distinct species, its spination and flowers agreeing with *E. ferreirianus* in most respects. The chief differences apart from its habit concern the higher central spine count and the rather short, darker green stigmas of the flower. It also flowers in spring, before *E. ferreirianus*, which usually blooms in late summer, but similar phenological variations are known between varieties of other Baja cactus species (e.g. *Ferocactus gracilis*) and should not be over-emphasized. The conspicuous difference in the habit of *E. lindsayi*, namely the short, solitary stem, as opposed to the cylindric, branching form of *E. ferreirianus*, is completely paralleled in the allied *E. fendleri* complex. It is perhaps indicative of the difference between well-marked varieties than distinct species. Furthermore, as shown by Moran, *E. ferreirianus* is quite variable, and some forms have much stouter spines approaching, though not equalling, those of *E. lindsayi*. The habitat of *E. lindsayi* is a little to the north of the range of *E. ferreirianus*, but both are commonly associated with rocks of volcanic origin, which are of frequent occurrence in the central third of Baja California.

The almost *Ferocactus*-like *Echinocereus ferreirianus* var. *lindsayi* is one of those extraordinary plants that every enthusiast wants to own. It is now gradually becoming available to connoisseurs through intensive propagation by seed and grafting. However, this supply of material came too late to save the original and only wild population, discovered in the spring of 1975. Publication of its whereabouts (Lindsay, 1976) permitted American collectors to drive down the Baja peninsula and decimate the plant in its roadside habitat, to the extent that it has been claimed as virtually extinct in the wild. Although it is probably not extinct, further populations are yet to be reported, but if they are, one sincerely hopes that its placement on Appendix 1 of the Convention on International Trade in Endangered Species (CITES) will ensure its protection from ruthless collectors. Such protection is more likely to be successful if artificial propagation can be achieved on a sufficient scale to meet horticultural demand.

DESCRIPTION. *Stem* solitary, or branched near base and sometimes forming clumps to 50 cm in diameter, to 30(-40) cm high, 4-10 cm in diameter, globose to cylindric, green, grey-green, bluish or purplish, very spiny. *Ribs* (9-)11-14, 1-2.5 cm high, somewhat tuberculate. *Areoles* circular to oval, 4-12 mm long, 3-10 mm wide, 0.7-3 cm apart, with white or yellowish wool at first. *Radial spines* 8-14, 8-45 mm long, whitish or darker tipped; centrals 4-7, 1.5-10 cm long, 0.5-2.5 mm thick, perfectly terete, variously directed, curved or straight, red at first then brown to black, pale at base, finally grey. *Flowers* funnelform, 6-10 cm long, 4-9.5 cm in diameter, arising just below stem apex or lower. *Receptacle-tube* 2.5-5 cm long, ovary occupying basal half or more, 1.2-2 cm in diameter, tube expanded above to 2.5 cm in diameter at apex, exterior green below, bronze to purplish above, bearing circular, woolly areoles, 1-3 mm in diameter, with 5-15, to 3.5 cm long, white to dark, bristle-like spines. *Nectar chamber* not described. *Perianth-segments* in 2 rows, the largest cuneate-oblanceolate, to 5 cm long and 1.6 cm wide, acute to obtuse or rounded and apiculate at the somewhat lacerate apex, outer segments with purplish to brown midribs, inner pale to deep or purplish-pink, contrasted darker orange to red in the throat. *Stamen filaments* 8-20 mm long, often purplish near base, paler above. *Style* 1.8-3.3 cm long, to 2 mm in diameter; stigmas 8-12, 5-14 mm long, whitish or pale to deep green. *Fruit* ± globose, to 4 cm long, 2-3.5 cm thick, green to purplish, spiny, splitting down one side to expose sweet white pulp. *Seeds* ovoid, 1.2-1.35 mm long, tuberculate, black.

DISTRIBUTION. NW Mexico: Central & E Baja California between c.27° 30' N – 29° 30' N; Sonoran Desert from near sea-level to 1850 m altitude.

Echinocereus ferreirianus H. Gates in Saguaroland Bull. 7: 8-11, with figs. (1953); G. Lindsay in Cact. Suc. Mex. 12: 78-79, 87, figs. 34, 38 & 47 (1967); Moran in Cact. Succ. J. (US) 44: 162-167, figs. 1-6 (1972); Supthut in Kakt. and. Sukk. 29: 117, with fig. (1978). Type: Mexico, Baja California Norte, Isla Piojo in the Isla Smith group, Bahia de los Angeles, 1934, *H.E. Gates* (DS).

6a. var. **ferreirianus**

Stems branched, to 30(-40) cm high and 8 cm in diameter. *Central spines* mostly 4. *Flowers* (in late summer) with pale green to whitish stigmas 7-14 mm long.

DISTRIBUTION. Central E Baja California (vicinity of Bahia de los Angeles, including islands in the bay, and Sierra San Borja to Volcan Las Tres Virgenes); near sea-level to 1850 m altitude.

6b. var. **lindsayi** (Meyran) N.P. Taylor, stat. nov.

Echinocereus lindsayi Meyran in Cact. Suc. Mex. 20: 80-81, figs. 40-42, 52 (1975); G. Lindsay in Cact. Succ. J. (US) 48: 51, fig. 14 (1976); K.W. Beisel in Kakt. and. Sukk. 34: 223 (1983) (superb colour pl.). Type: Baja California Norte, between Cataviña and Laguna Chapala, 8 May 1975, *Meyran et al.* in *H. Sanchez-Mejorada* 2424 (MEXU).

Stem solitary, to 13 cm high and 10 cm in diameter (eventually much taller in cultivation). *Central spines* 4-7. *Flowers* (in spring) with deep green stigmas c. 5mm long.

DISTRIBUTION. At present known only from the type locality (where it is thought to be extinct due to unscrupulous collecting).

7. ECHINOCEREUS FENDLERI

Like *Echinocereus engelmannii*, the name *E. fendleri* represents a wide-ranging and highly variable complex, here divided into seven rather diverse varieties. These form a series the extremes of which, e.g. var. *boyce-thompsonii* and var. *fendleri*, could easily be taken for quite distinct species but are, in fact, clearly interconnected by morphologically and ecologically intermediate taxa.

The variety including the type of the species, var. *fendleri*, was discovered by a young German collector, Mr A. Fendler, at Santa Fe, New Mexico in 1846. It forms dwarf, scarcely branched, few-spined stems and is found at high altitudes in open woodland or grassland, particularly in the eastern and northern portions of the species' range. Further west and at lower altitudes this 'alpine' plant is replaced by the larger-growing semi-desert varieties, var. *fasciculatus* and var. *boyce-thompsonii*, with conspicuous clusters of cylindric, densely spiny stems somewhat resembling those of the sympatric *E. engelmannii* (but with terete, not angular, central spines).

The first-named of these desert varieties has a complicated nomenclatural history. At the rank of variety it first became known as *E. rectispinus* var. *robustus* Peebles (1938). In 1944 Lyman Benson referred both *E. rectispinus* and its variety to *E. fendleri*, making the combination *E. fendleri* var. *robustus* (Peebles) L. Benson for the plant considered here. However, this combination had already been used for a different member of the *E. fendleri* complex (*E. fendleri* var. *robustus* Fobe 1911) and cannot be legitimately employed again for Peebles' taxon. Then, in 1969, Benson published the results of an investigation into the identity of *Mammillaria fasciculata* Engelm. (1848) and put forward a convincing argument that this name, hitherto employed for a true *Mammillaria* species (*M. thornberi* Orcutt 1902), should be applied to Peebles' *Echinocereus rectispinus* variety instead. Fortunately, it turns out that Engelmann's name was provisional* and, therefore, not validly published in 1848. Otherwise the well-known *Echinocereus fendleri*, based on *Cereus fendleri* Engelm. (1849), would be lost in the synonymy of *E. fasciculatus* (Engelm.) L. Benson, unless an artifical classification retaining them both as separate species is adopted, as in Benson (1969). In fact Engelmann's *Mammillaria fasciculata* was not validly published until 1895, but it is still the oldest name for Peebles' taxon, and is also the correct epithet to use at varietal rank, although its confused history makes this unavoidable action highly undesirable.

Echinocereus fendleri var. *fasciculatus* is of particular systematic interest as the closest relative of *E. ferreirianus* H. Gates, a vicariant of *E. fendleri* from across the Gulf of California in central E Baja California. Both inhabit the Sonoran Desert region, but var. *fasciculatus*, which ranges east of the Gulf, from central Sonora northwards, has fewer central spines (1-3 vs. 4-7) and flowers in spring (*E. ferreirianus* in late summer). Variety *fasciculatus* could also be considered as the central taxon within the *E. fendleri* complex. In one direction it is linked to the densely-spined, low altitude var. *boyce-thompsonii*, the short-spined var. *bonkerae* and the yellow-spined, high altitude var. *ledingii*, all of which have stems with more ribs; and in another to the smaller-growing, fewer-ribbed var. *rectispinus* and its highly specialized allies, var. *fendleri* and var. *kuenzleri*.

Of these, var. *bonkerae* is worthy of mention for its unusually short armament, which almost gives it the aspect of one of the finely-spined, so-called 'pectinate echinocerei'. Indeed, the vague similarity of its stems to *E. pectinatus* may not be

*See appended Nomenclatural Note (p.51)

entirely superficial, for on floral morphology both belong in section *Erecti*, the 'pectinate echinocerei' being an arbitrarily defined grade of no systematic significance.

Previous authors have maintained *E. fendleri* var. *ledingii* as a distinct species, *E. ledingii* Peebles (1936). At first sight it certainly appears to differ, especially in its bright yellow spines, with the largest central in each areole down-curved from near the base, but it agrees closely with var. *fasciculatus* in other respects. It is found at higher elevations, however, preferring chaparral and open oak woodlands in SE Arizona.

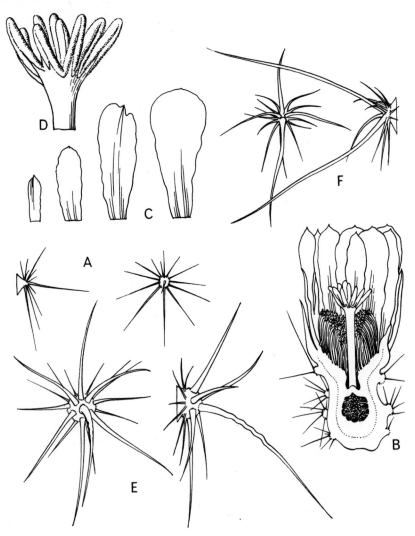

Echinocereus fendleri var. **fasciculatus**. A, stem areole, two views, × 1⅓; B, half-flower, × 1; C, outer (left) to inner (right) perianth segments, × 1; D, top of style with stigmas, × 3 (ex Hort. G. E. Cheetham). **E. ferreirianus** var. **lindsayi**. E, stem areole, × 1 *(G. Lindsay s.n.)*. **E.f.** var. **ferreirianus**. F, stem areole, × 1 *(N.P. Taylor 49)*.

Plate 1

Echinocereus fendleri var. *fasciculatus* (top) *E. engelmannii* var. *engelmannii* (bottom)

Plate 2

Echinocereus pectinatus var. *dasyacanthus* (upper)   *E. rigidissimus* var. *rubispinus* (lower)

Echinocereus fendleri var. *rectispinus* is common in living collections and the popular literature, where it was, and often still is, mistaken for typical *E. fendleri*. It intergrades with var. *fasciculatus*, but can generally be distinguished by its solitary, perpendicular central spines, maximum of only nine radial spines, and shorter stems with 9-10 ribs. Typical var. *fendleri* has even shorter ovoid stems and an upward-curving central spine. Both its usual magenta-flowered and less common white- or pale pink-flowered forms are in cultivation. Albino forms of var. *rectispinus* and var. *fasciculatus* are also known, and Backeberg (1960) has a photograph of one of these labelled as var. *albiflorus* (Weingart) Backeb. However, *E. albiflorus* Weingart (1933) correctly belongs in the synonymy of var. *fendleri*, as the original illustration of its type clearly indicates.

Closely related to var. *fendleri*, and perhaps not worthy of separate status, is var. *kuenzleri*, which provisionally includes *E. hempelii* Fobe. The latter was first described and illustrated in 1897, but has only recently been located in the field, in the Mexican state of Chihuahua (Schreier, 1982). The elongate, dark green stems of var. *kuenzleri* are the least armed in the *E. fendleri* complex, each areole having only 2-6 stout spines, the central normally absent. This variety has the capacity for producing remarkably large flowers for its size – up to 11 cm in length and diameter, the maximum for the species – making it one of the most sought-after echinocerei in cultivation. The final systematic position of var. *kuenzleri*, the type of which is from New Mexico, must await a better understanding of the complex in the field further south, in W Texas and Chihuahua. The degree of relationship between var. *fendleri*, var. *kuenzleri*, and the latter's suggested synonym, *E. hempelii*, unfortunately cannot be resolved here.

In general *E. fendleri* seems easy to grow, and to propagate, from either seeds or cuttings. The spinier varieties, from the Sonoran Desert and its margins, should receive plenty of sunlight, and are unlikely to fully develop their spines or flower freely without it.

DESCRIPTION. *Stem* solitary or with up to 20 or more branches, 7.5-50 cm long, 3.8-8 cm in diameter, ovoid to cylindric, pale yellowish- to dark green, sometimes dull reddish, purplish or brownish in winter. *Ribs* 8-18(-22), strongly to weakly tuberculate. *Areoles* circular, c 4.5 mm in diameter, 1-2.5 cm apart, wool soon disappearing. *Spines* not or almost obscuring stem, variously coloured; radials (2-)5-13, to 9-20 mm long, straight or one curved; centrals 0-3(-5), very short or to 7.5(-10) cm long, terete, variously directed, straight or curved, slender or stout. *Flowers* broadly funnel-shaped, (5-)6-11 cm long and in diameter, borne on upper half of stem, sometimes from near apex. *Receptacle-tube* 2.5-4 cm long, abruptly expanding to 2.5 cm wide at apex, to 1.5 cm wide in ovary region, hardly contracted above ovary which occupies basal 1.5 cm, tube exterior bearing areoles with up to 10 stout whitish spines, to 1-2 cm long. *Nectar chamber* c 2 mm long and 3 mm in diameter, almost filled by base of style. *Perianth-segments* in c 2 rows, loose and widely separated at base; outer segments oblong-lanceolate, 1-3 cm long, rather thick and fleshy, dark brownish-crimson or with a green midrib, entire; inner segments elliptic-oblanceolate, cuneate, 3-5 cm long, to 1.5 cm wide, pointed to nearly rounded at apex, slightly lacerate to almost entire, shades of magenta to pure white, deep crimson in the throat, sometimes green at the very base. *Stamen filaments* 9-11(-16) mm long, green to pinkish; anthers yellow, oblong, to 1.5 mm long. *Style* 1.6-2.5 cm long, c 2.5 mm in diameter; stigmas 8-15, 3-7 mm long, deep green. *Ovary locule* almost spherical, c 7 mm in diameter at anthesis, ovules very numerous. *Fruit* ± globose, to 3 cm long, green turning reddish, fleshy and juicy, edible. *Seeds* 1-1.5 mm long, broadly ovoid, tuberculate black (see Frank, loc.cit.).

DISTRIBUTION. NW Mexico, in Sonora and N Chihuahua; SW U.S.A., in Arizona, S Colorado, New Mexico and W Texas; semi-desert, grasslands and woodlands, 30-2400m altitude.

Echinocereus fendleri (Engelm.) Ruempler in Foerster, Handb. Cacteenk. ed. 2, 801 (1885); L. Benson, Cacti of Arizona, ed. 3, 129-131 (1969) and Cacti US & Can. 625-627, 626 (map), 942, figs. 665-666 (1982); G.R.W. Frank in Kakt. and. Sukk. 35: 150, Abb. 14-31(1984).

Cereus fendleri Engelm. in Mem. Amer. Acad. ser. 2, 4: 51 (1849). Type (*fide* Benson, 1982): U.S.A., New Mexico, Santa Fe, 1846, *A. Fendler* 3 (MO).

Echinocereus albiflorus Weingart in Kakteenk. 1933: 156-157 (1933).

7a. var. **fasciculatus** (Engelm. ex B.D. Jackson) N.P. Taylor in Kew Mag. 2: 252 (1985).(PLATE 1, PRO PARTE)

Mammillaria fasciculata Engelm. ex B.D. Jackson, Ind. Kew. 2: 157 (1895); Engelm. in Emory, Notes Milit. Reconn., App. 2, 156, fig. 2 (1848), nom. inval. (Art. 34.1(b)). Type: Emory, loc. cit. fig. 2 (1848).

Echinocereus fasciculatus (Engelm. ex B.D. Jackson) L. Benson, tom. cit., 21, 132, figs. 3.9-3.11 (1969) et tom. cit., 631-633, 942, figs. 671 & 672, colour pl. 93 (1982).

E. rectispinus var. *robustus* Peebles in Amer. J. Bot. 25: 675 (1938).

E. fendleri var. *robustus* (Peebles) L. Benson in Proc. Calif. Acad. Sci. ser.4, 25: 259 (1944), non Fobe in Monatsschr. Kakteenk. 21: 55 (1911) (see Benson, 1982: 942, *sub* var. *fendleri*).

E. abbeae S.H. Parsons in Desert Pl. Life 9: 6, with figs. (1937). Type: Mexico, Sonora, District of Hermosillo, 28°49'N, 111°51'W, 30m altitude, 2 March 1932, *S.H. Parsons* (preserved ?).

Stems 5-20, 17.5-45 cm long. *Ribs* 8-13. *Spines* 10-15; centrals 1-3, the lowermost to 7.5 cm, porrect to slightly deflexed, dark-coloured.

DISTRIBUTION. W & S Arizona and SW New Mexico; Mexico in N & cent. Sonora (to SW of Hermosillo); Sonoran Desert and desert grassland, 30-1050 (-1500)m altitude.

Intergrades with var. *rectispinus*.

7b. var. **boyce-thompsonii** (Orcutt) L. Benson in Proc. Calif. Acad. Sci. ser. 4, 25: 260 (1944); E. & B. Lamb, Colourful Cacti, t.98 (1974).

E. boyce-thompsonii Orcutt, Cactography, 4 (1926). Type: apparently not preserved. Neotype (Benson, 1969: 21): Arizona, c 5 miles W of Boyce-Thompson Arboretum, 2400 feet, 17 Oct. 1950, *L. Benson* 14621 (POM 278845).

E. fasciculatus var. *boyce-thompsonii* (Orcutt) L. Benson, tom. cit., 21, figs. 3.11 & 3.12 (1969).

Stems 3-12, to 25 cm long. *Ribs* (12-) 14-18(-22). *Spines* 13-17; centrals 3, the lowermost to 5(-10) cm long, strongly deflexed, very slender, mostly light-coloured (often yellowish).

DISTRIBUTION. Central Arizona; Sonoran Desert, (300-)600-900m altitude.

7c. var. **bonkerae** (Thornber & Bonker) L. Benson, loc. cit. (1944); E. & B. Lamb, tom. cit., tt. 123 & 124 (1974).

E. bonkerae Thornber & Bonker, Fantastic Clan, 71-73, 85, with pl. (1932). Type: 'nearing the Pinal Mountains in southeastern Arizona' [near Oracle ?] (living plants only). Neotype (Benson, 1969, as 'lectotype'): one of the original living plants, preserved in 1940 by Benson (ARIZ 156240).

E. fasciculatus var. *bonkerae* (Thornber & Bonker) L. Benson, tom. cit., 22, fig. 3.13 (1969). *Stems* 5-35, to 20 cm long. *Ribs* (11-)13-16. *Spines* 12-15; central(s) 1(-3), <1 cm long, porrect.

DISTRIBUTION. Central & SE Arizona; desert grassland, 900-1500 (-1800)m altitude.

7d. var. **ledingii** (Peebles) N.P. Taylor in Kew Mag. 2: 253 (1985).
Echinocereus ledingii Peebles in Cact. Succ. J. (US) 8: 35, with figs. (1936); L. Benson, tom. cit., 136, fig. 3.15 (1969) et tom. cit., 637, 638 (map), 943, figs. 678 & 679, colour pl. 96 & 97 (1982). Type: Arizona, Graham Co., Pinaleno (Graham) Mts, Mt Graham, 4500 feet, 11 July 1935, *Louis Wankum* (US 1634004).

Stems 4-12, to 50 cm long. *Ribs* 12-14(-16). *Spines* 10-13(-16), all yellow; central(s) 1-3(-5), the principal one to 2.5 cm long, strongly down-curved from near base.

DISTRIBUTION. SE Arizona; grassland, chaparral and woodland, 1200-2000m altitude.

7e. var. **rectispinus** (Peebles) L. Benson, loc. cit., 259 (1944) et tom. cit., 626-627, figs. 667-670, colour pl. 90 (1982).
E. rectispinus Peebles, loc. cit., figs. 1 & 3d (1938). Type: Arizona, hills nr Nogales, 3900 feet, 5 May 1935, *Peebles* SF 905 (US 1729266).

Stems 1-10, to 18(-25) cm long. *Ribs* 9-10. *Spines* 8-10; central 1, to 3.8 cm long, porrect.

DISTRIBUTION. SE Arizona, SW New Mexico and W Texas; adjacent parts of Sonora and (?) Chihuahua; margins of Sonoran & Chihuahuan Deserts and desert grassland, 900-1650(-2040)m altitude.

This variety connects var. *fasciculatus* with the following.

7f. var. **fendleri**
Stems 1-2(-5), 7.5-15(-25) cm long (ovoid to ovoid-cylindric). *Ribs* 8-10. *Spines* 5-10; central (0-)1, to 3.8 cm long, curved upward.

DISTRIBUTION. Central & E Arizona, S Colorado, New Mexico (except in E) and W Texas (nr El Paso); Mexico in adjacent Chihuahua; Great Plains grassland, and woodlands, 1800-2400m altitude.

7g. var. **kuenzleri** (Castetter *et al.*) L. Benson, tom. cit. 942 (1982).
E. kuenzleri Castetter *et al.* in Cact. Succ. J. (US) 48: 77-78, figs. 1 & 2 (1976). Type: New Mexico, Otero Co., Sacramento Mts, Elk, 5 May 1968, *H. Kuenzler* 3585 (UNM 55571).
E. hempelii Fobe in Monatsschr. Kakteenk. 7: 187, with fig. (1897); M. Guerke in ibid. 17: 187-188 (1907); Vaupel in Bluehende Kakt. 3: t.142 (1912); Schreier in Kakt. and. Sukk. 33: 187, with fig. (1982); H. Hecht, BLV Handb. der Kakteen, 255 (1982)(superb colour pl.).

Stems 1-4(-8), to 25(-30) cm long (conical to cylindric). *Ribs* 9-10(-12). *Spines* 2-6(-7); central 0(-1), when present to 2.9 cm long.

DISTRIBUTION. S New Mexico (Otero Co.), Juniper-Pinyon woodland at 1830-2130m altitude; Mexico in N Chihuahua (Santa Clara valley and northwards).

Doubtfully distinct from the preceding variety.

NOMENCLATURAL NOTE ON MAMMILLARIA FASCICULATA ENGELM. (1848). The name *Mammillaria fasciculata* Engelm. first appeared in a letter written to Lieut. Col. W. H. Emory, published in Appendix 2 of his 'Notes of a Military Reconnoissance from Fort Leavenworth in Missouri to San Diego in California' (Emory, 1848). In this letter Engelmann provides brief diagnoses for nine new species of cacti, basing them on rather poor sketches drawn in the field by J.M. Stanly, artist to Emory's expedition. Not surprisingly the subsequent application of some of these names was problematical and at least three are now known to have been applied in the wrong sense for long periods. In the case of *Mammillaria fasciculata* even the genus to which the plant belonged was uncertain from Stanly's sketch. Engelmann wrote, 'Apparently a *mammillaria*, though the habit of the plant is more that of an *echinocereus*, but all *echinocerei* have the bunches of spines disposed in vertical ridges, which is not the case in the figure in question.' Engelmann's numerous later publications on the Cactaceae do not mention this species again, and its identity remained in doubt until the monograph of Britton & Rose (Cactaceae, vol. 4, 1923)*. The American monographers (tom. cit., 162) took up Engelmann's binomial for *M. thornberi* Orcutt (1902), a true *Mammillaria* from Arizona, the state in which *M. fasciculata* was encountered by Emory's expedition. Their interpretation, although made with some reservation, was accepted by subsequent botanists and horticulturists, the name *M. fasciculata* becoming established in both literature and living collections for Orcutt's species. However, in 1969 Lyman Benson (Cacti of Arizona, ed. 3, 21) reported on what was to be found at the type locality of *M. fasciculata* Engelm. and, without any hesitation, pronounced the plant to be an *Echinocereus* instead. This sudden about turn, while confusing enough, is made worse by the fact that *M. fasciculata* Engelm. (1848) threatens to replace the well-known name *Echinocereus fendleri* (Engelm.) Ruempler, based on *Cereus fendleri* Engelm. (1849). Both taxa belong to the same species complex, Benson having treated the former as *E. fendleri* var. *robustus* (Peebles) L. Benson prior to 1969. This classification is taxonomically sound and is accepted here, but the problem of the priority of the name *Mammillaria fasciculata* remains. To submerge the botanically and horticulturally familiar *E. fendleri* into a taxon known by a name previously applied to a species in an altogether different genus is unacceptable and likely to be ignored by amateur growers, who form the majority among those concerned with cacti and their names. No doubt with this in mind, Benson (1969), apparently without advancing any systematic justifications, decided to recognize *E. fasciculatus* as specifically distinct from *E. fendleri*, but while this avoids the loss of the name *E. fendleri*, it results in an equally unacceptably weak taxonomy, arbitrarily separating two halves of an intergrading complex of six geographical varieties.

Fortunately there is a solution to this unhappy state of affairs. As noted by D.R. Hunt (J. Mamm. Soc. 9: 38. 1969), *Mammillaria fasciculata* Engelm. (1848) could be considered a provisional name, invalid under Art. 34 of the International Code. Hunt draws attention to the prefixing remarks in Engelmann's letter to Emory, which indicate that he was uncertain about accepting the names he was proposing. Engelmann writes (loc. cit. 155) 'I have ventured to describe some of the species from the drawing; my descriptions, however, and the names given by me, must remain doubtful till we are able to obtain some more data to characterize the species.' He goes on to say that the letter is mainly for Emory's benefit, but that it can be published if desired, providing Emory makes any amendments that his recollection of the plants in the field might permit. However, this permission to publish does not alter the fact that Engelmann considered his 'descriptions' and 'names' would 'remain doubtful' until more information about the plants was forthcoming. The only additional fact supplied by Emory in his report was that Stanly's drawings were natural size unless stated to the contrary but, though this information was specifically requested by Engelmann, there is no published reply from him to the effect that Emory's statement (given in a footnote to Engelmann's letter) had removed all earlier expressed doubts about the taxa being named. Thus, as Engelmann's letter reads, it is difficult to escape the conclusion that his new species were provisional in the sense of ICBN Art. 34.1(b) and

---

* See, for example, the equivocal treatment of *M. fasciculata* Engelm. by S. Watson, Bibl. Index to N. Amer. Bot. 397, 402, 404 (1878).

their names, therefore, were not validly published in 1848. This being so, *Mammillaria fasciculata* must be attributed to the next author who definitely accepted the name. Engelmann, as already noted, did not subsequently employ it, and it appears to have escaped validation until its acceptance by B. Daydon Jackson in *Index Kewensis*, vol. 2 (1895). This date is fortunately after that for *Cereus fendleri* Engelm. (1849) and so *Echinocereus fendleri* (Engelm.) Ruempler is no longer endangered by taxonomic union with *E. fasciculatus* (Engelm. ex B.D. Jackson) L. Benson.

Though Benson (1969, 1982) has convincingly identified the plant observed and drawn on Emory's Reconnoissance, the nomenclatural type of *M. fasciculata*, as validated by Jackson's reference back to Engelmann's diagnosis, remains the poor illustration by Stanly, published in Emory's report. Benson's provision of a neotype, though desirable, may be inadmissible under Art. 32.2 of the Code (NB. Ex.3). This is an unsatisfactory situation since, at varietal rank, *fasciculatus* is the earliest priorable epithet for the taxon treated here (*E. fendleri* var. *robustus* (Peebles) L. Benson 1944, *non* Fobe 1911, cf. Art. 64.3). Nevertheless, in the absence of information contradicting Benson's identification of *M. fasciculata*, this epithet must be employed.

The consequences of rejecting Engelmann's published letter to Emory (1848) as a source of valid names have been taken into account with respect to the other species he described. The outcome will be reported on elsewhere.

8. ECHINOCEREUS PECTINATUS

Echinocereus pectinatus (Scheidw.) Engelm. needs little introduction. It was the first of the popular pectinate-spined echinocerei to reach Europe and was figured in Curtis's Botanical Magazine as long ago as 1845 (tab. 4190). Nowadays it is seen in cultivation less often than its pectinate rivals, *E. reichenbachii* and *E. rigidissimus*, though its flowers are, if anything, more spectacular. It is, however, of slow growth, and only old plants seem to flower freely. Nevertheless, it should be in every collection.

The species was first named *Echinocactus pectinatus* by Scheidweiler in 1838. He was sent material by the famous French collector, Henri-Guillaume Galeotti (1814-1858), though, as usual, it seems that none was preserved. Galeotti is said to have obtained his material near a settlement called 'Pennasco', which may be the Penasco marked on modern maps to the north of the city of San Luis Potosi. According to McVaugh (1978) Galeotti visited this region in December 1837. Benson (1982) prefers to believe that the type of the species was collected by John Potts in Chihuahua, as suggested by Salm-Dyck to Engelmann (see Wislizenus, 1848), but this is surely an error, since Scheidweiler's original description of 1838 was in a paper entitled 'Descriptio diagnostica nonnullarum Cactacearum quae a domino Galeotti in provinciis [San Luis] Potosi et Guanaxuato regni Mexicani inveniuntur', and Scheer (1856) records that Potts first sent plants from Chihuahua only in 1842. Thus Benson's designation of a Chihuahuan neotype for *Echinocactus pectinatus* Scheidw. can be regarded as 'in serious conflict with the protologue' (ICBN, 1983, Art. 8.1) and may be superseded. A more appropriate choice of neotype is the early and characteristic figure of the species in Curtis's Botanical

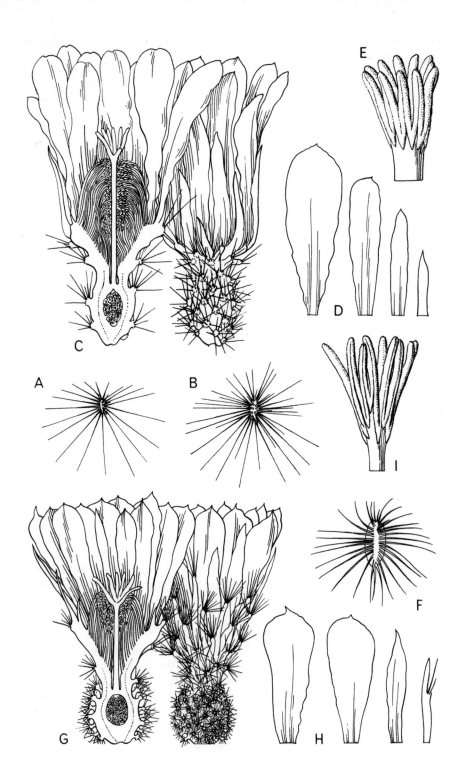

Magazine (1845), which represents a plant from San Luis Potosi, 'the region of Galeotti's type' (Britton & Rose, 1922). The Bot. Mag. plate clearly shows the large, bowl-shaped flowers, which are unique among the various pectinate-spined members of the genus.

Despite its unusual flowers the true systematic affinity of this well-known plant has not been realized by previous authors. It is not at all related to the other pectinate-spined species when their flowers are compared, and has almost certainly evolved such spination convergently. Three floral characters immediately identify its systematic position. These are the broad throat of the flower, the long, dark, narrow outer perianth-segments and, most important, the very widely spaced and loosely inserted petaloid segments whose bases are remarkably fleshy and invariably green. Compare these features with E. fendleri and E. engelmannii and it becomes obvious that, like them, E. pectinatus is referable to section Erecti, where it is the most specialized representative and the only member to have successfully colonized much of the Chihuahuan Desert region. The spination of E. pectinatus suggests its inclusion in the E. FENDLERI GROUP of sect. Erecti, where it should be compared with E. fendleri var. bonkerae in particular.

Echinocereus pectinatus is a wide-ranging and variable species. The type variety, var. pectinatus, occurs throughout the Chihuahuan Desert area, in central northern and NE Mexico, and has been recorded near the Rio Grande in Texas. Benson and others also record var. pectinatus from a number of sites outside the Chihuahuan Desert, in southern Arizona. However, the plant involved (see Kearney & Peebles, Ariz. Fl. tab. 28. 1951) is not E. pectinatus, but a variety of E. bristolii, a distinct species originally described from adjacent Sonora. The flowers of var. pectinatus are pinkish to lavender, with either a darker maroon, or, more commonly, a white throat, the very centre being green. They are very similar in Benson's variety wenigeri, an endemic of Texas which differs chiefly in having fewer spines per areole. Its status may prove to be less than that of variety when the diversity of var. pectinatus in Mexico is better understood.

The plant figured here is a form of var. dasyacanthus (Engelm.) N. P. Taylor. This variety has often been considered a distinct species on account of its very different spination and yellow flowers. It was first described as Echinocereus dasyacanthus by Engelmann, ten years after Scheidweiler named E. pectinatus. The type was collected by Wislizenus near El Paso, Texas, on the border between the United States and Mexico. Its extensive range includes the northern part of the Chihuahuan Desert, and it overlaps with var. pectinatus in Texas, N Coahuila and N Chihuahua. However, it also extends outside this area into the desert grasslands of central Texas and New Mexico, and into the Sonoran Desert in S Arizona and N Sonora.

Echinocereus pectinatus var. dasyacanthus. A, stem areole, × 2; B, stem areole, × 1½ (C. Wright, New Mexico in 1851); C, half-flower, exterior and interior views, × 1; D, outer (r) to inner (l) perianth-segments in series, × 1; E, top of style with stigma-lobes, × 3 (ex Hort. G. E. Cheetham). E. rigidissimus var. rubispinus. F, stem areole, × 6; G, half-flower, exterior and interior views, × 1; H, outer (r) to inner (l) perianth-segments, the outermost bearing an areole and two bristle-like spines, × 1; I, top of style with stigma-lobes, × 3 (Lau 88).

In its typical state it is easily distinguished from var. *pectinatus*. The radial spines and numerous central spines are much longer and diverge at various angles, giving the taller stems a bristly appearance. The yellow flowers are striking and can reach 15 cm in diameter. But both these distinguishing features are known to break down, there being specimens whose spination more nearly resembles var. *pectinatus*, and those with purplish flower pigments beginning to replace the yellow, or completely replacing them as in the form described as *E. steereae* Clover (1938). Furthermore, the flower's shape and construction are extremely similar to that in var. *pectinatus*, and this, together with the existance of forms such as that figured here, justify the referal of *E. dasyacanthus* to varietal status under *E. pectinatus*, as advocated by Benson (1944, 1968). Unfortunately his classification has proved unpopular in some quarters, no doubt in part because he was obliged, under the International Code of Botanical Nomenclature then in operation, to use the unfamiliar varietal epithet *neomexicanus* (J. Coulter) Benson at this subordinate rank. Happily a recent change in the rules concerning autonyms (Art. 57.3) means that *dasyacanthus* is now the correct varietal epithet.

The form of var. *dasyacanthus* illustrated corresponds to *E. ctenoides* (Engelm.) Lemaire, which is recorded from both sides of the international border in Texas and Coahuila (Weniger, loc. cit. infra). Its stem is transitional in appearance to var. *pectinatus*, but the radial spines are longer and interlaced with those of adjacent ribs as in var. *dasyacanthus*.

Two further varieties of *E. pectinatus* have been recognized by Benson (1982). The first, var. *rigidissimus,* is a good species, discussed on page 120. The second, var. *minor* (Engelm.) L. Benson (syn. *E. roetteri* (Engelm.) Ruempler*), is of uncertain status at present. In synonymy Benson (1968) includes no less than three amply distinct species from the E. RIGIDISSIMUS GROUP. (sect. *Reichenbachii).* These are *E. bristolii* W. T. Marsh., from the uplands of Sonora, and *E. scopulorum* Britton & Rose and *E. floresii* Backeb. (a synonym of *E. sciurus* (K. Brandegee) Dams), from the coasts around the Gulf of California. With these excluded Benson's concept of Engelmann's var. *minor* is restricted to plants found near the Rio Grande, in S New Mexico and Texas (near El Paso and in the Big Bend). They resemble var. *dasyacanthus,* but are smaller in all respects and have orange to magenta flowers. A flowering specimen is figured by Weniger (1970: tab. 10, as *E. roetteri*) and could be interpreted as a hybrid between var. *dasyacanthus* and a variety of *E. triglochidiatus.* The entire, rounded apices of the perianth-segments, in Weniger's plant are particularly suggestive of influence from the latter, and the original material of Engelmann's taxon (*C. Wright* in 1851-52, K) also displays characters of *E. triglochidiatus.*

Another plant of possible hybrid origin is *E. lloydii* Britton & Rose (1922). Photographs of flowering plants taken by Steven Brack at Tuna Springs, Texas,

---

* *Cereus roetteri* Engelm. in Proc. Amer. Acad. 3:345-346 (1857) is based on the same material (collections of *Bigelow* and *Wright*) as *C. dasyacanthus* var. *minor* Engelm., Syn. Cact. US. 23 (1856) and they are thus absolute synonyms.

the type locality, suggest that once again *E. pectinatus* var. *dasyacanthus* and a variety of *E. triglochidiatus* could be involved. Breeding experiments are needed to help resolve the status of both *E. pectinatus* var. *minor* and *E. lloydii*.

DESCRIPTION. *Stem* solitary, sometimes branched when old, globose to cylindrical, 8-35 cm long, to 13 cm in diameter, broadest near base, ± obscured by spines. *Ribs* 12-23, composed of low tubercles. *Areoles* elliptic, 2.5-6 mm long, c 6 mm apart, with much white wool at first. *Radial spines* 12-30, 5-15 mm long, with tips of spines from adjacent ribs nearly touching or considerably interlaced, adpressed or directed away from the stem surface, white, yellowish, brownish, pinkish or grey; central spines (1-)2-5 or more, (1-)2-15(-25) mm long, in 1 or 2 porrect rows or diverging at various angles and like the radials, but stouter, yellow to pinkish or dark brown. *Flowers* commonly from the sides of the stem, occasionally nearer apex, (5-)6-12(-15) cm in diameter; buds sharply pointed. *Receptacle-tube* c 3-4 cm long, basal 2-3 cm ± cylindric, enclosing ovary and nectar chamber, distal 1 cm expanded into a broad funnel-shaped section; areoles on tube well separated on low tubercles, spines 3-11 per areole, 5-11 mm long, stout, white tipped brown; uppermost areoles subtended by linear scales to 10 mm long. *Nectar-chamber* c 5-6 mm long, completely occupied by base of style. *Perianth-segments* in 2 rows, well separated from each other at the base, outermost segments narrowly linear-oblanceolate with a very dark midrib, c 3-5 cm long, inner segments cuneate-oblanceolate, to 6 cm long and 1.5 cm broad, apex acute to rounded, apiculate, with a ± irregularly serrate margin, pink to lavender, yellow or whitish, basal half maroon, yellow or white, but green at the very base. *Stamen filaments* 1.5-2.5 cm long, pink or yellow; anthers oblong, yellow, 1.5 mm long. *Style* to 4 cm long, 1.5-3 mm in diameter; stigmas 11-21, c 3-5 mm long, dark green. *Fruit* globose to ellipsoid, to 6 cm long and 4.5 cm in diameter, green to purplish, fleshy, with clusters of deciduous spines. *Seeds* to 1.3 mm long, black.

DISTRIBUTION. N Mexico and SW USA: from N Guanajuato to S Arizona, NE New Mexico & Cent. Texas; Chihuahuan Desert and desert grasslands at 800-1900 m.

Echinocereus pectinatus (Scheidw.) Engelm. in Wislizenus, Mem. Tour North. Mex. 110, in adnot. (1848); D. Herbel, Alles ueber Kakteen, 156 (1978); H. Hirao, Colour Encycl. Cacti, 156, fig. 612 (1979); H. Hecht, BLV Handbuch der Kakteen, 256 (1982); W. Cullmann et al., Kakteen, ed. 5, 156 (1984).
Echinocactus pectinatus Scheidw. in Bull. Acad. Sci. Brux. 5: 492 (1838). Type (see McVaugh in Contrib. Univ. Mich. Herb. 11: 293-297. 1978): Mexico, [San Luis Potosi], 'prope l'ida del Pennasco [El Penasco] in locis temperatis', [Dec. 1837], *Galeotti* (apparently not preserved). Neotype (superseding that designated by Benson, 1982): Curtis's Bot. Mag. 71: tab. 4190 (1845), depicting a plant flowering at Kew, which had been sent from 'San Luis, Mexico, by Mr Staines' (Taylor in Kew Mag. 1: 179. 1984).

8a. var. **pectinatus**
Stem globular to shortly cylindric, 8-15 cm long, to 20-23-ribbed. *Radial spines* c 22-30, not interlaced, adpressed to stem; central spines 3-5, to c 3 mm long, porrect. *Flowers* pinkish to lavender, maroon to white in the throat.

DISTRIBUTION. N Mexico: N Guanajuato, W San Luis Potosi, N Zacatecas, E Durango, SW Tamaulipas, S Nuevo Leon, Coahuila and N & E Chihuahua; and Texas, near the Rio Grande; mostly in the Chihuahuan Desert.

8b. var. **wenigeri** L. Benson in Cact. Succ. J. (US) 40: 124-125, fig. 3 (1968) and Cacti US & Can. 657, 658 (map), 661, fig. 697, colour plate 106 (1982); Weniger, Cacti of the Southwest, 29-30, t. 7 (1970). Type: USA, Texas, Val Verde Co., nr Langtry, April 1965, *L. & E. L. Benson* 16521 (POM 311338).

Stem to 25 cm long, to 13-18-ribbed. *Radial spines* 14-20; centrals 1-3. Otherwise similar to var. *pectinatus*.

DISTRIBUTION. Texas (Sutton to Brewster, Terrell and Val Verde Counties) near the Rio Grande; Chihuahuan Desert at 800-1200 m altitude.

8c. var. **dasyacanthus** (Engelm.) N. P. Taylor in Kew Mag. 1: 179 (1984). (PLATE 2, PRO PARTE)

Echinocereus dasyacanthus Engelm. in Wislizenus, Mem. Tour North. Mex. 100, in adnot.
(1848); Britton & Rose, Cact. 3: 19, fig. 19 (1922); Weniger, Cacti of the Southwest, 32, t. 9 (1970); G. R. W. Frank in Kakt. and. Sukk. 33: 217 (many figs.) (1982). Type: USA, Texas, El Paso, August 1846, *Wislizenus* (not found at MO according to Benson, 1968). Neotype (Benson, l.c.): Texas, between San Antonio and El Paso, Oct. 1849, *C. Wright* (MO).

E. pectinatus var. *neomexicanus* (J. Coulter) L. Benson in Proc. Calif. Acad. Sci. 25: 256 (1944), in Cact. Succ. J. (US) 40: 127, fig. 5 (1968) and Cacti US & Can. 664, 945-946, 659 (map), figs. 701 & 702, colour plates 108 & 109 (1982); G. Lindsay in Shreve & Wiggins, Veg. & Fl. Sonoran Des. 2: 999 (1964).

'*E. pectinatus* var. *ctenoides*' (Engelm.) Weniger, tom. cit. 31, t. 8 (1970), nom. inval. (ICBN Art. 33.2).

Stem cylindric, tapering towards apex, to 35 cm long, 12-21-ribbed. *Radial spines* 12-25, interlaced with those from areoles on adjacent ribs, adpressed or spreading outwards; centrals 2-5 or many, 2-25 mm long, porrect or diverging like the radials and scarcely distinguishable from them. *Flowers* commonly yellow, but sometimes whitish, orange, pink or purplish.

DISTRIBUTION. N Mexico: N Sonora, N Chihuahua & N Coahuila; USA: S Arizona, New Mexico (N to San Miguel Co.), Cent. & W Texas; Chihuahuan Desert, Sonoran Desert and desert grassland at 1200-1500 m altitude.

Section III. Triglochidiatus

Echinocereus sect. **Triglochidiatus** H. Bravo-H. ('Triglochidiata') in Cact. Suc. Mex. 28: 109 (1973). Type: *E. triglochidiatus* Engelm.

The three exceptionally variable and rather ill-defined species which make up this section are immediately recognizable by their floral syndrome, here assumed to be indicative of hummingbird pollination. Accordingly the receptacle-tube is long and only gradually flared, enclosing a large or very elongate nectar chamber, which produces and can store considerable quantities of nectar. The perianth-segments are relatively short, often bluntly rounded or entire, and mostly bright orange to pure red. In certain plants, especially forms of *E. polyacanthus* var. *densus*, the perianth limb is slightly oblique, making the flower somewhat zygomorphic and better shaped for bird visitation. The flowers either remain open both day and night, or close during the warmer parts of the day to re-expand in the afternoon. At first this semi-nocturnal rhythm may seem inconsistent with diurnal pollination by birds, and doubts about this are reinforced by the occurrence of pink flowers, seemingly atypical of the bird

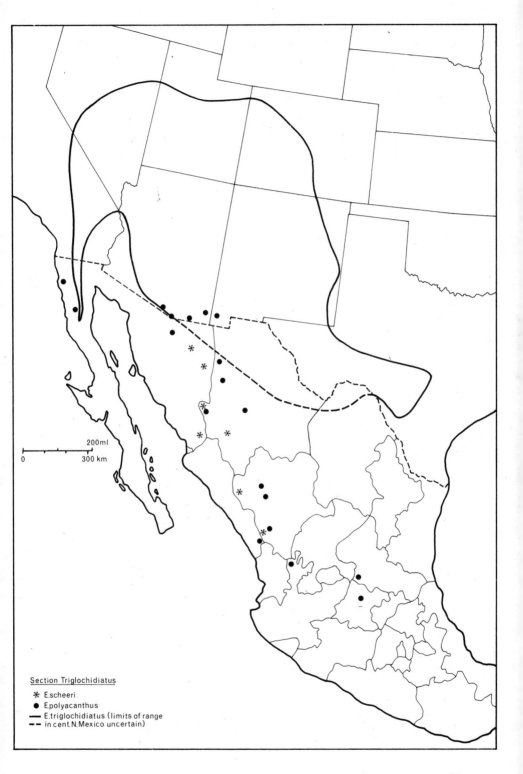

Section Triglochidiatus

* E.scheeri
● E.polyacanthus
— E.triglochidiatus (limits of range
-- in cent.N.Mexico uncertain)

59

syndrome, in *E. scheeri*, which may remain closed for much of the day*. However, in hot, dry regions, where cacti occur, it seems likely that vectors such as birds will be more active during the cooler parts of the day, e.g. in the late afternoon when these flowers are opening. This would appear to be so in the documented parallel case of *Melocactus macracanthos* and its hummingbird visitor (see Rodgers & Evans in Cact. Succ. J. (GB) 43: 36. 1981). Also, the forms with pink perianths often have an orange 'flash' in the throat, which is a colour favoured by hummingbirds. In any case these colours and the absence of a detectable sweet fragrance tend to rule out nocturnal pollination by hawkmoths–the only other pollinators compatible with this elongate flower shape. (Although some fragrances may not be noticed by the human nose, many other cactus flowers displaying the hawkmoth syndrome have readily detected perfumes.)

Vegetatively, sect. *Triglochidiatus* is generally rather unspecialized, the 4-14-ribbed stems sharing various characteristics with those of the least derived members of sections II & IV. The elongate ('cereoid') stems and extravagant flowers of *E. scheeri* suggest that it is the least specialized representative. However, like its allies, the flower-buds arise within the stem and tend to scar it badly when they burst out through the epidermis. The juicy fruits which follow often smell slightly of strawberries. The section has a wide geographical range, especially through the mountains of central N & NW Mexico and the SW United States, at altitudes of up to 3000 metres.

Apart from the obvious floral syndrome there appears to be little else to distinguish this section from the next, which is presumed to be insect-pollinated.

* The names 'E. noctiflorus' and 'E. nocturniflorus' have been used for a variety of this species.

9. ECHINOCEREUS SCHEERI

Echinocereus scheeri (Salm-Dyck) Scheer has long been a familiar plant, both in cultivation and in the literature, where it is often encountered under its synonyms *E. salm-dyckianus* Scheer (1856) and *E. salmianus* Ruempler (1885). It was first collected by the Potts brothers and sent to Frederick Scheer, a resident of Kew, who forwarded a specimen to the great cactologist Prince Joseph Salm-Reifferscheid-Dyck of Dusseldorf (Salm-Dyck, 1850). John Potts was manager of the mint at Chihuahua and, despite many difficulties (notably with Mexican Indians), succeeded in sending parcels of cacti to Scheer 'almost annually' from 1842 onwards (Scheer, 1856). Britton & Rose (1922) and others have assumed that these were all gathered in the vicinity of Chihuahua city, but it seems that some at least were obtained from far to the southwest, towards the border with the state of Sonora, where John Potts' brother Frederick resided (cf. Lindsay, 1944). *Echinocereus scheeri* was evidently one of these, for today it is found only on the Pacific slope of the Sierra Madre Occidental, from E Sonora to W Durango.

Echinocereus scheeri is a polymorphic species closely allied to *E. polyacanthus* Engelm., from which it is most readily distinguished by its more elongate stems, the ribs with closely set areoles only 2-7 mm apart. The large flowers at first seem very like those of *E. polyacanthus* var. *densus* (formerly *E. acifer*) but the developing buds are sharply pointed. Typical *E. scheeri* has slender, spiny stems 1.5-3.0 cm. in diameter, with about 7-10 ribs, but is extremely variable, especially in flower size and colour, habit and spination. It was figured in Curtis's Botanical Magazine in 1906 (tab. 8096). Application of the basionym, *Cereus scheeri* Salm-Dyck (1850), and of its synonyms mentioned above, rests entirely on interpretation of the original descriptions, there being neither type material nor contemporary illustrations to aid typification. It is also to be regretted that with the exception of three Sonoran collections of Alfred Lau (L. 84 from Alamos, L. 603 from Agua Blanca and L. 613 from Nacozari) the provenance of the many forms in cultivation is largely unknown. Another exception, however, is a form recently collected near La Bufa, SW Chihuahua, by Herr G. Unger of Austria. Further south, in the state of Durango, typical *E. scheeri* has been found in the Rio Tamazula valley at an elevation of only 800 metres. A photograph of a flowering specimen from this locality is preserved in the Kew Herbarium and appears to represent the type of *E. ortegae* Rose ex J. G. Ortega (1929), an additional synonym.

The varieties of *E. scheeri* form a series in which rib number and density of spination increase together. At one extreme is the variety figured here. Its mature stems have only 4-5 ribs and spination is poorly developed or entirely absent. It was discovered in 1932 by Howard Scott Gentry at Cañon Saucito, located between the Rio Bavispe and Nacori Chico in the Rio Yaqui watershed of E Sonora. Clover (1938) named it *E. gentryi* and published photographs of the type plant in flower. A year earlier, Werdermann, of the Berlin botanic garden, had received an almost spineless form from Hummel, a Californian nursery-man. The origin of this form was not known but, when it eventually flowered, Werdermann (1949) decided to describe it, being unaware of Clover's pre-war publication. He chose the name *E. cucumis*, since he thought the older, spineless stems bore a close resemblance to a cucumber. This remarkable plant has recently been located in the field by Alfred Lau, who came upon it in the Sierra Oscura of W Chihuahua in 1972. The plant illustrated derives from his collection, which bears the number *Lau* 87. It is being vegetatively propagated and is becoming more freely available and although, in botanical terms, it is scarcely distinct from the type of var. *gentryi*, its curious appearance makes it worthy of treatment as a cultivar, 'Cucumis'.

Echinocereus scheeri var. *gentryi* is particularly distinct on account of a peculiar developmental phenomenon. Seedlings and young branches have six or seven ribs at first (cf. var. *scheeri*) but, as the stems elongate and become mature, rib number actually decreases and in 'Cucumis' there are commonly only four ribs, giving an almost square cross-section near the stem apex. This is in stark contrast to the other *E. scheeri* varieties, where rib number tends to increase with stem age. However, the flowers of var. *gentryi* are typical of the species as a whole and there can be little doubt that it is conspecific. In its native environment the plant sprawls over or hangs from rocks, as photographs published by Lau (1974) clearly show. It seems sensitive to strong sun, turning purple if fully exposed, no doubt because it occurs in the shade of forest in the wild (Gentry, 1942). This environment may also explain its weak spination, which is presumably not needed to shade the plant.

An undescribed variety is represented by *Lau* 1143, collected *en route* between Mazatlan (Sinaloa) and the city of Durango, at an altitude of 1800 metres. The stems, with up to 14 ribs, are clothed in a dense armament of fine whitish spines, which lend the plant an attractive appearance. A flowering specimen was figured in a recent catalogue of the Belgian nursery firm of De Herdt, and propagations are now becoming available under the unpublished name '*E. koehresianus*'. It will be formally described as a variety of *E. scheeri* once complete material has been studied.

DESCRIPTION. *Stem* soon sprouting near base and plant becoming caespitose, sprawling, creeping or erect, cylindric, tapering towards apex, 10-60 cm or more long, 1.5-4 cm in diameter. *Ribs* 4-14, well-defined and even-edged or tuberculate, obtuse, sinuses shallow. *Areoles* circular, small, to 2 mm in diameter, 2-6(-7) mm apart, at first with white wool. *Spines* acicular to shortly subulate, 0-17 per areole; radials (0-)6-13, white, dirty white or pale brownish, 1-7 mm long; centrals (0-)1-4, white to dark brownish, stouter, 1-20 mm long, variously directed. *Flowers* tubular-funnelform, (6-)7-12 cm long, expanding to 4.0-8 cm in diameter; flower-buds sharply pointed at apex. *Receptacle-tube* 4.5-7.5 cm long, ovary occupying basal 1-1.5 cm, tube narrowing to 0.7-1.5 cm in diameter at c. 1 cm above ovary, flared in upper half, mouth of tube c. 1 cm in diameter, ± straight, exterior green, bearing 1-5 mm long, narrowly triangular scales, these subtending areoles with spines and often tufts of wool, in ovary region areoles closely spaced, spines to c. 20 per areole, 1-8 mm long, bristle-like, white tipped brownish, upper areoles few, 1-2 cm apart, spines few, to 10(-15) mm long. *Nectar chamber* 7-19 mm long, 4-7 mm wide. *Perianth-segments* in 4-5 rows, pink, salmon-pink, orange or vermillion-scarlet, paler, orange or yellowish in the throat; outermost segments narrowly triangular, like the scales on receptacle-tube but to 1 cm long, ± reflexed; outer segments oblanceolate 2.5-3.5 cm long, 0.7-1.0 cm wide, with a greenish or darker midrib, attenuate-apiculate, margins somewhat irregular; inner segments similar or longer, the innermost almost rounded at apex, margins entire. *Stamens* inserted on upper part of tube, above nectar chamber and to within 0.7 cm of tube apex; filaments very slender, to c. 5 cm long, white, coloured at distal end; anthers oblong, pinkish-purple to red before dehiscence, 1.5-2 mm long, pollen yellow. *Style* 6-8 cm long, to 2.5 mm thick, exceeding stamens by c. 5 mm, whitish; stigmas 7-15, pale emerald green, c 6 mm long. *Ovary locule* globose, 5-7 mm in diameter. *Fruit* shortly ovoid, c. 2 cm long, bright green, covered in easily detached bristle-bearing areoles, splitting along one side, filled with white funicular flesh and smelling slightly of strawberries. *Seeds* black, broadly ovoid, c. 1 mm long.

DISTRIBUTION. NW Mexico: E Sonora, W Chihuahua and W Durango; on rocks and cliffs, mostly in forest, at 800-2000 m altitude.

Echinocereus scheeri (Salm-Dyck) Scheer in Seemann, Bot. HMS Herald, 291 (1856); Schumann, Gesamtb. Kakt. fig. 48 (1897) and Bluehende Kakt. 1: t. 14 (1901); Werderm. in Nat. Cact. Succ. J. 4: 2-3 (1949); Backeb., Die Cact. 6: 3845, Abb. 3482 (1962).
Cereus scheeri Salm-Dyck, Cact. Hort. Dyck. 1849, 190 (1850); N.E. Br. in Curtis's Bot. Mag.

132: t. 8096 (1906). Type: cult. Hort. Dyck. 1849; original material sent to Salm-Dyck via F. Scheer at Kew, from NW Mexico by *Potts* (not known to have been preserved). Neotype (see Kew Mag. 1: 154. 1984): Sonora, Alamos, San Antonio, c. 1972, *A. Lau* 84, cult. at Holly Gate Nurseries, Ashington, W. Sussex, U.K., 5 May 1984 (K, spirit coll.).

9a. var. **gentryi** (Clover) N. P. Taylor in Kew Mag. 1: 154 (1984). (PLATE 3, PRO PARTE)

Echinocereus gentryi Clover in Bull. Torrey Bot. Club 65: 565, figs. 1-3 (1938); H. Gentry, Rio Mayo Plants, 193 (1942). Type: Mexico, Sonora, Cañon Saucito, 1932, *H. S. Gentry* (MICH).

Mature stems to 3 cm in diameter, 4-5-ribbed (in cultivation sometimes retaining the juvenile growth with 6-7 ribs). *Ribs* almost without tubercles. *Spines* absent or to 2 mm long. *Flowers* pink, throat pale or orange; spines on lower part of receptacle-tube and fruit to 3 mm long.

DISTRIBUTION. E Sonora and W Chihuahua; mostly hanging from cliffs, at 1000-2000 m altitude.

The form illustrated (*Lau* 87) is treated as cultivar 'Cucumis':
E. cucumis Werderm., loc. cit. 3-4, with fig. (1949); Krainz, Die Kakteen, Lfg. 12, with fig. (1959); A. Lau in Cact. Succ. J. (US) 46: 132, figs. 3 & 4 (1974).

9b. var. **scheeri**

Stems to 3 cm in diameter, (6-)7-10-ribbed; ribs tuberculate. *Spines* 9-13, conspicuous, 1(-4) central. *Flowers* pink, orange or scarlet; spines on lower part of receptacle-tube and fruit to 8 mm long.

DISTRIBUTION. E Sonora, W Chihuahua & W Durango.

9c. var. (unnamed; *Lau* 1143)

Stems c. 2.5-4 cm in diameter, 10-14-ribbed. *Ribs* strongly tuberculate. *Spines* 16-17, fine and dense, 3-4 central. *Flowers* not yet described.

DISTRIBUTION. W Durango, between Mazatlan and Cd. Durango, at 1800 m altitude.

10. ECHINOCEREUS POLYACANTHUS

Echinocereus polyacanthus Engelm. is a poorly understood species, which links the Mexican *E. scheeri* to the better-known, smaller-flowered *E. triglochidiatus*, whose varieties abound in the mountains of the SW United States. Like *E. scheeri* it ranges through the Sierra Madre Occidental of NW Mexico, but at higher altitudes (usually above 1700 metres) and extending further north, across the international border into SE Arizona and SW New Mexico. Its varieties reach still further afield—into Baja California Norte (var. *pacificus*), and southeast-wards into north-central Mexico, as far as San Luis Potosi and Guanajuato (var. *densus*). As is characteristic of species in this section, *E. polycanthus* is highly variable, especially in flower size and habit, though its spination usually lives up to its well-chosen name.

The botanical history of *E. polyacanthus* and its varieties is one of uncertainties and misidentifications. Recent treatments by American botanists (e.g. Weniger, 1970; Benson, 1982) either apply the name in a broad and meaning-less sense, or dispose of it completely in the synonymy of *E. triglochidiatus*

Engelm. However, these studies have been largely concerned with the cacti of the United States, whereas *E. polyacanthus* is primarily a Mexican species and should not be reduced to synonymy until an overall study of this section has been completed in the field. Earlier accounts, such as Wooton & Standley (1915) and Britton & Rose (1922), although employing rather narrow species concepts, did draw attention to the feature which distinguishes *E. polyacanthus*, namely the flower with its woolly receptacle-tube. This characteristic seems reliable despite the geographical range and variability of the plant in Mexico. Their treatments represented important clarifications, since earlier authors had been confused about the identity of the species, largely because Engelmann's original description (1848) omitted mention of the flowers and his later writings and illustrations (1859) relate to a different plant (*E. triglochidiatus* var. *neomexicanus*).

Here, typical *E. polyacanthus* is circumscribed as in Britton & Rose (1922), and is well represented in the plate recently published in Curtis's Botanical Magazine (N.S. tab. 818. 1981). From SE Arizona and adjacent New Mexico it ranges south as far as southern Durango, and *E. durangensis* Poselger ex Ruempler (1885) and *E. acifer* var. *durangensis* Schumann (1897) are synonyms which belong here. A fine illustration of a plant in habitat was recently identified as the latter by Frank (1983a).

Echinocereus polyacanthus var. *polyacanthus* has flowers ranging from 4-8 cm long and forms small clumps of stems with fairly even-edged ribs. The two species which follow *E. polyacanthus* in Britton & Rose's monograph are very similar and can be conveniently treated as geographical varieties. The first is *E. pacificus* Engelm., until recently a plant poorly known in cultivation; the second is *E. acifer* (Salm-Dyck) Hort. F. A. Haage, a confused taxon whose identity is clarified below.

Echinocereus polyacanthus var. *pacificus* is geographically isolated from var. *polyacanthus* in the mountains of northern Baja California, where it was discovered by C. C. Parry and H. C. & C. R. Orcutt in 1883. The type locality is at rather low altitude in the valley of the Rio San Carlos, which drains the western flank of the Sierra Juarez into Bahia de Todos Santos south of Ensenada. (A recent introduction from this locality is *Lau* 1350.) Ten years later it was found again by T. S. Brandegee, on the western slopes of the higher Sierra San Pedro Martir, further to the south east. Subsequently it has been collected in this range of a number of occasions*, the most recent being that of Alfred Lau, who records it growing at elevations between 1900-2800 metres (*Lau* 1248). It differs from var. *polyacanthus* chiefly in its highly caespitose habit, sometimes forming clumps of hundreds of stems with a diameter of a metre or more (Lindsay, 1967). The flowers tend to be smaller (3-5 cm long), though they are still quite eye-catching, as shown by the illustration in Hirao (1979).

Echinocereus acifer, based on *Cereus acifer* Otto ex Salm-Dyck (1850), is often encountered in the literature, but considerable doubt surrounds its typifica-

---

* It is omitted, presumably through an oversight, from the *Flora of Baja California* (I.L. Wiggins, 1980).

Plate 3

Echinocereus scheeri var. *gentryi*

Plate 4

Echinocereus polyacanthus var. *densus*

tion. The name *Cereus acifer* first appeared, without description, in the horticultural work *Handbuch der Cacteenkunde* of C. F. Foerster (1846), but unfortunately the origin of the plant was not stated. Salm-Dyck's later validating description omits mention of the flowers and his herbarium has been lost. However, Lemaire is quoted by Labouret (1853) as saying that the flowers were very large and red, and this agrees with a plant figured in an article by Regel (1852). Regel stated that his plant was purchased as *Cereus acifer*, though not being familiar with the echinocerei he re-identified it as a variety of *Echinopsis valida* Monv. ex Salm-Dyck, and published the varietal epithet *densa* for it. His coloured plate of var. *densa* is the only contemporary illustration available to help clarify the identity of *Cereus acifer* Otto ex Salm-Dyck and, in the absence of authentic herbarium material, is a suitable choice of neotype for Salm-Dyck's name. Fortunately this same illustration can be matched with a wild plant from the state of Guanajuato, where Meyran (1972) has photographed it in flower.

Thus Regel's varietal epithet represents the large-flowered plant figured here, which is at present known from Guanajuato (as recorded by Meyran), SW San Luis Potosi (*Parry & Palmer* 278, K), and then, disjunctly, from southern Durango (*Lau* 1082), where it grows in close proximity to typical *E. polyacanthus**. It differs primarily in flower size, the largest flowers reaching 14 cm in length, but the stems are also distinctive for their rather tuberculate ribs. At varietal rank the name *E. acifer* is antedated by Regel's epithet *densa* (1852) and must therefore be lost in the synonymy of the combination, *E. polyacanthus* var. *densus*. The disappearance of the epithet *acifer*, however, is a bonus, since it has been frequently misapplied in both literature and horticulture, and would otherwise remain a source of confusion.

The plant figured here, from the collection of Mr G. E. Cheetham, is exceptional for its very broad and spectacular flowers (to 7 cm in diameter). It also displays long needle-like spines (hence Otto's epithet *acifer*, i.e. needle-bearing) and is a most attractive addition to any *Echinocereus* collection. Mr Cheetham (1977) believes this form is identifiable with Friedrich Schwarz's '*E. marksianus*' (Backeberg, 1960, 1966), and were this name valid it would be useful to use it at cultivar rank, since the plant is known only in cultivation at present.

The relationship between the large-flowered *E. polyacanthus* var. *densus* and small-flowered var. *polyacanthus*, where both occur in southern Durango, merits further investigation. From the field collections of Hunt and Lau it is clear that plants which differ in flower size by a factor greater than two grow in close proximity in habitat. The significance of flower-tube length in relation to the pollinating agents, here assumed to be hummingbirds, is a question of particular interest.

A taxon of somewhat uncertain status, that is probably to be referred to *E. polyacanthus*, is *E. leeanus* (Hook.) Lemaire, based on *Cereus leeanus* Hooker in

---

* *Note added in proof.* It seems likely that the little-known *E. huitcholensis* (F.A.C. Weber) M. Guerke from NW Jalisco (c.1800 m alt.) is referable here. Cultivated plants under Lau's no. 768, from SE Sinaloa, which agree with '*E. matthesianus*' Backeb., may belong here too.

Curtis's Bot. Mag. 75: t. 4417 (1849). The original illustration which represents the type, and Hooker's description of the flowers, strongly suggest *E. polyacanthus* var. *polyacanthus*, but the stem, with up to 14 ribs, is much larger (30 × 10 cm) than has so far been recorded for this species. Britton & Rose (1922) mention a plant of *E. leeanus* received from the Berlin botanic gardens in 1914, which they supposed to be correctly named. Through the kindness of Dr B.E. Leuenberger of Berlin I have received photographs of what may be the same taxon, still in cultivation there today. It has the stout, many-ribbed stem described by Hooker, but lacks the long central spines illustrated for the type and has narrower, pinkish flowers. The wild provenance of *E. leeanus* has always been a mystery and without this information its systematic placement will remain difficult. The name has sometimes been linked erroneously with *E. polyacanthus* var. *densus* (*E. acifer*) by previous authors, e.g. W. Sterk, loc. cit.

DESCRIPTION. *Stem* solitary or more often caespitose, sometimes forming a clump of up to c. 400 branches, cylindric, tapering towards apex and at point of origin, 10-20 cm or more long, 2-6(-7.5) cm in diameter, erect not creeping, epidermis bright to dark green. *Ribs* (9-)10-13, well-defined, tuberculate or even-edged, c. 12 mm apart, the sinuses 3-7 mm deep. *Areoles* circular, 7-10 mm apart, 3 mm in diameter, at first with much pale yellow wool, this later becoming grey and eventually almost disappearing. *Spines* all acicular, bulbous-based, (9-)11-21 per areole; radials 6-14, dirty white, lowermost 3 and laterals longest, to 15(-20) mm long, overlapping with those of adjacent rib, uppermost 2-3 only 4-9 mm long; centrals (1-)2-4(-7), pale to dark brown or yellowish, the lowermost porrect to deflexed, to 50 mm long, the lateral pair slightly ascending, only ½ to ⅓ as long, the others, when present, 3-10(-20) mm long, resembling the radials but darker. *Flower* tubular-funnelform, (3-)4-14 cm long, expanding to (2-)3-6(-8) cm in diameter and remaining ± open for several (7-10) days and nights (or closing somewhat during hottest part of day); flower-buds rounded at apex. *Receptacle-tube* 2-8 cm long, the ovary occupying up to 1-2 cm at its base, tube contracted to only 0.7 cm in diameter immediately above ovary, flared in upper half, mouth to c. 1.0 cm in diameter, straight, or curved and making the flower slightly zygomorphic, exterior bearing 2 mm long triangular scales, these subtending areoles with spines and floccose wool, tube in ovary region green, with 15-20, 5-9 mm long bristle-like spines per areole, upper part reddish-brown to dark red, areoles more spaced, with 10-16, 7-16 mm long acicular spines. *Nectar chamber* 4-12 mm long, 2 mm wide. *Perianth-segments* in 2-3 rows, brilliant pinkish-, orange- or deep red, fading to yellowish or whitish in the throat; outer segments obovate, 10-35 mm long, 5-12 mm wide, apex rounded to broadly acute, apiculate; inner segments similar to outer but smaller, apex broadly acute to bluntly rounded, with an entire or finely fimbriate margin. *Stamens* inserted on upper part of tube, above nectar chamber; filaments very slender, white, pale pinkish at distal end; anthers oblong, c. 2 mm long, pink, pollen yellow. *Style* 1-1.5 mm thick, yellowish-white, slightly exceeding stamens; stigmas 7-10, 3.5-9 mm long, bright green, not spreading. *Ovary locule* 7 mm long, 4 mm in diameter. *Fruit* ovoid, 2.3 cm long, 1.6 cm in diameter, green, apparently indehiscent, filled with white funicular flesh and smelling of ripe strawberries. *Seed* black, broadly ovoid, 1 mm long.

DISTRIBUTION. N-Cent. & NW Mexico; USA: SE Arizona and SW New Mexico; open montane forest, mostly above 1700 m altitude.

Echinocereus polyacanthus Engelm. in Wislizenus, Mem. Tour North. Mex. 104, in adnot. (1848); Britton & Rose, Cact. 3: 11-12, figs. 8 & 12 (1922); H. Bravo-H., Las Cactaceas de Mexico, 361, fig. 194 (1937); C. Glass & R. Foster in Cact. Succ. J. (US) 41:

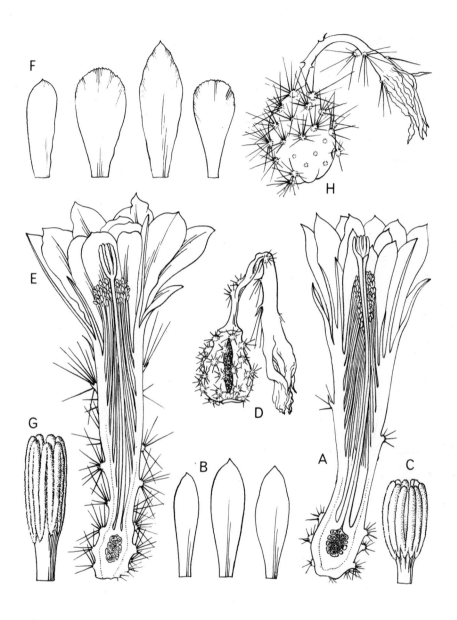

Echinocereus scheeri var. **gentryi**. A, half-flower, × 1; B, outer (l) to inner (r) perianth-segments, × 1; C, top of style with stigma-lobes, × 3; D, ripe fruit, × 1 (*Lau* 87). **E. polyacanthus** var. **densus**. E, half-flower, × 1; F, outer (l) to inner (r) perianth-segments, × 1; G, top of style with stigma-lobes, × 3; H, ripe fruit, × 1 (ex Hort. G. E. Cheetham).

260, fig. 1 (1969); D. Hunt in Curtis's Bot. Mag. 183, 3: 104-106, t. 818 (1981). Type: Mexico, Chihuahua, Cusihuiriachic [Cosihuiriachi], 1846, *Wislizenus* (MO).

10a. var. **densus** (Regel) N. P. Taylor in Kew Mag. 1: 159 (1984). (PLATE 3, PRO PARTE)

Echinopsis valida Monv. ex Salm-Dyck var. *densa* Regel in Gartenflora 1: 295, t. 29 (1852).
  Type: a cultivated plant purchased '*unter dem Namen Cereus acifer*'. Lectotype (Taylor, l.c.): Regel, loc. cit., t. 29 (representing the type, which is assumed not to have been preserved).
Cereus acifer Otto ex Salm-Dyck, Cact. Hort. Dyck. 1849, 189 (1850); Otto ex C. F. Foerster, Handb. Cacteenk. 433 (1846), *nom. nud.*; Lemaire in Labouret, Monogr. Cact. 315 (1853).
  Type: cult. Hort. Dyck. 1849 (not preserved). Neotype (Taylor, l.c.): Regel, loc. cit., t. 29 (1852).
Echinocereus acifer (Otto ex Salm-Dyck) Hort. F. A. Haage, Cacteen-Verzeichniss, 19 (1859); Guerke, Bluehende Kakt. 2: t. 106 (1908); Meyran in Cact. Suc. Mex. 27(2): fig. 29 (1972).
E. acifer var. *trichacanthus* Hildmann in Monatsschr. Kakteenk. 1: 44, with tab. (1891).
[*E. leeanus* sensu W. Sterk in Succulenta (NL) 61: 136-139, with figs. (1982) non (Hook.) Lemaire.]
  Flowers 8-14 cm long, to 6(-8) cm in diameter, sometimes slightly zygomorphic with an oblique limb.
  DISTRIBUTION. N-Cent. & W Mexico: S Durango to SW San Luis Potosi and Guanajuato; NW Jalisco and SE Sinaloa if *E. huitcholensis* is synonymous.

10b. var. **polyacanthus**
  Stems in clumps of 5-100. *Central spines* 1-4, merging with the radials. *Flowers* 4-7(-8) cm long, 3-4 cm in diameter, ± regular.
  DISTRIBUTION. NW Mexico: N & E Sonora, W Chihuahua and W Durango in the Sierra Madre Occidental; SW USA: SE Arizona and SW New Mexico.

10c. var. **pacificus** (Engelm.) N. P. Taylor in Kew Mag. 1: 160 (1984).
Cereus phoeniceus Engelm. var. *pacificus* Engelm. apud Orcutt in West Amer. Sci. 2: 46 (1886).
  Type: Mexico, Baja California Norte, Rio San Carlos (E of Bahia de Todos Santos), 25 Jan. 1883, *Parry et al.* (MO?).
Echinocereus pacificus (Engelm.) Hort. F. A. Haage, Special Offer [catalogue], 12 (1897); Britton & Rose, Cact. 3: 12, fig. 9 (1922); G. Lindsay in Cact. Suc. Mex. 12: 82, 84, 87, figs. 34 & 43 (1967); Hirao, Colour Encycl. Cacti, 157, fig. 620 (1979).
  Stems to 400, in a clump to 1.3 m in diameter. *Central spines* (3-) 4(-7), distinct. *Flowers* 3-5 cm long, 2-3 cm in diameter.
  DISTRIBUTION. NW Mexico, Baja California Norte: W drainage of the Sierra Juarez (Rio San Carlos at low elevation); W slopes of Sierra San Pedro Martir, to 2800 m altitude.

11. ECHINOCEREUS TRIGLOCHIDIATUS

A proper understanding of this complex species is still some way off and no significant contribution to its classification can be offered here. Even with *E. polyacanthus* excluded, the name still covers a bewilderingly diverse assemblage of plants, and Benson's delimitation of eight varieties (Benson, 1982) is only a partial solution to the problem, a significant proportion of field-collected specimens not falling clearly within the circumscription of any of these infraspecific taxa. However, Benson's treatment is accepted here, and the size of the task to revise the system he has developed means that it is likely to remain a standard for some time to come. His very thorough documentation of the immense synonymy of *E. triglochidiatus* represents a great achievement, without which this account would be much the poorer.

In the United States the *E. triglochidiatus* complex can be resolved into two, or perhaps three, basic units. The most widespread of these is centred around the well known specific name *E. coccineus* Engelm. (1848), the type of which belongs in Benson's *E. triglochidiatus* var. *melanacanthus*. It is a small-stemmed, highly caespitose plant with 8 or more stem ribs and terete spines. Like it, but with progressively larger though fewer stems, are the varieties *neomexicanus, arizonicus* and *gurneyi*. This unit ranges into Mexico and has much in common with the primarily Mexican *E. polyacanthus*. An additional taxon from south of the international border in NW Chihuahua, which may belong here, is *E. matudae* H. Bravo-H. (1960). It is somewhat intermediate between var. *neomexicanus* and var. *gurneyi*, but differs from all of the above in having stems with only 7 ribs.

The second unit ranges in the eastern half of the area occupied by var. *melanacanthus* and its allies, and is hardly recorded from south of the Mexican border. This is centred on var. *triglochidiatus*, a plant with only 5-8 ribs and few, angular spines, and includes the similar, but more spiny, var. *gonacanthus* and var. *paucispinus*. The third basic unit is var. *mojavensis*, the westernmost representative of the species. It combines some aspects of each of the other two units, having a higher rib count but a tendency for angular spines, which are, however, much longer than in the other varieties, and also curved or twisted.

Flower morphology does not obviously reinforce the groupings just noted, but appears to correlate to some degree with the stems in size. As elsewhere in the genus, it is possible that valuable floral characters have been ignored in favour of the more easily compared vegetative features, but, apart from the wide range in size, the flowers seem, on present knowledge, to be fairly uniform.

The origin of the infraspecific diversity within *E. triglochidiatus* outlined above can only be speculated on. In certain localities in New Mexico the extreme taxa representing var. *triglochidiatus* and var. *melanacanthus* are found growing in close proximity, but apparently do not intergrade (introgress) with one another. Elsewhere, however, intermediates between these two basic varieties, or their geographical/ecological vicariants, are frequent, and have led to the naming of many ill-defined taxa (now mostly referred to the synonymy of var. *melanacanthus* by Benson). Are we trying to classify the product of widespread and long term hybridization between two formerly distinct species, or merely observing a complex pattern of infraspecific variation within one genetically diverse taxon? Since species are defined by man the answer one way or the other is perhaps of limited importance anyway. Certainly much field and laboratory study awaits the scientist who wishes to answer these questions, but such work is definitely worthwhile in the hope that a better taxonomy can be arrived at.

Echinocereus triglochidiatus is well represented in cultivation, where most of the varieties recognized here can be found in their many differing forms. Although considered as uniformly red-flowered, some plants of horticultural origin have sported pink or lilac forms, which at first sight might be taken for hybrids, although for no reason other than flower colour. It is possible that this variation is inherent in the species, but normally suppressed in habitat by selection pressure from their presumed ornithophilous pollinators, which seem to favour brilliant reds, particularly in N America.

Pollination of *E. triglochidiatus sens. lat.* in habitat also deserves careful investigation in view of the suspected occurrence of hybrids with other *Echinocereus* species with quite dissimilar flowers. As mentioned under *E. pectinatus*, hybrids between members of the complex and *E. pectinatus* var. *dasyacanthus* may be represented by the plants known as *E. roetteri* (Engelm.) Ruempler *(Cereus dasyacanthus* var. *minor* Engelm.) and *E. lloydii* Britton & Rose. The variety of *E. triglochidiatus* most likely to be involved is var. *gurneyi*, and it would be valuable if attempts to re-create these putative hybrids* from their suggested parents were initiated by enthusiasts.

The cultivation and propagation of *E. triglochidiatus* is easy, but it does not always flower freely unless quite old or large. Most forms of the species are extremely cold resistant.

DESCRIPTION. *Stem* occasionally solitary, but commonly ± branched and sometimes forming mounds of up to 500 heads to 40 cm high and 1.2 m in diameter, largest branches ovoid to cylindric, 5-30(-40) cm long, to 5-15 cm in diameter, light to bluish-green. *Ribs* 5-12, high and even-edged to low and ± tuberculate, sometimes spiralled. *Areoles* ± circular, 3-4.5 mm in diameter, 6-12 mm apart, wool persistent. *Spines* (0-)3-16(-22), minute, or up to 7 cm long, terete or flattened-angular, shades of yellow, grey, or brown, or blackish, centrals, when distinguishable from the radials, 1-4(-6). *Flowers* tubular-funnelform, to 3-9 cm long, 2.5-7 cm in diameter, arising below apex and remaining permanently open for a number of days following anthesis. *Receptacle-tube* to 4 cm or more long, ovary occupying basal third or less, to 1.5 cm in diameter, tube contracted above to 1.2 cm or less, then flared to 1.7 cm in diameter at apex, exterior green to brownish, bearing conspicuous scales subtending areoles with up to c. 7, to c. 1 cm long, white, brown-tipped spines. *Nectar chamber* large, to 8 mm long and 4 mm in diameter. *Perianth-segments* oblong to cuneate-oblanceolate, to 3 cm long and 1.3 cm wide, bluntly rounded or even emarginate, the outermost mucronate, margins entire, in habitat usually brilliant orange-red to blood-red (sometimes pink to lilac in cultivation), paler to whitish in the throat. *Stamen-filaments* 9-30 mm long, white to pale green below, pink above; anthers oblong, c. 1.5 mm long, pollen pink to purplish. *Style* 1.2-4 cm long, 1-2 mm in diameter, pale greenish; stigmas c. 7-10, to 5 mm long, pale to dark green. *Fruit* globose to obovoid, to 2.5 cm long and 1.5 cm in diameter, eventually pink to red, spines deciduous. *Seeds* 1.5-2 mm long, tuberculate, black.

DISTRIBUTION. SW USA (S & E California, S & E Nevada, Utah, Arizona, Colorado, New Mexico and W & Cent. Texas) and adjacent Mexico (doubtfully reported as far S as Durango & San Luis Potosi); diverse habitats between 150-3000 m altitude.

Echinocereus triglochidiatus Engelm. in Wislizenus, Mem. Tour North. Mex. 93, in adnot. (April 1848); L. Benson in Proc. Calif. Acad. Sci. ser. 4, 25: 253-255 (1944) et Cacti US & Can. 604 (map), 606-607, 618, figs. 658 & 659 (1982). Type: U.S.A., New Mexico, 1846, collections of *Wislizenus* and *Fendler*. Lectotype (Benson, 1944): 'On Wolf Creek', *Wislizenus* (MO).

* Or hybrid, since *E. lloydii* B. & R. may not be distinct from Engelmann's taxon.

11a. var. **melanacanthus** (Engelm.) L. Benson, loc. cit. (1944) et tom. cit., 606-611, 937-939, figs. 638-644, colour pl. 81-84 (1982); W. Cullmann et al., Kakteen, ed. 5, 158, with colour pl. (1984).

Cereus coccineus (Engelm.) Engelm. var. *melanacanthus* Engelm. in Mem. Amer. Acad. 4: 51 (1849). Type: New Mexico, Santa Fe, *Fendler*. Lectotype (Benson, 1982): loc. cit., 26 Nov. 1846, *A. Fendler* (MO).

C. roemeri Muehlenpfordt in Allg. Gartenz. 16: 19 (Jan. 1848).

Echinocereus roemeri (Muehlenpfordt) Rydb. in Bull. Torrey Bot. Club 33: 146 (1906), non Hort. F.A. Haage, Cacteen-Verzeichniss, 20 (1859) (based on *Cereus roemeri* Engelm. 1849, non Muehlenpfordt 1848).

E. coccineus Engelm. in Wislizenus, loc. cit. (April 1848)*.

Further synonymy and details of typification can be found in Benson (1982).

Stems in mound-like clumps of up to 500 branches, to 7.5(-15) cm long, 2.5-5(-6.2) cm in diameter. *Ribs* 8-10. *Spines* 6-14, including 1-3 centrals, to 6.2 cm long, straight, smooth, rarely angled.

DISTRIBUTION. As for species, but the typical form absent from Baja and most of California; diverse habitats at 1000-2400 (-2900) m altitude.

A popular, cultivated, ± spineless form of this variety from Utah and Colorado is treated as cultivar 'Inermis':

E. phoeniceus (Engelm.) Lemaire var. *inermis* Schumann in Monatsschr. Kakteenk. 6: 150-153, with pl. (1896).

E. triglochidiatus var. *inermis* (Schumann) G. Arp in Cact. Succ. J. (US) 45: 132-133, figs. 1-4 (1973); G.R.W. Frank in Kakt. and. Sukk. 35(9): inside front cover (1984) (with superb cover illustration).

11b. var. **neomexicanus** (Standley) W.T. Marsh. in Marshall & Bock, Cactaceae, 118 (1941).

E. neo-mexicanus Standley in Bull. Torrey Bot. Club 35: 87-88, figs. 3-5 (1908). Type: New Mexico, Dona Ana Co., mesa W of Organ Mts, *P.C. Standley* 383 (MO, lectotype, *fide* Benson, 1982).

E. rosei Wooten & Standley in Contrib. US. Nat. Herb. 19: 457 (1914). Type: New Mexico, Agricultural College, 1907, *P.C. Standley* 1235 (US 535093).

[*E. polyacanthus* sensu Engelm., Cact. Mex. Bound. tt. 54 & 55 (1859), non Engelm. 1848.]

Stems in clumps of up to 45 branches, to 30 cm long, 7.5-10 cm in diameter. *Ribs* 8-12. *Spines* 11-22, including up to 4 much longer centrals, to 1 mm thick at base and 4 cm long, ± straight, terete.

DISTRIBUTION. SE Arizona, S & W New Mexico, W Texas (W of Pecos River to nr El Paso) and N Mexico in adjacent Chihuahua; woodlands and grasslands at 800-2000 m altitude.

11c. var. **arizonicus** (Rose ex Orcutt) L. Benson, Cacti of Arizona, ed. 3, 21, 129, fig. 3.3 (1969) et tom. cit., 607, 617, figs. 654 & 655, colour pl. 87 (1982).

E. arizonicus Rose ex Orcutt, Cactography, 3 (1926). Type: Arizona, on the Superior-Miami highway, nr boundary between Pinal and Gila Counties, 4700 feet, July 1922, *C.R. Orcutt* (NY, lectotype, Benson, 1969).

Stems few, to 40 cm long. *Spines* 6-14, radials often slightly curved, the 1-3 centrals to 1.5 mm thick at base. Otherwise like var. *neomexicanus*.

---

* Under ICBN Art. 57.3 (1983) the autonym, var. *coccineus*, established by *Cereus coccineus* var. *melanacanthus* Engelm., would normally have priority here. However, the name *Cereus coccineus* (Engelm.) Engelm. (1849) is an illegitimate later homonym of *C. coccineus* DC. (1828) and its epithet cannot be employed according to Art. 57.1.

DISTRIBUTION. Type locality and vicinity; woodland and chaparral at c. 1000-1400 m altitude.

11d. var. **gurneyi** L. Benson in Cact. Succ. J. (US) 41: 126 (1969) et tom. cit., 606, 615, figs. 650-652, colour pl. 86 (1982). Type : Texas, Brewster Co., igneous rocks S of Marathon, 4100 feet, 4 April 1965, *D.S. & H. Correll & L. & E. Benson* 16488 (POM 317078).

Stems few, 10-15 cm in diameter. *Spines* 8-10(-11), including 1(-2) centrals ± equal to radials, to 2 cm long. Otherwise like var. *neomexicanus*.

DISTRIBUTION. Central-S New Mexico, W Texas (in the Big Bend) and N Mexico in adjacent Chihuahua; Chihuahuan Desert and desert grassland, on limestone and granite, 1200-1500 m altitude.

11e. var. **paucispinus** (Engelm.) W.T. Marsh., loc. cit. (1941); L. Benson, tom. cit., 607, 617, 940, fig. 653 (1982).

Cereus paucispinus Engelm., Syn. Cact. US. 29 (1856) et Cact. Mex. Bound. 37-38, t. 56 (1859); Hook.f. in Bot. Mag. 110: t. 6774 (1884). Type: 'W Texas from the San Pedro to

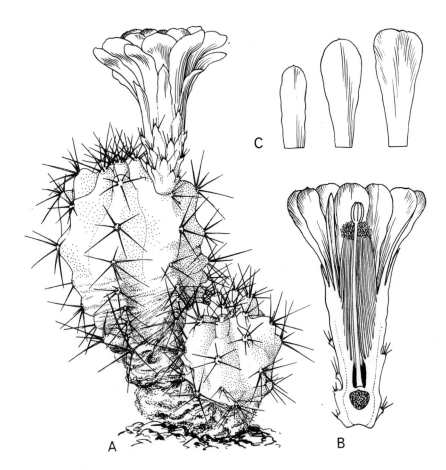

Echinocereus triglochidiatus var. **paucispinus**. A, plant in flower, × ⅔; B, half-flower, × 1; C, outer (l) to inner (r) perianth-segments, × 1 (ex Hort. C. King).

the mouth of the Pecos'. Lectotype (Benson, 1982): 'Cultivated from the original seeds' (MO).

Stems few, to 20 cm long, 6-10 cm in diameter. *Ribs* 5-7. *Spines* 4-6(-7), 3-4 cm long, terete or angled, centrals 0(-1).

DISTRIBUTION. S Texas; Chihuahuan Desert at c. 150-300 m altitude.

11f. var. **triglochidiatus**

Stems solitary or few, to 30 cm long and 7.5 cm in diameter. *Ribs* 5-8. *Spines* 3-4(-7), to 2.5 cm long, 3-angled, centrals 0(-1).

DISTRIBUTION. New Mexico (except in E), NE Arizona (Apache Co.) and S Colorado; Juniper-Pinyon woodland at 1300-2070 m altitude.

11g. var. **gonacanthus** (Engelm. & Bigelow) Boissev. in Boissev. & Davidson, Colorado Cacti, 36 (1940); L. Benson, tom. cit., 607, 618, 940-941, fig. 657 (1982).

Cereus gonacanthus Engelm. & Bigelow in Engelm., Syn. Cact. US. 27 (1856) et Descr. Cact. 33-34, t. 5, figs. 2 & 3 (1856). Type: [Arizona] 'about 40 miles W of Zuni, nr the 109th degree'. Lectotype (Benson, 1982): Cedar woods 35 miles W of Zuni, 29 Nov. 1853, *J.M. Bigelow* (MO).

Stems few, or in mound-like clumps of up to 200 branches, to 12.5 cm long, 5-7.5 cm in diameter. *Spines* 6-9(-11), centrals (0-)1(-2), to 4.4 cm long, 3-6-angled.

DISTRIBUTION. New Mexico (except E edge), NE Arizona (Apache Co.) and S Colorado; in or near Juniper-Pinyon woodland at 1680-2370 m altitude.

11h. var. **mojavensis** (Engelm. & Bigelow) L. Benson, loc. cit. (1944) et tom. cit., 606, 612-613, 939, figs. 645-648, colour pl. 85 (1982).

Cereus mojavensis Engelm. & Bigelow in Engelm., Syn. Cact. US. 25 (1856) et Descr. Cact. 33, t. 4, fig. 8 (1856); N.E. Br. in Bot. Mag. 126: 7705 (1900). Type: (*fide* Benson, 1982): California, 'Mojave Creek', 4 March 1854, *J.M. Bigelow* (MO).

Stems in mound-like clumps of up to 500 branches, to 7.5 (-15) cm long, 2.5-5(-6.2) cm in diameter. *Ribs* 9-10. *Spines* 6-10, including 1-2 centrals, to 7 cm long, curving and twisting, terete or angled.

DISTRIBUTION. Mexico in NE Baja California (E flanks of Sierras San Pedro Martir & Juarez); SW U.S.A. in E & S California, S Nevada, SW Utah and (?) NW Arizona (W Mohave Co.); woodlands, chaparral and upper Mojavean Desert at 1000-2400(-3000) m altitude.

Extensively intergrades with var. *melanacanthus*.

Section IV. Echinocereus

This section includes *E. viridiflorus*, lectotype of the name *Echinocereus* Engelm. (1848). The following are sectional synonyms:

Cereus sect. *Costati* Engelm. in Mem. Amer. Acad., ser. 2, 4: 50, in adnot. (1849). Lectotype (designated here): *C. enneacanthus* (Engelm.) Engelm.

Cereus sect. *Sulcati* Engelm., loc. cit. (1849). Lectotype (designated here): *C. viridiflorus* (Engelm.) Engelm.

This is the second largest section with 12 species, but one, *E. pentalophus*, is only placed here provisionally. The flowers range from very large to very small (i.e. to only 2.5-3 cm long), the larger flowers being distinguishable from those of section *Erecti* by the broader, less fleshy outer perianth-segments. The flower-buds mostly burst through the epidermis above the areole and usually arise well away from the stem apex. Vegetatively, they range from unspecialized, with 4-12 ribs and open spination, to rather specialized, with up to 24 ribs and short dense, or long hair-like spination. The fruits are mostly very juicy and often smell of strawberries. An entirely eastern group, ranging east of the Sierra Madre Occidental, with the centre of diversity around the northern parts of the S.M. Oriental. Three species groups can be defined:

The vegetatively unspecialized E. PENTALOPHUS GROUP is monotypic and of uncertain affinity within the genus. It is readily distinguished from the remainder of the section by its conspicuously woolly receptacle-tube. From E & NE Mexico and S Texas.

The E. CINERASCENS GROUP (species 13-19) represents an eastern parallel of the less specialized species of sect. *Erecti*. They have generally rather large flowers with broad perianth-segments and very stout, fleshy receptacles. The stems of these highly caespitose plants have 5-17 ribs and can be either erect or partly prostrate, often with long, but usually ± terete, spines (excepting *E. enneacanthus*). There are seven highly variable and taxonomically difficult species, from central-E to cent.-N & NE Mexico and the immediately adjacent parts of the United States.

The E. VIRIDIFLORUS GROUP (species 20-23) seems to be a specialized derivative of the last group characterized by proportionately much narrower perianth-segments, more stem ribs and much denser and finer spination. The most derived species pair, *E. chloranthus* and *E. viridiflorus*, have solitary or few-branched stems and very small flowers, representing the height of economy. The group ranges from the northern parts of the Chihuahuan Desert and Sierra Madre Oriental, to the high and cooler Great Plains of the United States (to South Dakota), *E. viridiflorus* being the most northerly distributed and hardiest member of the genus.

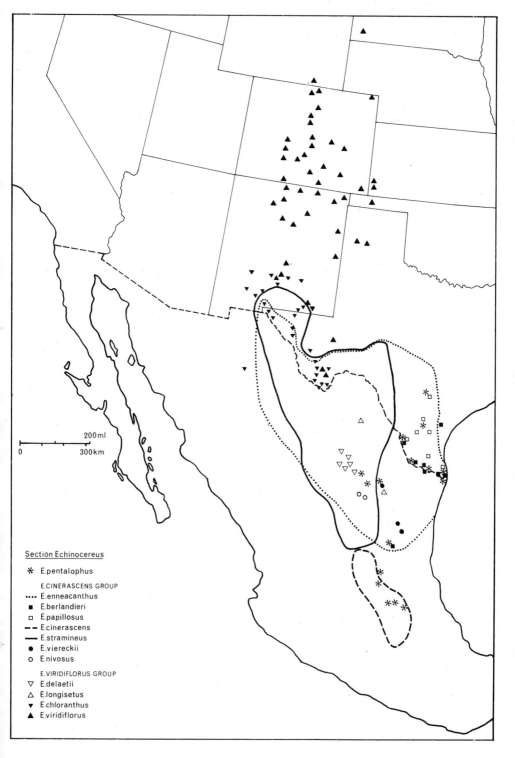

Section Echinocereus

* E.pentalophus

E.CINERASCENS GROUP
•••• E.enneacanthus
■ E.berlandieri
□ E.papillosus
– – E.cinerascens
—— E.stramineus
● E.viereckii
○ E.nivosus

E.VIRIDIFLORUS GROUP
▽ E.delaetii
△ E.longisetus
▼ E.chloranthus
▲ E.viridiflorus

12. ECHINOCEREUS PENTALOPHUS

Together with *E. cinerascens*, this popular species was the first member of the genus discovered and described. It was christened *Cereus pentalophus* by De Candolle in 1828, who based the name on material collected by the Irishman, Thomas Coulter during 1827-28, when working in the E Mexican state of Hidalgo, at Zimapan (very likely the plant came from the nearby Barranca de Toliman; cf. McVaugh, 1943). Soon after, it was recorded from the same region by Carl Ehrenberg (1846) under the name *Cereus propinquus* Otto, one of many synonyms for this variable plant. Unfortunately, Coulter's type material is no longer extant, or perhaps was prized as a living plant and never preserved, so that the original form remains somewhat uncertain. However, Benson's solution to this problem (loc. cit. 1982), that of providing a neotype from distant Texas (!), is far from satisfactory. The species does range into S Texas, but its northern forms are almost certainly not taxonomically identical with those from Central E Mexico. Quite apart from this it could be argued that Benson's neotype is 'in serious conflict' (ICBN Art. 8.1) with De Candolle's protologue, which specified 'Mexico' for Coulter's type. A representative collection from NW Hidalgo should now be chosen and Benson's neotype superseded.

Early authors, such as Engelmann, compared the 4-5-ribbed *E. pentalophus* (or its northern form, *E. procumbens*) with *E. berlandieri* (q.v.), a plant of similar prostrate habit and slender few-ribbed stems. They are also frequently confused today (cf. Weniger, 1970), especially in living collections, although their floral differences are considerable. Indeed, the flowers of *E. pentalophus* cannot be confused with those of any other species from section *Echinocereus*, where it is placed purely on its superficial vegetative resemblance. The areoles on the receptacle-tube produce much diffuse cobwebby wool and the receptacle itself is not so massively constructed as in many members of the otherwise similar E. CINERASCENS GROUP, to which *E. berlandieri* belongs. Furthermore, when preserved in alcohol, its perianth fails to turn brown, unlike all the species from this same group (an interesting question of phytochemistry for someone to investigate). If its vegetative characteristics are ignored, it could even find a position within section *Reichenbachii*. Much further study of this species is required if its true affinity is to be established.

Included in a broadened concept of *E. pentalophus*, as a variety here, is *E. leonensis* Mathsson (1891), another plant confused, and even synonymized, with *E. berlandieri* (or '*E. blanckii*') during its early botanical history. It is distinguishable only on vegetative characters, the flowers being all but identical with those of typical *E. pentalophus*. It emanates from the Sierra Madre of NE Mexico and has rhizomatous, then erect, stems with more (6-8) ribs, but close inspection of its spination shows additional similarities. In cultivation it is one of the plants most often encountered under the wrong name, and its name is also widely misapplied.

Another plant which may deserve varietal recognition is *E. procumbens*, a form from Texas with more slender stems, less well-defined ribs and deep purplish green or reddish stem pigmentation (light or yellow-green in typical Mexican plants of the species). Its flowers are smaller and have bristle-like rather than stiff spines at the receptacular areoles. The name combination for it at varietal rank has been made, but its use should depend on a careful investigation of the plant in the field. Benson (1982) does not recognize it. There are also other forms perhaps worthy of examination. One such is a very stout almost terete-stemmed plant occasionally seen in living collections. Its origin is not known.

Echinocereus pentalophus is among the easiest species to grow, flower and vegetatively propagate. A large clump is a fine sight in flower, the large yellow- to white-throated, pinkish-magenta perianths having few equals within the genus.

DESCRIPTION. *Plant* freely caespitose, forming low clumps to 1 m or more in diameter, the branches arising above ground or as subterranean rhizomes. *Stems* to 20-60 cm or more long, 1-6 cm in diameter, cylindric towards apex, stiff, erect or ± procumbent, yellowish- to reddish-green or grey-green. *Ribs* 4-8, acute or later rounded, straight or somewhat disorganized and then quite tuberculate. *Areoles* circular, 1.5-3 mm in diameter, mostly 1-2 cm apart. *Radial spines* 3-8, short or to 2 cm long, the uppermost 1-3 very small, acicular, straight, dirty white to yellowish when mature; central spine 0-1, very short or to 3 cm long, acicular, porrect or often ascending, yellowish to dark brown. *Flowers* broadly funnelform, to 8-10 cm long, 10-15 cm in diameter, arising away from stem apex. *Receptacle-tube* 2.5-4 cm long, ovary occupying basal half or more but locule base to 9 mm above base of receptacle, to 1.5 cm in diameter in ovary region, constricted above to 1 cm and then flared to c. 2 cm in diameter at apex, exterior green below, reddish above, bearing areoles with 4-8, to 1.3 cm long, straight light to dark bown, sometimes white-tipped, stout to bristle-like spines, and much loose wool. *Nectar chamber* 3-4 mm long, 2-2.5 mm in diameter. *Perianth-segments* in 1-2 rows, cuneate-oblanceolate, to 6 cm long and 9-18 mm wide, bluntly rounded to mucronate at the entire or slightly toothed apex, bright pink to pinkish-magenta in upper half, white to yellow in the throat, rarely completely white. *Stamen-*

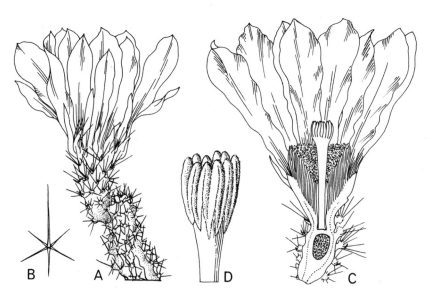

Echinocereus pentalophus var. **pentalophus** (*E. procumbens*). A, stem with flower, × ⅔; B, stem areole, × 4; C, half-flower, × 1; D, top of style with stigmas, × 4 (ex Hort. Holly Gate).

filaments to 12 mm long, whitish to green; anthers oblong, 1.5 mm long. *Style* to 2.5 cm long, 2-3 mm in diameter; stigmas 7-14, to 6 mm or more long, stout to slender, dark green. *Ovary locule* ovoid, to 11 mm long at anthesis. *Fruit* ovoid, to 1.8 cm long, green, with brownish spines and loose wool, irregularly dehiscent. *Seeds* ovoid, c. 1 mm long, tuberculate, black (see Sterk, loc. cit.).

DISTRIBUTION. Central E to NE Mexico (Hidalgo, Querétaro, E Guanajuato, San Luis Potosi, Tamaulipas, Nuevo Leon & SE Coahuila) and adjacent S Texas; sandy brushlands and grassy places, or on rocks in barrancas, from sea-level to c. 1400 m altitude.

Echinocereus pentalophus (DC.) Lemaire, Cactées, 56 (1868); Weniger, Cacti of the Southwest, 51-52, t. 16 (1970); W. Sterk in Succulenta (NL) 59: 224-226, with figs. (1980); K.W. Beisel in Kakt. and. Sukk. 32: 210 (1981); L. Benson, Cacti US & Can. 623-624, 942, figs. 662 & 663, colour pl. 88 & 89 (1982).

Cereus pentalophus DC. in Mem. Mus. Hist. Nat. Paris 17: 117 (1828); Hook. in Bot. Mag. 65: t. 3651 (1838). Type: 'Mexico [Hidalgo, environs of Zimapan, 1827-1928 (cf. McVaugh in J. Wash. Acad. Sci. 33: 65-69. 1943)], *Coulter*' (apparently not preserved). The neotype designated by Benson (1982) should be superseded under Art. 8.1, since the specimen cited (*Benson* 16545, POM) is from Texas, not 'Mexico', and may differ taxonomically from that described by De Candolle.

C. propinquus Salm-Dyck ex Otto in Allg. Gartenz. 1: 366 (1833); C.A.Ehrenb. in Linnaea 19: 362 (1846). (Based on *C. pentalophus simplex* DC., loc. cit. 1828.)

C. procumbens Engelm. in Mem. Amer. Acad. ser. 2, 4: 50, in adnot. (1849) et Cact. Mex. Bound. 38-39, t. 59, figs. 1-11 (1859); Hook.f. in Bot. Mag. 117: t. 7205 (1891). Type: Mexico, NE Tamaulipas, 'Matamoras'. Lectotype (Benson, 1982): 'Burita nr the mouth of the Rio Grande below Matamoras by the Missouri Volunteers, 1846, cultivated at St. Louis, fl. May 1848' (MO).

E. procumbens (Engelm.) Lemaire, loc. cit. (1868); W. Sterk, loc. cit. 225, 227, with figs. (1980).

E. pentalophus var. *procumbens* (Engelm.) P. Fournier, Cactees & Pl. Grasses, 25 (1935); Krainz, Die Kakteen, Lfg. 14, with fig. (1960).

[*E. berlandieri* sensu Weniger, tom. cit., 52-53, t. 17 (1970), non (Engelm.) Hort. F.A. Haage.]

[*E. tulensis* H. Bravo-H. in Cact. Suc. Mex. 18: 110 (1973), tantum quoad fig. 63.]

12a. var. **leonensis** (Mathsson) N.P. Taylor, stat. nov.
Echinocereus leonensis Mathsson in Monatsschr. Kakteenk. 1: 66, with pl. (1891). Type: Mexico, Nuevo Leon, nr Monterrey [Huasteca canyon?], 1800 feet, *Runge* (assumed not to have been preserved). Lectotype (designated here): Mathsson, loc. cit. (tab.).

[*E. dubius* sensu Borg, Cacti, ed. 2, t. 27(a) (1951), non (Engelm.) Ruempler.]

Stems ± erect, often tapered towards apex from base and branching by means of subterranean rhizomes, grey-green. *Ribs* 6-8. *Spines* up to 9 per areole.

DISTRIBUTION. NE Mexico: SE Coahuila, W & S Nuevo Leon in the Sierra Madre Oriental, at or above 550 m altitude.

12b. var. **pentalophus**
Stems erect or prostrate, cylindric, branched above ground, reddish-purple to dark- or yellowish-green. *Ribs* 4-5. *Spines* 3-7.

DISTRIBUTION. As for species; nr sea-level to c. 1400 m altitude.

The form included here, which was originally described as *Cereus procumbens* Engelm., may deserve recognition as a separate variety.

13. ECHINOCEREUS ENNEACANTHUS

Since the publication of misidentified plates in Engelmann's *Cactaceae of the Boundary* in 1859, the name *Echinocereus enneacanthus* Engelm. has been employed for a plant found on the Edwards Plateau, Texas, and in brushlands along the Rio Grande and on its lowland plain, north and south of the Mexican border. This familiar plant has relatively slender stems to 5 cm in diameter and areoles to c. 2 cm apart on the ribs. However, the type of Engelmann's species, described eleven years earlier, came from central Chihuahua and had stout stems 7.5-10 cm in diameter with areoles spaced 2.5 cm apart. The type was collected by Wislizenus in 1847 and consisted of living stems and pressed flowers, of which only the latter are extant today. Nevertheless, the description itself and specimens subsequently collected from the same region (between Cd. Chihuahua and Cd. Camargo) indicate that the original *E. enneacanthus* was the same as that later described by Engelmann (1856) as *Cereus dubius*, and not the '*E. enneacanthus*' of modern authors. Thus *Echinocereus dubius* (Engelm.) Ruempler, and also *E. merkeri* Schumann (1897) and *E. sarissophorus* Britton & Rose (1922), are synonyms of the true *E. enneacanthus* Engelm. (1848), a very variable and widespread member of the Chihuahuan Desert flora.

The '*E. enneacanthus*' of authors and of horticulture (since 1859) is not a distinct species, but intergrades with the true *E. enneacanthus (E. dubius)* along the Rio Grande in Brewster County, Texas (Breckenridge & Miller, 1982). Benson (1969, 1982) has treated both as varieties of one species, i.e. *E. enneacanthus*, and this seems a satisfactory classification to follow (the var. *stramineus* is a separate species, however). His var. *enneacanthus* must now be renamed and the epithet chosen here is var. *brevispinus* (W.O. Moore) L. Benson (1969), based on the clearly typified *E. enneacanthus* forma *brevispinus* W.O. Moore (1967). This variety is taxonomically almost identical with var. *enneacanthus sensu* Benson, and the epithet *brevispinus* is also very apt for the plant concerned, since the true *E. enneacanthus (E. dubius)* has much longer spines.

There are at least two earlier names for the taxon called var. *brevispinus* here (var. *enneacanthus* of Benson), but none of these is adequately typified. The oldest has also been the cause of much confusion, namely *Cereus blanckii* Poselger (1853). Although the original description and type locality are extremely suggestive of var. *brevispinus*, the epithet *blanckii*, as *Echinocereus blan(c)kii*, has long been misapplied to *E. berlandieri*, a related but quite distinct species. The name *Cereus blanckii* is best forgotten, as its type was never preserved, and its use in place of var. *brevispinus*, over which it has priority at varietal rank, would create confusion of the worst kind. Another priorable name for var. *brevispinus*, recently employed by Weniger (1970), is *E. carnosus* Ruempler (1885) (*E. enneacanthus* var. *carnosus* Quehl 1898). Once again the type specimen was not preserved, nor was its precise origin known.

Leaving nomenclatural considerations aside, *E. enneacanthus* is of considerable systematic interest. Within section *Echinocereus* it seems to provide a link between the creeping, slender *E. berlandieri*, with similar dark-throated flowers, and the more erect, thicker-stemmed species such as *E. cinerascens*, *E. stramineus* and *E.*

viereckii, with paler or white-throated flowers. It exhibits few, if any, derived characters and could be considered as the taxon closest to the hypothetical ancestor of the section. It has angular central spines, in common with certain species in the equally unspecialized sections *Erecti* and *Triglochidiatus*, and amongst sect. *Echinocereus* is geographically one of the species closest to the W Mexican region from which the various infrageneric groups appear to have radiated.

The cultivation of *E. enneacanthus* presents no problems, but it does best when afforded plenty of room, such as when planted out in a sunny greenhouse bed. Propagation by seed or cuttings (usually the latter) is straightforward.

DESCRIPTION. *Plants* caespitose, forming low flat clumps of up to 30-200 stems. *Stems* cylindric, rarely globose, decumbent except towards the erect apex, to 2 m long, 3.5-15 cm in diameter, the erect part to 25 cm high, dull to pale green. *Ribs* 7-10, scarcely tuberculate or the tubercles broad and flat. *Areoles* circular, 3-4.5 mm in diameter, 1.6-4.5 cm apart. *Radial spines* 6-13, to 4 cm long, ± straight, whitish to brownish, often with darker tips; centrals 1-4, to 8 cm long, straight or curved, terete to strongly flattened, angled or grooved, yellow, brown or bluish. *Flowers* funnelform, to 8 cm long and 10 cm or more in diameter, arising below stem apex. *Receptacle-tube* to 4 cm long, ovary occupying basal 1.7 cm, c. 1.2 cm in diameter, locule base 9 mm above receptacle base, tube contracted to 0.9 cm above ovary, then flared to 2.2 cm in diameter at apex, exterior with narrowly triangular, 2-5 mm long scales subtending areoles with 0-7, to 2.2 cm long, ± straight, whitish spines. *Nectar chamber* 5 mm long, c. 2 mm in diameter, ± filled by style base. *Perianth-segments* in 2-3 rows, oblanceolate, to 5.5 cm long, 1-2 cm wide, quite fleshy at base,

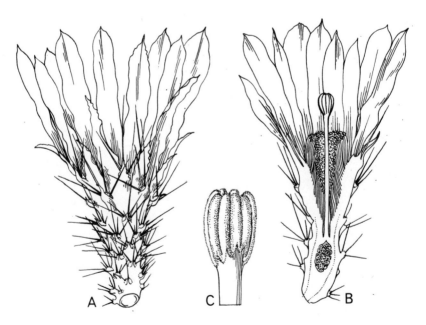

Echinocereus enneacanthus. A, flower, × 1; B, half-flower, × 1; C, top of style with stigmas, × 3 (ex Hort. A. J. Ward).

Plate 5

Echinocereus stramineus

Plate 6

Echinocereus viereckii var. *viereckii*

apex acuminate, serrate, magenta deepening to crimson in the throat. *Stamen filaments* to c. 10 mm long, greenish to pink; anthers oblong, scarcely 1 mm long. *Style* to 3.1 cm long, 1.5-2 mm in diameter; stigmas 6-10, 5-6 mm long, green. *Ovary locule* oval, to c. 8 mm long at anthesis, ovules very numerous. *Fruit* globular to ovoid, to 3.8 cm long and 2.5 cm in diameter, flesh pink, strawberry flavoured. *Seeds* ovoid, 1-1.4 mm long, tuberculate, black.

DISTRIBUTION. Central N & NE Mexico and adjacent Texas and New Mexico, sea-level to 1200(-1700) m altitude.

Echinocereus enneacanthus Engelm. in Wislizenus, Mem. Tour North. Mex. 111, in adnot. (1848). Holotype: Mexico, Chihuahua, 'nr San Pablo' [nr Delicias, Chihuahuan Desert at c. 1100 m alt.], 8 April 1847, *Wislizenus* 244 (MO 83707, flowers only). NB. the 'paratypes' cited by W.O. Moore (1967) and Benson (1982) are not relevant for typification of this name as they are not mentioned in Engelmann's protologue (cf. ICBN, p. 80, T.4(c), in adnot.).

Cereus dubius Engelm., Syn. Cact. US. 26-27 (1856) et Cact. Mex. Bound. 36, t. 50 (1859). Lectotype (J. Coulter in Contrib. US. Nat. Herb. 3: 390. 1896): Texas, Hudspeth Co., nr the Rio Grande, 19 June 1852, *C. Wright* (MO) (cf. Benson, loc. cit. infra).

Echinocereus dubius (Engelm.) Ruempler in Foerster, Handb. Cacteenk., ed. 2, 787 (1885); Weniger, Cacti of the Southwest, t. 15 (1970); E. & B. Lamb, Colourful Cacti, 183, t. 54 (1974).

E. enneacanthus var. *dubius* (Engelm.) L. Benson in Cact. Succ. J. (US) 41: 127 (1969) et Cacti US & Can. 649, 650 (map), 654, 944, figs. 692 & 693 (1982); Breckenridge & Miller in Syst. Bot. 7: 367-371, figs. 1, 4 & 5 (1982).

E. merkeri Hildmann ex Schumann, Gesamtb. Kakt. 277-278 (1897); Britton & Rose, Cact. 3: 35, fig. 43 (1922). Syntypes: Mexico, Durango, Ciudad Lerdo, and S Coahuila, in the Sierra Bola and nr Parras, *Mathsson* (B ? †).

E. sarissophorus Britton & Rose, Cact. 3: 38-39, fig. 47 (1922). Type: SE Coahuila, nr Saltillo, April 1898, *Palmer* 100 (US).

13a. var. enneacanthus

Stems 5-15 cm in diameter. *Areoles* 1.9-4.5 cm apart on the ribs. *Radial spines* to c. 4 cm long; centrals 1-3(-4), to 8 cm long, divergent, curved, often very stout.

DISTRIBUTION. Central N Mexico (Central & E Chihuahua, Coahuila, NE Durango & N Zacatecas; (?) N San Luis Potosi & SW Nuevo Leon) to W Texas (in the Big Bend and along the Rio Grande W of the Pecos River to El Paso); Chihuahuan Desert on limestone in valleys and washes, 600-1200(-1700) m altitude.

13b. var. brevispinus (W.O. Moore) L. Benson, loc. cit. (1969) et tom. cit. 649, 650 (map), 654, 944 (1982).

E. enneacanthus f. *brevispinus* W.O. Moore in Brittonia 19: 93-94, fig. 34 (1967). Type: cultivated plant ex Texas, Starr Co., 8 miles E of Rio Grande City, *Moore* 508, originally collected on 31 Dec. 1953 by *E.U. Clover* (MICH).

? *Cereus blanckii* Poselger in Allg. Gartenz. 21: 134 (1853). Type: Mexico, N Tamaulipas, nr Camargo (apparently not preserved).

? *E. berlandieri* var. *blanckii* (Poselger) P. Fournier, Cactées & Pl. Grasses, 21 (1935).

? *E. carnosus* Ruempler, tom. cit. 796 (1885). Type: Texas, sine loc. (not preserved).

? *E. enneacanthus* var. *carnosus* (Ruempler) Quehl in Monatsschr. Kakteenk. 18: 114 (1908).

[*E. enneacanthus* sensu Engelm., tom. cit. (1859) tantum quoad t. 48 fig. 2 & t. 49, et auctt. omnium.]

[*E. enneacanthus* var. *enneacanthus* sensu Benson, tom. cit. 649-651, 650 (map), 944, figs. 688 & 689 tantum (1982) et Breckenridge & Miller, loc. cit., figs. 1-3 (1982).]

[*E. tulensis* H. Bravo-H. in Cact. Suc. Mex. 18: 109 (1973) tantum quoad fig. 62.]

Stems to 5 cm in diameter. *Areoles* to 2(-2.4) cm apart on the ribs. *Radial spines* mostly < 1.5 cm long; centrals 1(-3), to 4(-5) cm long, porrect, straight.

DISTRIBUTION. S New Mexico (Ash Canyon, Dona Aṇa Co.), S Texas (along the Rio Grande, Edwards Plateau and Rio Grande Plain) and Mexico in N & E Coahuila, N Nuevo Leon, Tamaulipas and (?) NE Chihuahua; Chihuahuan Desert, grassland and brushland, near sea-level to c. 900 m altitude (higher in the S?).

14. ECHINOCEREUS BERLANDIERI

In the literature and in living collections this species has long been mistakenly known as '*E. blan(c)kii*', a name based on *Cereus blanckii* Poselger (1853). The original description of the latter, which calls for stems with 8-10 ribs, cannot apply to this species, but probably refers to a variety of the allied *E. enneacanthus* (q.v.). Although it was not described until 1856, *E. berlandieri* is probably among the four earliest discovered species of *Echinocereus*. It is named for Jean Louis Berlandier, a French explorer who travelled in NE Mexico between 1827 and 1830 before moving to Texas, where he found our species in flower by the Nueces River, in April 1834. There is a representative herbarium collection from this date, but he also sent living material or seeds to Engelmann at St. Louis, where a plant flowered and was subsequently figured in the *Cactaceae of the Boundary*, plate 58 (1859). This illustration, even today, is amongst the finest published of the species, and leaves no excuse for the misapplication of its name by Weniger (1970), who uses *E. berlandieri* for a Texas form of *E. pentalophus* also found along the Nueces. These two are not confusable when seen in flower, the pinkish perianth of the latter having a conspicuous pale yellow to white throat, whereas the purple perianth of *E. berlandieri* is darker in the throat.

Echinocereus berlandieri is wide-ranging and extremely variable, though its stems are always more or less creeping. The common form in cultivation has rather slender branches, the 5-7 ribs composed of small tubercles. It seems to be a northern plant, probably from Texas. Forms from further south, in ṆE Mexico, seem to have stouter stems and spines. Included here is a giant form from near Tula, Tamaulipas, with stems to 5 cm thick. It may be the plant described as *E. tulensis* by Helia Bravo-Hollis (1973). Here we must emphasize the word *described*, since the illustrations accompanying her article seem to depict two other species (*E. pentalophus* and *E. enneacanthus*). This and other forms may deserve recognition at varietal rank, but at present the species is still very poorly understood in the field. This may in part be due to its preferred habitat, beneath thorny brushland, which does not solicit close investigation by cactophiles.

In cultivation the sprawling *E. berlandieri* needs plenty of room and cannot be grown to its best unless bedded-out or placed in a very wide pan. Large specimens flower abundantly and are well worth the space they occupy. Propagation is almost entirely by cuttings, the longer prostrate stems sometimes having adventitious roots already developed. It is probably a little tender, since much of the species' range is at relatively low altitudes, and it should therefore be protected from frost. It does not need full sun.

DESCRIPTION. *Plant* caespitose, forming low clumps to 1 m or more in diameter, the branches arising above or below ground, tapered at base. *Stems* cylindric, 5-60(-200) cm long, 1.5-5 cm thick, soft, prostrate, or erect near apex, light to dark or purplish-green. *Ribs* 5-7, low, conspicuously to finely tuberculate, sometimes ill-defined. *Areoles* circular, 2.5-4 mm in diameter, 8-20 mm apart. *Radial spines* 6-9, to 1(-2.5) cm long, mostly acicular, dirty white, sometimes brown-tipped; centrals 1-3, to 2.5-5 cm long, stouter, porrect to deflexed, yellowish to dark brown. *Flowers* like those of the preceding species, but broadly funnelform; *receptacle-tube* areoles bearing up to 12 spines, the upper ones sometimes curved or twisted; *perianth-segments* narrower, mostly not exceeding 1 cm wide, darker coloured, especially in the throat. *Stigmas* more slender, to 9 mm long. *Fruit* ovoid, 2-2.5 cm long and 1.5 cm in diameter, green, with numerous brownish, deciduous spines. *Seeds* broadly ovoid, c. 1 mm long, tuberculate, black.

DISTRIBUTION. S Texas (nr the Nueces River SE of Mathis and along the Rio Grande) and NE Mexico (Nuevo Leon & Tamaulipas); mesquite thickets and grassland, near sea-level, to 1200 m altitude (in the S).

Echinocereus berlandieri (Engelm.) Hort. F.A. Haage, Cacteen-Verzeichniss, 19 (1859); Schumann in Bluehende Kakt. 1: t. 37 (1903); H. Hirao, Colour Encycl. Cacti, 159, fig. 631 (1979); L. Benson, Cacti US & Can. 618-622, 941, figs. 660 & 661 (1982); E. Haustein, Der Kosmos-Kakteenfuhrer, 222, with pl. (1983).

Cereus berlandieri Engelm., Syn. Cact. US. 30 (1856) et Cact. Mex. Bound. 38, t. 58 (1859). Type: 'On the Nueces [River], in Southern Texas: fl. May and June' [*Berlandier*]. Lectotype (cf. Benson, 1982): 'flumen . . . las Nueces [SE of Mathis], Abrilo 1834', *Berlandier* 2423 (MO, flowers) (no. '2433' according to Benson, but the duplicate at K is clearly marked '2423'). Although the month of this collection does not agree with Engelmann's protologue it appears to be the only material eligible. Engelmann's description was probably, at least in part, drawn up from material cultivated at St. Louis (hence the later flowering date?) which Berlandier originally provided. The plate 58 in Engelmann (1859) was more than likely drawn from the same living material and clarifies the name's application considerably.

Echinocereus blanckii var. *berlandieri* (Engelm.) Backeb., Die Cact. 4: 1999 (1960) (basionym given on p. 1997); W. Rauh, Kakt. an ihren Standorten, Farbtafel 3.8 (1979) (excellent colour pl.).

E. poselgerianus A. Linke in Allg. Gartenz. 25: 239-240 (1857). Type: Mexico, 1849-1852, *Poselger* (not preservered).

'*E. cereiformis*' W. v. Roeder in Kakteenkunde 1935: 2, with figs. pp. 1 & 3 (1935), nom. inval. (Art. 36).

? *E. tulensis* H. Bravo-H. in Cact. Suc. Mex. 18: 110-111 (1973) tantum quoad descr.

[*E. blanckii* sensu auctt. omnium: F. Palmer ('blankii') in Rev. Hort. 36: 92, with pl. (1865); Britton & Rose, Cact. 3: 20, t. 3.4 (1922); Weniger, Cacti of the Southwest, 53-54, t. 17 (1970), etc., non *Cereus blanckii* Poselger.]

This distinctive, and when in flower, unmistakable species is closely related to the last, and together with its more caespitose, dwarf variety *angusticeps*, has indeed been sunk into *E. berlandieri* by Benson (1969)*. However, in addition to its unusual yellow flowers, strikingly spotted with red in the throat, it is amply distinct for its much broader, spatulate perianth-segments and short, erect stems with more numerous ribs. The ribs are more or less dissolved into fine tubercles, which can sometimes be as much as 9 mm long but only 3 mm wide at base.

As noted by Weniger (1970), 'the plant itself is insignificant and not particularly attractive in its growth, but is highly prized for its beautiful flowers'. Persuading it to flower is, unfortunately, not always easy, although greater warmth in winter may be the solution to this deficiency. It originates from low

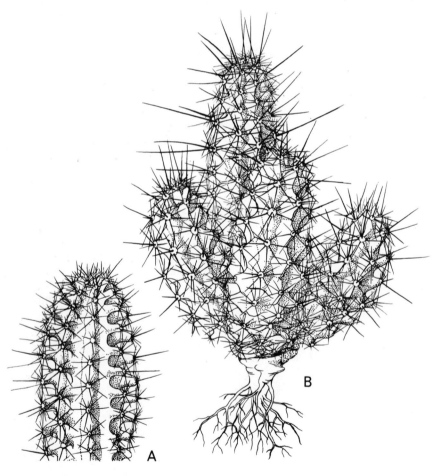

Echinocereus papillosus var. **papillosus**. A, stem apex, × 1. **E. p.** var. **angusticeps**. B, plant, × 1 (both ex Hort. D. Parker).

altitude brushlands in S Texas, where it grows in fine sandy loam overlying limestone. This well drained substrate and subtropical climate give the clues as to how it should be grown. Probably a minimum winter temperature of 7-10°C would suit it best, but it will survive if kept cooler. A very open largely mineral compost is desirable, if it is to be watered without fear of rot appearing during inevitable dull summer spells. As yet it is uncommon, though not rare, in cultivation, where vegetative propagation of the less caespitose var. *papillosus* has been slow. As a result it is very much in demand by would-be connoisseurs of the genus.

DESCRIPTION. Like the preceding species, but stems mostly ± erect, occasionally to 7 cm in diameter, often brownish-green. *Ribs* (6-)7-10, tubercles much more prominent to papilliform, to 9 mm long and 2-3 mm wide at base; spines not exceeding 2 cm long. *Flowers* funnelform, 8-12 cm in diameter, fragrant. *Receptacle-tube* to 4.5 cm long. *Perianth-segments* in 2-4 rows, broader, to 2 cm wide, bright yellow contrasted with orange-red to purple in the throat. *Fruit* ± globose to 1.5 cm in diameter.

DISTRIBUTION. S Texas (S from San Antonio & E from Laredo to the coast N of the Rio Grande); Rio Grande plain at low elevations; reported from adjacent NE Mexico (Tamaulipas).

Echinocereus papillosus A. Linke ex Ruempler in Foerster, Handb. Cacteenk. ed. 2, 783 (1885); M. Guerke in Bluehende Kakt. 2: t. 115 (1909); Clover in Rhodora 37: 77-79, t. 327, fig. 1 (1935); Weniger, Cacti of the Southwest, 49-50, t. 16 (1970); E. & B. Lamb, Ill. Ref. Cact. Succ. 5: t. 303 (1978) (superb colour pl.). Type: cultivated plants of unknown origin (not preserved). Neotype (Benson in Cact. Succ. J. (US) 41: 126. 1969): Guerke, loc. cit., tab. 115 (1909).

15a. var. **papillosus**
Stems few to 10, to 10 cm or more long, 3-5(-7) cm in diameter.
DISTRIBUTION. As for species; under dense acacia-mesquite chaparral.

15b. var. **angusticeps** (Clover) W.T. Marsh. in Marshall & Bock, Cactaceae, 119 (1941); Weniger, loc. cit., t. 16 (1970).
E. angusticeps Clover, loc. cit., 78-79, t. 327, figs. 1 & 2 (1935) (reprinted in Cact. Succ. J. (US) 7: 173-174, with plate, 1936). Type: Texas, Hidalgo Co., N of Edinburgh, nr Linn, [*Clover*] no. 15261 (MICH).
Stems 5-95, 4-8 cm long, 2-3 cm in diameter.
DISTRIBUTION. Type locality and vicinity; exposed in grassy, open mesquite woodland.

* *Note added in proof.* Fresh flower material (studied May 1985) indicates that *E. papillosus* is misplaced here. Its basally thickened and widely spaced perianth-segments indicate a relationship with sect. *Erecti*, where its closest ally would seem to be *E. fendleri*.

16. ECHINOCEREUS CINERASCENS

This wide ranging E Mexican species is not as well known as the distinctive *E. pentalophus*, though both were discovered by Thomas Coulter and named before 1830. De Candolle's original diagnosis of Coulter's material called for a plant with 8 ribs and areoles with ten radial and four central spines. Such plants are common in Hidalgo, where Coulter is believed to have collected, but the variation of the species is immense, especially in respect to rib number and stem thickness. One of the more distinctive Hidalgo forms, with 10-12 ribs, was described and figured long ago in Curtis's Botanical Magazine (t. 4373) as *Echinocactus chlorophthalmus* Hook. (1848). It and many other variants may be worthy of varietal recognition, but detailed field study is required first. Here, only var. *ehrenbergii* (Pfeiffer)· H. Bravo-H. is accepted, and mainly, it is to be admitted, for psychological reasons, as the plant is extremely distinctive in cultivation.

Echinocereus cinerascens ranges across the high central Mexican plateau and may be a southern vicariant of the Chihuahuan Desert species, *E. stramineus*. Their massively constructed flowers seem to agree in most details. It is often confused with the vegetatively similar *E. enneacanthus* (q.v.), but has white or pale, not dark-throated flowers to distinguish it. Its many synonyms are not listed here but can be found in the index. The variety *ehrenbergii* was discovered by Carl Ehrenberg in Hidalgo during the 1830's, and is in cultivation at present, but rare. The name is often misapplied to var. *cinerascens* in collections, while a stout form

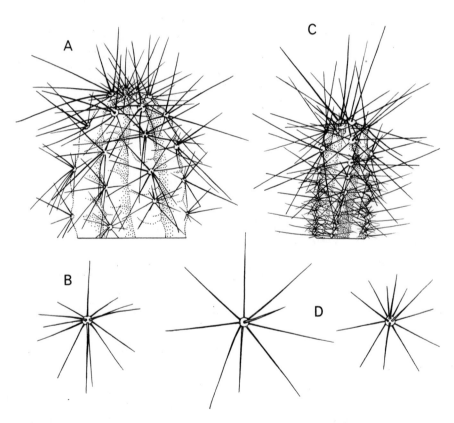

Echinocereus cinerascens var. **cinerascens**. A, stem apex, × ⅔; B, stem areole, × ⅔ (ex Barranca de Toliman, Hidalgo). **E.c.** var. **ehrenbergii**. C, stem, × ⅔; D, stem areoles, × ⅔ (cult. D. Minnion ex vicinity of Barranca de Metztitlan, Hidalgo).

of var. *ehrenbergii* can be found labelled '*E. spinibarbis*' (a name which properly applies to a species of *Eulychnia!*). It has mostly very slender stems, with 5-6 ribs and is covered in attractive, very long glassy white spines. The flowers are enormous for the size of the stems, but are produced only by large, old clumps. In its typical state it is known only from the great Barranca of Metztitlan, which was one of the localities reported for *Cereus propinquus* by Ehrenberg (1846), under which name he included Pfeiffer's *C. ehrenbergii* as a synonym. Elsewhere in Hidalgo and Querétaro are forms which seem to connect it to var. *cinerascens*, but the typical Metztitlan plant may be ecologically distinct, coming from lower altitudes than the type variety of the species. If not, then it is certainly worthy of treatment as a cultivar for horticultural purposes.

DESCRIPTION. *Plant* caespitose, forming mats or mounds of prostrate to erect stems. *Stems* cylindric, to 30 cm or more long, 1.5-12 cm in diameter, bright green. *Ribs* 5-12, usually with pronounced tubercles, but sometimes even-edged. *Areoles* circular, 2-3 mm or more in diameter, with creamy-white wool at first, 8-15 mm or more apart. *Radial spines* 6-10, 1-3.5 cm long, acicular, dirty yellowish- to glassy-white; centrals 1-6, to 4.5 cm long, porrect to divergent-cruciform, pinkish to orange at first, then yellow, brown or glassy-white, darker at the bulbous base. *Flowers* broadly funnelform, 7-10 cm long, 6-12 cm or more in diameter, mostly arising well below stem apex. *Receptacle-tube* to 4.5 cm long, walls to 6 mm thick in region of nectar chamber, ovary occupying basal 2.4 cm or less, 1.5-2 cm in diameter, tube contracted above to 1.2-1.7 cm, then flared to 3-4 cm in diameter at apex, exterior green, bearing few areoles with up to 12, to 2 cm long, white, straight or curved spines. *Nectar chamber* 6-9 mm long, 2.5-3 mm in diameter. *Perianth-segments* cuneate--

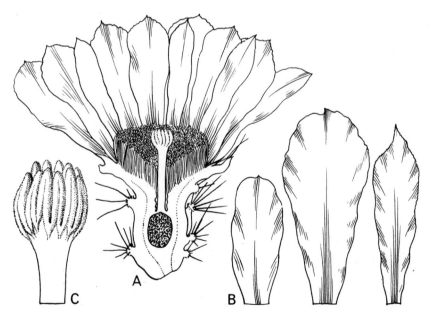

Echinocereus cinerascens. A, half-flower, × 1; B, outer (1) to inner (r) perianth-segments, × 1; C, top of style with stigmas, × 3 (ex Hort. Holly Gate).

oblanceolate, to 5 cm or more long, 1.5-2.5 cm wide near the rounded to acuminate, serrate apex, pinkish-magenta, but white or paler in the throat or at base. *Stamen filaments* to c. 9 mm long; anthers oblong, 2 mm long. *Style* 2.7-3.3 cm long, 2-3 mm in diameter; stigmas 10-15, to 6 mm long, very stout, dark green. *Ovary locule* globose to obconic, c. 6 mm long at anthesis. *Fruit* 2-3 cm in diameter, green, spiny, strawberry or raspberry-flavoured. *Seeds* broadly ovoid, 1.2 mm long (see Sterk, loc. cit.).

DISTRIBUTION. Central E Mexico: states of Mexico, Distrito Federal, Hidalgo, Querétaro, E Guanajuato & W San Luis Potosi, at or above 1600 m altitude.

Echinocereus cinerascens (DC.) Lemaire ('cinerescens'), Cactées, 56 (1868); Sanchez-Mej., Man. Cact. Suc. Metztitlan, 27-28, 103, fig. 24 (1978); W. Sterk in Succulenta (NL) 50(5): 102-104, with figs. (1980) (excellent cover illustration).
Cereus cinerascens DC. in Mem. Mus. Hist. Nat. Paris 17: 116 (1828); C.A. Ehrenb. in
  Linnaea 19: 362 (1846). Type: 'Mexico'[environs of Zimapan, 1827-1828 (cf. McVaugh
  in J. Wash. Acad. Sci. 33: 65-69. 1943)], *Coulter* 23' (apparently not preserved).
Echinocactus chlorophthalmus Hook. in Bot. Mag. 74: t. 4373 (1848). Type: a cultivated plant
  ex Mexico, Hidalgo, 'Real del Monte' (not preserved). Lectotype (designated here):
  Hook., loc. cit. t. 4373.
[*Echinocereus pentalophus* var. *ehrenbergii* sensu Backeb., Die Cact. 4: Abb. 1907 (NB. almost
  certainly not natural size as stated, probably × ¼-½) (1960) et E. Kleiner in Kakt. and.
  Sukk. 33(8): inside front cover, excellent cover illustration (1982), non *Cereus ehrenbergii*
  Pfeiffer.]

16a. var. **cinerascens**
Stems 4-10(-12) cm in diameter, 6-12-ribbed. *Central spines* equal to or less than stem diameter in length, yellowish to brown.
DISTRIBUTION. As for species, mostly at or above 2000 m altitude.

16b. var. **ehrenbergii** (Pfeiffer) H. Bravo-H. in Cact. Suc. Mex. 19: 47 (1974).
Cereus ehrenbergii Pfeiffer in Allg. Gartenz. 8: 282 (1840). Type: 'Mexico' [Hidalgo], *C.A.
  Ehrenberg* (presumed not to have been preserved).
Echinocereus ehrenbergii (Pfeiffer) Ruempler in Forester, Handb. Cacteenk. ed. 2, 775 (1885);
  Sanchez-Mej., loc. cit., fig. 51 (1978).
E. spinibarbis Haage f. sec. Backeb., tom. cit., 2052, Abb. 1947 (1960), non (Pfeiffer)
  Schumann (1897).
Stems 1.5-4(-6) cm in diameter, 5-6-ribbed. *Central spines* exceeding stem diameter in length, glassy white to pale yellow.
DISTRIBUTION. E Hidalgo (upper part of Barranca de Metztitlan and vicinity), 1600-2000 m altitude.

17. ECHINOCEREUS STRAMINEUS

This species inhabits the Chihuahuan Desert region where it is commonly found on rocky limestone slopes in full sun. The plants form large mounds of many stems, covered in long, straw-coloured to white, needle-like spines. In the field these 'mounds of straw' are sometimes almost hidden in summer by the large magenta flowers, as pictures in E. & B. Lamb (1974) and Benson (1982) amply testify. Flowering in cultivation, however, is achieved less easily since the plants must be grown to a fair size before they will oblige, and are then rather space-consuming. But as our plate shows the event is worth waiting for!

Echinocereus stramineus (Engelm.) Ruempler was first described in the genus *Cereus* by Engelmann in 1856. The material upon which he based the name came from southern New Mexico and western Texas where the Chihuahuan Desert has its northern limit. Southwards the species ranges through parts of Chihuahua, Coahuila and Nuevo Leon to E Durango, N Zacatecas and N San Luis Potosi. In the southeastern part of its range it is represented by a smaller-flowered form, previously distinguished as *E. conglomeratus* Schumann, but scarcely even worthy of varietal status.

The immediate affinity of *E. stramineus* is with the allopatric *E. cinerascens* and *E. viereckii*, which range further south and east, respectively, and with the partially sympatric *E. enneacanthus* (*E. dubius*), which generally occurs at lower elevations and often in less exposed situations. Lyman Benson (1969, 1982) has treated *E. stramineus* as a variety of the last-named, but this is refuted in a recent study by Breckenridge & Miller (1982). Their conclusions, which emphasize differences in flower-pigment chemistry and the existence of a partial reproductive barrier between the two taxa, are also supported by divergences in habit (*E. enneacanthus* is not mound-forming), rib number, spination, and flower shape and colour (in *E. stramineus* much broader and often paler in the throat). It is to be admitted that intermediates or hybrids between them are occasionally found in the field, but

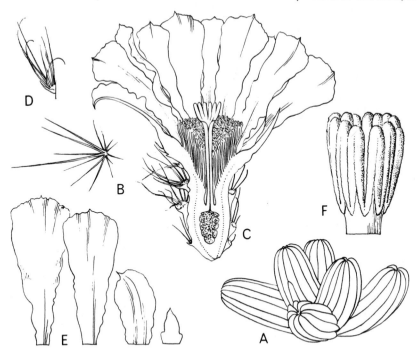

Echinocereus stramineus. A, habit, × ⅙; B, stem areole, × ⅔; C, half-flower, × ⅔; D, areole from receptacle-tube, × 1; E, outer (r) to inner (l) perianth-segments, × ⅔; F, top of style with stigma-lobes, × 3 (ex Hort. G. E. Cheetham).

otherwise their differences seem greater than those which can be found to differentiate *E. stramineus* and *E. cinerascens*. The flowers of *E. cinerascens* are very similar indeed, and the latter's var. *ehrenbergii*, at least in cultivation, looks and behaves like a miniature *E. stramineus*. The relationship between this allopatric species pair needs investigation in N San Luis Potosi, where their ranges appear to meet. However, on present knowledge there can be no question of recognizing *E. stramineus* at other than specific rank.

DESCRIPTION. *Plant* caespitose, forming hemispherical mounds of up to 500 stems, to a metre or more in diameter. *Stems* to 45 cm long and 8 cm in diameter near base, tapering gradually towards apex. *Ribs* (10-)11-17, somewhat tuberculate. *Areoles* 7-15(-18) mm apart, with abundant white wool at first, later naked. *Spines* pink, dirty straw-coloured or brownish at first, later glassy white, acicular; radials 7-14, to 30 mm long; centrals (1-)2-4, 4-8.7 cm long, much stouter, terete to somewhat flattened, straight or slightly curved, variously directed. *Flowers* broadly funnel-shaped, 6-12.5 cm long and in diameter, mostly arising well away from stem apex. *Receptacle-tube* to c 5 cm long, ovary occupying basal 2 cm, to c 1.7 cm in diameter at apex of nectar chamber, but scarcely or not contracted above ovary, expanding above nectar chamber to 4 cm in diameter at apex, very fleshy and thick, exterior bearing 4-5 mm long, pointed, widely spaced scales subtending white-woolly areoles with 6-9 glassy white spines, spines to 3 cm long, uppermost longest and usually curved. *Nectar chamber* c 5 mm long, 4 mm in diameter, mostly filled by the base of the style, surrounded by a very thick section of the receptacle. *Perianth-segments* in about 2 rows, outermost varying from pointed and scale-like to obovate-apiculate, with a green midrib, inner segments cuneate-oblanceolate, longest to 6 cm long, 2.5 cm wide near apex, margins entire or somewhat wavy, at apex raggedly toothed, apiculate, bright magenta, often paler towards base. *Stamen filaments* short, only 8-10 mm long, purplish-red; anthers oblong, yellow, 1-1.5 mm long. *Style* c 2.7 cm long, to 2.5 mm in diameter, reddish, expanding at apex into 10-13, c 8 mm long, deep green stigmas. *Ovary locule* oblong, at anthesis 13 mm long, 8 mm in diameter. *Fruit* globular, to 5 cm long, red when ripe, with glassy deciduous spines, very fleshy, smelling and tasting of strawberries. *Seeds* black, ovoid, c 1.5 mm long (see Sterk, loc. cit.).

DISTRIBUTION. SW USA: S New Mexico & W Texas; Cent N Mexico: N Chihuahua, Coahuila, Nuevo Leon, E Durango, N Zacatecas & N San Luis Potosi; Chihuahuan Desert on limestone, (600-)1200-1600 m altitude.

Echinocereus stramineus (Engelm.) Ruempler in C. F. Foerster, Handb. Cacteenk. ed. 2, 797 (1885); E. & B. Lamb, Colourful Cacti, 187, tt. 27-30 (1974); W. Sterk in Succulenta (NL) 59: 164-167, with figs. (1980); Breckenridge & Miller in Syst. Bot. 7, 4: 369-377, figs. 1, 6 & 7 (1982); H. Hecht, BLV Handbuch der Kakteen, 257 (1982). (PLATE 5)

Cereus stramineus Engelm., Syn. Cact. US. 26 (1856) and Cact. Mex. Bound. 35, tt. 47-48 (1859). Type: 'mountain slopes, from El Paso to the Pecos and Gila Rivers'. Lectotype (J. Coulter in Contrib. US. Nat. Herb. 3: 390. 1896): *C. Wright* in 1851 (MO).

E. enneacanthus Engelm. var. *stramineus* (Engelm.) L. Benson in Cact. Succ. J. (US) 41: 127 (1969) and Cacti US & Can. 649, 654, 944, 650 (map), figs. 690 & 691, colour pl. 104 (1982).

18. ECHINOCEREUS VIERECKII

Echinocereus viereckii Werderm. is one of the best of the spreading, clump-forming echinocerei for cultivation. In a sunny position it grows easily and with luck will produce its stunning magenta flowers when still in a small pot. It is also readily propagated by cuttings and deserves to be seen in more collections than at present.

It is named for H. W. Viereck, a famous German cactus collector who discovered and introduced various species from NE Mexico in the 1920's and '30's. *E. viereckii* was described by Werdermann in 1934 after he had collected it himself, in habitat, the previous year. Apparently the original Viereck introduction had been mistaken for *E. scheeri*, an error sometimes encountered even today, but Werdermann rectified this blunder and correctly determined its relationship as near *E. enneacanthus* Engelm.

E. viereckii is certainly close to *E. enneacanthus* or at least to the latter's lowland forms from the dry brushlands of southern Texas and adjacent Mexico. However, its flowers, which have somewhat shorter, thicker receptacle-tubes and perianth-segments not darkened but usually paler at base, seem to indicate a closer affinity with *E. stramineus* and *E. cinerascens*, especially the latter. Nevertheless it occurs in wooded areas and its ecology, therefore, has more in common with that of the vegetatively similar *E. enneacanthus* var. *brevispinus*, rather than *E. stramineus*. Perhaps its closest relationship is with the next species (*E. nivosus*, q.v.), but a decision on its final systematic position must await a careful study of the E. CINERASCENS GROUP as a whole in the field.

The conspicuously yellow-spined original form of *E. viereckii*, as figured here, seems distinctive and unmistakable. It comes from the eastern edge of the Sierra Madre Oriental between Cd. Victoria and Jaumave, at altitudes of 1500-2000 metres. However, Alfred Lau's collection (no. 1295) from nearer the Nuevo Leon border to the northwest, at 1700 m, has much shorter whitish spines on less tuberculate stems, and seems dissimilar until it flowers. Though inferior from the horticultural standpoint, it is of considerable botanical interest as it provides a clear link between the spinier type form and *E. morricalii* Riha (1975), recently described from a cliff habitat further north in Nuevo Leon. Such a relationship may at first seem surprising, for *E. morricalii* is practically spineless and its ribs are quite devoid of tubercles, but there is, however, an almost exact parallel in the form of *E. scheeri* and its spineless variety *gentryi* (Clover) N.P. Taylor. *E. morricalii* is certainly not a distinct species, but rather a cliff-forest ecotype of *E. viereckii*, which has evolved a habit identical to *E. scheeri* var. *gentryi* and the type form of *E. subinermis* var. *subinermis*. All three are distinguishable from their 'normal' conspecific relatives by stems with fewer, straight-edged ribs, minute or absent spines, and a tendency for purple-tinging during drought or winter. In *Echinocereus* this would seem to represent a syndrome identifiable with a forested-cliff habitat in which all of the above are found, and its manifestations should not be mistaken for the characters distinguishing a new species. Accordingly *E. morricalii* Riha is here referred to varietal status under *E. viereckii*, there being no obvious floral differences to separate them. In taking this step the writer is aware of the apparently considerable altitudinal separation between typical var. *viereckii* (1500-2000 m) and var. *morricalii* (c. 350 m). However, this range is no greater than that recorded for the related *E. enneacanthus* (*sens. lat.*) and one's suspicion is that populations at intermediate altitudes do exist but have as yet not been recorded.

Riha (1976), in his later assessment of his species, suggests its affinity with *E. leonensis* Mathsson (= *E. pentalophus*), primarily on floral grounds. Careful comparison of their flowers, however, indicates that this is at best rather remote, the latter being a particularly isolated species within *Echinocereus*.

DESCRIPTION. *Stems* freely branching at the base, erect or somewhat decumbent, to 50 cm long and 2-7.5 cm in diameter, cylindric, tapering towards apex, light yellowish- to blackish-green or purplish. *Ribs* 6-9, 6-10 mm high, broken up into small tubercles or even-edged. *Areoles* 5-10 mm apart, 1.5-3 mm in diameter, at first with pale yellow wool but soon becoming glabrous. *Spines* whitish to yellow, acicular to bristle-like or absent; radials 7-11, 1-9 mm long, lowermost 5 longest; centrals 3-5, the lowermost to 20 mm long, like the radials but stouter and ± porrect. *Flowers* rather short-funnelform, but expanding to 7-11 cm in diameter. *Receptacle-tube* 2.5-3.5 cm long, ovary occupying basal 0.8-1.2 cm, 1.5 cm in diameter in ovary region, contracting to c 1.2 cm above ovary and then expanding to c 2.5 cm in diameter at apex, very fleshy and thick, exterior with closely set tubercles bearing triangular-apiculate scales subtending areoles with 3-12 straight, bristle-like, golden spines, 5-20 mm long. *Nectar chamber* 5 mm long, 2.5-3 mm in diameter, surrounding tissue very thick. *Perianth-segments* in about 2 rows, cuneate-oblanceolate, longest 3.5-5.5 cm long, 1.2-2 cm wide towards the rounded to subacute apex, apiculate, entire to finely serrate near apex, magenta, sometimes paler at base, outermost smaller segments with a green midrib. *Stamen filaments* short, 6-10 mm long; anthers scarcely 1 mm long, yellow. *Style* 1.3-2.6 cm

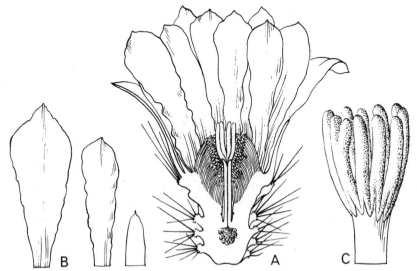

Echinocereus viereckii. A, half-flower, × 1; B, outer (r) to inner (l) perianth-segments, × 1; C, top of style with stigma-lobes, × 3 (ex Hort. G. E. Cheetham).

long, c 2mm in diameter, expanding into 10-11, to 10 mm long, bright green stigmas. *Ovary locule* very small, at anthesis c 3mm long and 4 mm in diameter. *Fruit* globular, to 2 cm in diameter, bright green, fleshy. *Seeds* (see Riha, 1976) ovoid, 1.5-2 mm long, tuberculate, black.

DISTRIBUTION. NE Mexico: SW Tamaulipas to Cent. W Nuevo Leon; wooded hills and cliffs on E flanks of the Sierra Madre Oriental at c. 350-2000 m altitude.

Echinocereus viereckii Werderm. in Kakteenk. 1934: 188-189, with fig. (1934) and in Bluehende Kakt. and. Sukk. Pfl., Lfg. 23, t. 89 (1935); Borg, Cacti, 181, t. 25(a) (1937); Backeb., Die Cact. 4: 2056, t. 211 (1960); Cheetham in Nat. Cact. Succ. J. 27: 5, with fig. (1972); H. Hecht, BLV Handbuch der Kakteen, 258 (1982). Type: Mexico, SW Tamaulipas, mountains between Jaumave and Ciudad Victoria, c 1500-2000 m.s.m, [no collector cited] (B †). Lectotype (Kew Mag. 1:165. 1984): illustration in Kakteenk., loc. cit. (1934) of flowering plant collected in Mexico by *Werdermann* in 1933 (cf. Werdermann, 1935). '*E. vatteri*' B. Botzenhart in Kakt. and. Sukk. 19 (7) front cover (1968) (superb colour pl.).

18a. var. **viereckii** (PLATE 6).
Stems yellowish- to mid-green, with 6-9 tuberculate ribs, spiny.
DISTRIBUTION. SW Tamaulipas and (*fide* Riha, 1976) adjacent Nuevo Leon, to 2000 m altitude.

18b. var. **morricalii** (Riha) N.P. Taylor, stat. nov.
E. morricalii Riha in Kaktusy (Prague) 11: 75, 78 (1975) and in Ashingtonia 2: 99-101, with
   excellent colour figs. (1976). Type: Mexico, Nuevo Leon, S of Monterrey, Barranca de
   las Garrapatas, La Boca Dam, *D.B. Morrical* (PRC).
Stems green to blackish-green or tinged reddish-purple in winter, with 6-7(-8) even-edged ribs, spineless when mature.
DISTRIBUTION. Cent. W Nuevo Leon (S of Monterrey), cliffs at c. 350 m (*fide* Lau, 1983, *sub num. L.* 1221).

19. ECHINOCEREUS NIVOSUS

This is the most specialized member of the E. CINERASCENS GROUP and tax-onomically its most distinct species. It forms compact mounds of many short stems, hidden under myriad glassy white spines, and produces rather small yet beautiful magenta flowers. Its habit, dense spination and less than extravagant flowers seem to reflect its harsh mountain habitat in SE Coahuila, where it grows amongst grass and limestone rocks exposed to sun and wind. It is unquestionably one of the choicest of Mexican cacti.

Its precise relationship is debatable. Here it is placed next to *E. viereckii*, which likewise inhabits the Sierra Madre Oriental but on its east side and in less xeric conditions. They share a number of points in common, both having rather slender spines, similar perianth-segments and stigmas, and very similar and unusually large seeds, though in receptacle-tube shape and vegetative habit they differ markedly. On this latter point *E. nivosus* resembles a dwarf version of *E. stramineus*, which occurs in the neighbouring Chihuahuan Desert, to the north and south of the ridge ESE of Parras where *E. nivosus* is found.

Echinocereus nivosus Glass & Foster (1978) was introduced to cultivation sometime before 1960, the year Backeberg invalidly described it as '*E. albatus*'. He allied the species with the poorly known *E. longisetus* and Frank (1981) discusses it in connexion with his *E. freudenbergeri* (= *E. delaetii* var. *freudenbergeri*). However, these Mexican members of the related, yet distinct E. VIRIDIFLORUS GROUP have proportionately much narrower perianth-segments, short, stout receptacle-tubes and differently shaped and ornamented seeds (see Frank, loc. cit.), and may merely be convergent with *E. nivosus* in their possession of dense whitish spination. They also differ in habit, there being no compact mound-forming taxa in that group.

Like *E. viereckii*, its suggested closest ally, *E. nivosus* is as yet imperfectly known in the field. Currently only two localities are recorded in the literature: the type locality of El Cinco, south of General Cepeda, and Lau's Cinco de Mayo (*Lau* 739) further east, to the south of Carneros. Lau's form appears to have more open spination (see Sterk, 1980) but its flowers are identical to that illustrated by Glass & Foster, whose all too brief description can now be amplified with details from a flower kindly preserved by Mr A.J. Ward of Scarborough, U.K.

The cultivation of this sought-after species presents no special problems, although abundant sunlight is essential. It does not seem to be particularly

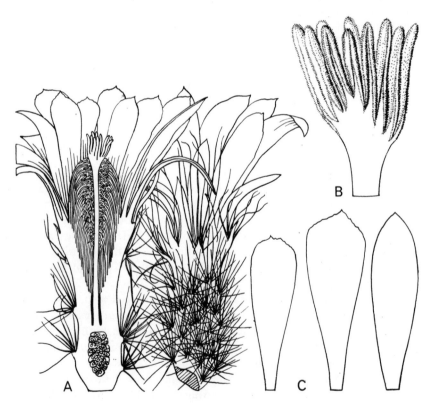

Echinocereus nivosus. A, half-flower and exterior, × 1½; B, top of style with stigmas, × 6; C, outer (l) to inner (r) perianth-segments, × 2 (ex Hort. A. J. Ward).

free-flowering, but in the absence of home-produced seeds, its propagation by cuttings is straightforward (so long as a friend, who does not mind removing a stem from a clump, can be found!).

DESCRIPTION. *Stems* branching freely and forming compact hemispherical mounds to c. 12 cm high and 30 cm in diameter, ovoid to shortly cylindric, to 4 cm in diameter, light green, but almost obscured by spines. *Ribs* c. 12, low, c. 3 mm high, somewhat tuberculate. *Areoles* 6-7 mm apart. *Spines* c. 35-50 per areole, mostly glassy-white, very slender, some radiating, 4-9 mm long, others ± porrect or deflexed, the centrals 10 or more, to 20 mm long, glassy or some brownish-tipped. *Flowers* to c. 6 cm long and 5 cm in diameter, slender funnelform, arising away from stem apex, and ovary therefore often immersed among the stems. *Receptacle-tube* to 3.3 cm long, ovary occupying basal 1.2 cm, there c. 1 cm in diameter, gradually flared above to 1.7 cm at apex, rather thick and fleshy, in ovary region exterior green, densely clothed in areoles with up to 35, to 3 cm long, glassy-white, upswept spines, upper part of tube deep crimson, with few triangular scales subtending areoles with fewer, curved or contorted spines. *Nectar chamber* c. 5 mm long, completely filled by base of style. *Perianth-segments* in about 2 rows, the largest obovate-oblanceolate, c. 2.3 cm long and 8.5 mm wide, apex nearly rounded to mucronate, deep pink to deep magenta, with a darker midline, paler to white at base. *Stamen filaments* c. 10 mm long; anthers oblong, 1 mm long, yellow. *Style* 3 cm long, 2 mm thick; stigmas 9-11, to 6 mm long, slender, bright green. *Ovary locule* ovoid, c. 7 mm long at anthesis. *Fruit* subglobose, 2 cm long, 2.5 cm in diameter, reddish-lavender, spiny. *Seeds* broadly ovoid, to 2 mm long.

DISTRIBUTION. SE Coahuila in the Sierra Madre Oriental (E of the Sierra de Parras); on limestone rocks at c. 2000 m altitude.

Echinocereus nivosus C. Glass & R. Foster in Cact. Succ. J. (US) 50: 18–19, figs. 1 & 2, 4 & 5, (1978); G.R.W. Frank in Kakt. and. Sukk. 32: 103–105, figs. C1–3 (1981). Type: Mexico, Coahuila, 'SE' [actually slightly SW] of General Cepeda, mountain pass 3 km N of El Cinco, Feb. 1972, *Glass & Foster* 3764 (POM).

'*E. albatus*' Backeb., Die Cact. 4: 2007–2009, Abb. 1910; ibid. 6: 3847, Abb. 3485 (1962); W. Cullmann in Kakt. and. Sukk. 16: 75, with fig. (1965); W. Andreae in ibid. 19: 81, with fig. (1968), nom. inval. (Arts. 9.5 & 37).

'*E. longisetus* var. *albatus*' W. Sterk in Succulenta (NL) 59: 12, with excellent colour pl. (1980), nom. inval. (based on the above).

20. ECHINOCEREUS DELAETII

To anyone interested in *Echinocereus* the name *E. delaetii* immediately has a meaning, for its typical form is a plant of extraordinary appearance, the stems obscured by long and sometimes wavy, hair-like spines. When it was introduced to cultivation and described, shortly after the turn of this century, the German cactologist Guerke at first thought it to be a *Cephalocereus*, such was its resemblance to a young specimen of the Old Man Cactus, *C. senilis* (Haw.) Schumann. However, the unusual spination of the original form should not be taken as the distinguishing feature of this species. In fact, large flowers and many-ribbed stems is the combination of characters which separates it from other members of the E. VIRIDIFLORUS GROUP. The long hair-like spines would appear to be an inconstant feature, since the recently described but synonymous *E. freudenbergeri* G.R.W. Frank (1981), with a nearly identical habit, flower and seed, has short, straight, dense, bristle-like spination akin to that seen in the related *E. chloranthus* var. *russanthus*. Here *E. freudenbergeri* is treated as a variety of *E. delaetii*, with which it grows in the Sierras de la Paila and de los Alamitos in the Chihuahuan Desert of central S Coahuila. It is being distributed in cultivation under Lau's number 1032 (Sierra de la Paila).

The closest relationship of *E. delaetii sens. lat.* is with *E. longisetus* (Engelm.) Lemaire, found further north and east, on the east side of the Sierra Madre Oriental. At present *E. longisetus* is too poorly understood in the field to evaluate its affinity with *E. delaetii* properly. However, apart from its generally smaller flowers, slightly fewer ribs and strongly deflexed, straight central spines to 5 cm long, there seems little to satisfactorily separate the two. Unfortunately, if the well-known *E. delaetii* is one day considered synonymous, then the older name *E. longisetus* will take its place.

In cultivation *E. delaetii* has a somewhat mixed reputation as far as flower production is concerned, this being reliable only in habitat-collected specimens in the season immediately following importation. However, the flowering specimen that enabled the accompanying line drawing and floral description to be made is a large, old plant with about 6 sprawling stems and flowers freely each year. It has been grown by Mr A.J. Ward of Scarborough, U.K., whose enviable success can probably be put down to a fully exposed greenhouse, which catches all available

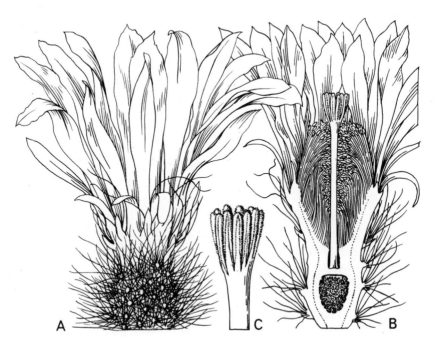

Echinocereus delaetii. A, flower, × 1; B, half-flower, × 1; C, top of style with stigmas, × 2 (ex Hort. A. J. Ward).

Plate 7

Echinocereus chloranthus var. *russanthus*

Plate 8

Echinocereus stoloniferus var. *stoloniferus*

sunlight (including during winter), although the considerable age of this clump, which is more than 40 cm in diameter, may be equally significant.

The much sought-after *E. delaetii* is commonly propagated by cuttings but, as it forms branches only slowly, these are in constant demand. The once frequent mass importation of habitat specimens is thankfully nowadays less common and should not be encouraged by would-be purchasers. Adequate stock of the species is in cultivation and there is no need to damage wild populations any further.

DESCRIPTION. *Stems* branched near base, forming loose open clumps of up to 50 stems, semi-prostrate, but apex ascending, cylindric, to 30 cm long, 4-8 cm in diameter, the green to pale green epidermis almost completely obscured by spines. *Ribs* (14-)17-24, narrow, tuberculate. *Areoles* orbicular to oval, to 6 mm in diameter, closely placed, to 1 cm apart. *Spines* 20-40, white to brown; radials bristle-like, some porrect, to 1 cm long; centrals 4-5, to 2.5-10 cm long, all straight, porrect and finely bristle-like, or some longer, shaggy and hair-like, hanging down around stem. *Flowers* broadly funnelform, 6-10 cm long, 6-12.5 cm in diameter, mostly arising well away from stem apex. *Receptacle-tube* to 4 cm long, very thick, ovary occupying basal 1.7 cm, 1.2-1.6 cm in diameter, tube contracted above then flared to 2.3 cm in diameter at apex, exterior thickly set with small areoles bearing 7-20, to 1.5 cm long, upswept, whitish, bristle-like spines, in the uppermost areoles curved or twisted. *Nectar chamber* to 4.5 mm long and 3 mm in diameter, partially filled by base of style. *Perianth-segments* in c. 2-3 rows, narrowly cuneate-oblanceolate, to 5.5 cm long and 1.5 cm wide, apex acute, fimbriate, bright pinkish-purple, white in the throat. *Stamen filaments* to 1.5 cm long, white; anthers oblong, to 1.7 cm long. *Style* to 3.5 cm long and 2.5 mm in diameter, white; stigmas 9-13, to 8 mm long, yellowish-green. *Ovary locule* ovoid, c. 1 cm long at anthesis. *Fruit* ovoid, to 2.5 cm long and 2 cm in diameter, carmine red, very spiny. *Seeds* (see Frank, loc. cit.) broadly ovoid, 1.5 mm long, dull black.

DISTRIBUTION. S Coahuila (especially in the Sierra de la Paila and Sierra de los Alamitos); Chihuahuan Desert, on limestone at or above 1800 m altitude.

Echinocereus delaetii (M. Guerke) M. Guerke in Monatsschr. Kakteenk. 19: 131 (1909); Britton & Rose, Cact. 3: 6, fig. 1 (1922); A. Berger, Kakteen, 175, Abb. 45 (1929); Backeb., Die Cact. 4: 2006, Abb. 1908 & 1909 (1960); H. Feiler in Kakt. and. Sukk. 20: 1, with fig. (1969); H. Wery in ibid. 30: 86-87, with figs. (1979); M. Pizzetti, Piante grasse le Cactaceae, no. 59, with excellent colour pl. (1985).
Cephalocereus delaetii M. Guerke in ibid. 116-121, with pl. (1909). Type not cited. Lectotype (designated here): Guerke, loc. cit. 119 (1909), an illustration of a flowering plant by De Laet who supplied the original material.

20a. var. **delaetii**
Stems to 30 cm long and 8 cm in diameter, clothed in shaggy hair-like spines to 10 cm long.
DISTRIBUTION. As for species.

20b. var. **freudenbergeri** (G.R.W. Frank) N.P. Taylor, stat. nov.
Echinocereus freudenbergeri G.R.W. Frank in Kakt. and. Sukk. 32: 105, with figs. (1981). Type: Mexico, Coahuila, 12 km S of Cuatrocienegas on road to San Pedro de las Colonias, *G. Freudenberger* (ZSS AA18–27).
Stems to 15 cm long, 4-6 cm in diameter, clothed in fine, straight, bristle-like spines to 2.5 cm long.
DISTRIBUTION. As for species.

21. ECHINOCEREUS LONGISETUS

Our knowledge of this very beautiful, long-spined Mexican species is far from complete at present, despite its discovery by J.M. Bigelow more than 130 years ago. This is largely because the type locality of 'Santa Rosa' (Coahuila) borders on the remote NE part of the Chihuahuan Desert, seldom visited it seems by botanists interested in cacti. An exception to this was the collecting trip of Del Weniger (1969), whose illustration of a plant from the type locality is the only documented figure of this form since that published by Engelmann (1859). Unfortunately, both these illustrations are of sterile plants and Weniger tells us only the size and colour of the flowers his specimens subsequently produced. However, from this limited information it is possible to believe that the excellent colour photograph of a flowering plant recently published by Haustein (1983) could represent the taxon originally described by Engelmann (1856)*. Its flowers appear to be quite large, with widely spread perianth-segments, and very similar to those of the preceding species in this account (whose claim to separate status begins to look doubtful).

Better known than the original form, just discussed, is a recent collection of Alfred Lau (no. 1101) from Rayones, Nuevo Leon (see Piltz, 1976). It has more slender stems and smaller flowers with very narrow perianth-segments, which sometimes open only partially and then resemble those of *E. chloranthus*. Indeed it is this form which originally drew the author's attention to the (now obvious) relationship of the otherwise isolated *E. viridiflorus* complex with *E. longisetus* and *E. delaetii*. Here *Lau* 1101 is treated as a probably new and very distinct variety of *E. longisetus*, but is not formally named pending the availability of more complete material and better field knowledge of this Mexican complex as a whole. It is the plant identified as *E. longisetus* and illustrated by Werdermann (1932).

A plant of uncertain identity to be mentioned here is that illustrated as *E. longisetus* by Backeberg (1962). The photograph in question was supposed to have been taken by Zehnder in the Sierra de la Paila, Coahuila – the classic habitat of *E. delaetii*. Unfortunately the illustration is too poor for positive recognition, but, if nothing more, it does highlight the desperate need for thorough field study in this cactus-rich region.

Experience of cultivating *E. longisetus* is limited to seedlings and a few imported habitat specimens at present. However, it seems likely that the comments concerning flower production under the preceding species will also apply here. Abundant sunshine at all times is certain to benefit such densely white-spined plants.

DESCRIPTION. *Stems* branching at base, forming clumps of up to 30 stems, cylindric, erect or sprawling, to 30 cm long, 2.5-7.5 cm in diameter, bright green but nearly obscured by dense spination. *Ribs* (8-)10-15, tuberculate. *Areoles* orbicular, 1.5-2 mm in diameter, with white wool, 8-13 mm apart. *Radial spines* 15-25, to 1.5 cm long, glassy-white; centrals 4-7,

---

* Another recent colour photo in M. Pizzetti, Piante grasse le Cactaceae, no. 63 (1985) (A. Mondadori, publishers, Milan) is a misidentification, the plant figured being *E. fendleri* var. *boyce-thompsonii*.

the lowermost 1-3 much longer than the others, to 5.5 cm, slender, strongly deflexed, glassy-white to yellowish, conspicuous. *Flowers* funnelform, 4-6 cm long, 3.5-6 cm in diameter, sometimes not opening fully, arising well below stem apex and sometimes from nearer stem base. *Receptacle-tube* at least 2 cm long, ovary 8-10 mm long, 7-8 mm in diameter, tube exterior green, bearing yellowish areoles with numerous whitish bristle-like spines to 2 cm long. *Nectar chamber* 3-4 mm long, 2 mm in diameter (*fide* Piltz, loc. cit.). *Perianth-segments* narrowly linear-elliptic to oblanceolate, at least 2-3 cm long and 4 mm or more wide, apex acuminate, fimbriate, pinkish-purple to claret-coloured with darker midstripes, white in the throat. *Stamen filaments* to c. 7 mm long, whitish to yellow. *Style* c. 1.5 cm long, white; stigmas 8-11, to 6 mm long, bright green. *Fruit and seed* not described.

DISTRIBUTION. NE Mexico: Central N Coahuila and Central W Nuevo Leon; E flanks of the Sierra Madre Oriental on limestone.

Echinocereus longisetus (Engelm.) Lemaire, Cactees, 57 (1868); Backeb., Die Cact. 4: 2006-2007 (1960) et ibid. 6: (?) Abb. 3484 (1962); D. Weniger in Cact. Succ. J. (US) 41: 42, fig. 6 (1969); E. Haustein, Der Kosmos-Kakteenfuhrer, 231-233, with colour pl. (1983). *Cereus longisetus* Engelm., Syn. Cact. US. 24-25 (1856) et Cact. Mex. Bound. 32-33, t. 45 (1859). Type: Mexico, Coahuila, mountains nr 'Santa Rosa' [W of Melchor Muzquiz], 1853, *J.M. Bigelow* (MO).

21a. var. **longisetus**
Stems 5-7.5 cm in diameter. *Flowers* at least 6 cm long and in diameter, opening widely. *Perianth-segments* > 5 mm wide, oblanceolate.
DISTRIBUTION. Central N Coahuila (W of Melchor Muzquiz).

21b. var. (unnamed; *Lau* 1101). See J. Piltz in Kakt. and. Sukk. 27: 32-34, with figs. (1976).
? *E. barcena* Rebut ex A. Berger, Kakteen, 175-176 (1929).
[*E. longisetus* sensu Werderm. in Bluehende Kakt. and. Sukk. Pfl., Lfg. 7, t. 25 (1932).]
Stems 2.5-4.5 cm in diameter. *Flowers* 4-6 cm long, 3.5-6 cm in diameter, sometimes not opening widely. *Perianth-segments* to c. 5 mm. wide, narrowly linear-elliptic.
DISTRIBUTION. Central W Nuevo Leon (nr Rayones).

22. ECHINOCEREUS CHLORANTHUS

Readers familiar with the current trend for conservative treatments in cactus taxonomy may be surprised to find *Echinocereus chloranthus* retained at species rank. Even the ultra-liberal Backeberg (1960) was content to reduce it to varietal status within his concept of the closely allied *E. viridiflorus* Engelm., and growers of this popular species complex are often heard to query how these two may be distinguished. On the other hand Benson (1982) prefers to keep them as separate species.

The problem, it seems, has been a reluctance to examine their floral morphology, where some clear divergences, correlated with stem and spination characters, can be observed. In typical *E. viridiflorus* the flowers open widely, the reflexed greenish petals generally having bluntly rounded or even emarginate apices. Above the ovary the receptacle-tube broadens and is conspicuous beneath the insertion of the perianth-segments. But in *E. chloranthus* and its varieties the yellowish-green, brownish or reddish flowers often appear as if only half-open, the petals remaining somewhat erect, even in bright sunlight, their apices gradually tapering and pointed. The receptacle-tube, viewed from the outside, seems very short, the insertion of the outer perianth-segments beginning just above the ovary. Also, Leuck & Miller (1982) have recently shown that the production of a lemon scent by the uniformly greenish-coloured flowers of *E. viridiflorus* and its varieties, *davisii* and *correllii*, correlates with the absorption pattern of ultraviolet light by the flower. Ultraviolet (UV) is absorbed in the throat, including the stamens and stigmas, but not near the ends of the petals, giving a dark centred, target-type flower when viewed through the eyes of a pollinator bee (for which UV is visible). However, in *E. chloranthus*, which has unscented flowers, the flower throat is visibly paler, but UV light is absorbed uniformly across the open surface of the perianth, making the whole appear dark to a bee (see Leuck & Miller, 1982, for illustrations).

According to these floral considerations, previous authors (including Benson, 1982) have consistently referred the taxon known as *E. viridiflorus* var. *cylindricus* (Engelm.) Ruempler to the wrong species. This is probably due to too much emphasis being placed on spination characters, since var. *cylindricus* has few or no central spines, as in *E. viridiflorus sens. str.* whereas in *E. chloranthus*, to which it properly belongs, there are normally three or more centrals. With var. *cylindricus* transferred to *E. chloranthus* the differences between the latter and *E. viridiflorus* become much more obvious, since, in addition to the floral characters, already explained, *E. chloranthus sens. lat.* is a much larger-growing taxon (to 20-25 cm high), with far more (15-45) radial spines per areole.

Surprisingly, Leuck & Miller, having drawn attention to the floral differences between this pair prefer to see only one species recognized. Their primary consideration seems to be the flavonoid compounds involved in UV absorbance by the flowers, which are the same for all taxa within the complex. While this may be so, the significance of flavonoids has still to be thoroughly investigated throughout the genus, and until more biosystematic information about these plants has been published it seems best and feasible, to continue to recognize two species.

Echinocereus chloranthus is here divided into four varieties, the limits of which deserve further investigation in the field. According to Weniger (1969, 1970), var. *chloranthus* itself is not widely distributed, being found only in a small area of westernmost Texas and adjacent New Mexico. Benson (1982) gives it a greater range, but this is partly because he includes var. *russanthus* in his concept.

Weniger's *E. russanthus* from the Big Bend region of W Texas, is not a distinct species, but does seem worthy of varietal status, even if it intergrades with var. *chloranthus* as Benson suggests. It has many more spines than var. *chloranthus* and a reddish flower. It also tends to form clumps of stems in time and is, in all respects, the variety which connects the small-flowered *E. viridiflorus* complex with the rest of the genus. In particular var. *russanthus* displays a clear relationship with an undescribed variety of *E. longisetus* (Engelm.) Lemaire from Nuevo Leon. Although its flowers are larger than those of var. *russanthus*, both have characteristically narrow, linear perianth-segments, which often remain more or less erect during anthesis. Recently the status of *E. chloranthus* as an endemic of the United States was lost when var. *russanthus* was discovered in Chihuahua, Mexico, in the Rio Santa Clara (Carmen) valley (*Lau* 1076). This disjunct form is now sometimes encountered in cultivation under the unpublished name '*E. finnii*'.

Echinocereus chloranthus var. *cylindricus* is the most widely distributed variety and the one most commonly misidentified in cultivation. It ranges from Lincoln Co., New Mexico to Brewster Co. in the Big Bend of Texas and appears to be quite variable. In the north its range overlaps with that of var. *chloranthus*, and in the south with var. *russanthus*, but in general it is found at higher elevations. Also, its flowers vary in colour from the brownish-greens of the former to the reddish shades of the latter. However, the few or frequently absent central spines immediately distinguish it from both.

In contrast to var. *cylindricus*, var. *neocapillus* has a very small range indeed. It is restricted to an interesting area in Brewster Co., Texas, to the south of Marathon, where various highly distinctive, and often dwarf Cactaceae are endemic. Although not dwarf, var. *neocapillus* is remarkable when small for its juvenile stems covered in long and dense hair-like, whitish spines. These prompt a comparison with the similarly clad stems of *E. delaetii* var. *delaetii*, from southern Coahuila, a species related to *E. chloranthus sens. lat.* via a mutual ally, *E. longisetus*. At maturity the stems of var. *neocapillus* develop spination similar to var. *chloranthus*, except that there are usually more spines per areole. In other respects they are difficult to distinguish, their flowers being more or less identical.

DESCRIPTION. *Stem* erect, cylindric, solitary, or branching near base to form clumps of up to c 12 stems, 7.5-20(-25) cm long, 5-7.5 cm in diameter, ± obscured by spines. *Ribs* 10-18, well-defined, tuberculate. *Areoles* circular to elliptic, c 3 mm long and 3-6 mm apart, wool soon disappearing. *Spines* acicular, red, cream or brownish (in one variety white or hair-like on juvenile specimens); radials (12-)15-45, to 12(-18) mm long, uppermost shortest; centrals 0-12, diverging, lowermost longest, to 25(-30) mm long and downwardly directed. *Flowers* numerous, in clusters from adjacent areoles, short-funnelform, 2.5-3.0 cm long, not opening widely, the perianth-segments remaining ± erect, not reflexed, unscented.

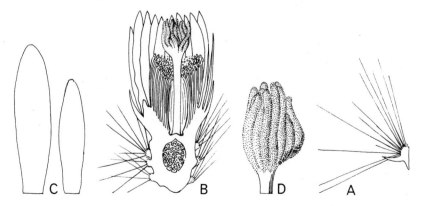

Echinocereus chloranthus var. **russanthus**. A, areole from receptacle-tube, × 4; B, half-flower, × 2; C, outer (r) to inner (l) perianth-segments, × 3; D, top of style with stigma-lobes, × 4 (*Hunt* 9576A).

Receptacle-tube c 1.2 cm long, lower 0.8 cm occupied by ovary and tapered fleshy base of receptacle, slightly contracted above ovary and then slightly expanding to a diameter of c 1.0 cm at point of insertion of perianth-segments, exterior tuberculate-ridged, bearing a few closely spaced areoles each with 4-12, 2-7 mm long whitish bristle-like spines, but little or no wool. *Nectar chamber* minute, scarcely 1 mm long and almost completely occupied by base of style. *Perianth-segments* in about 3 rows, grading from triangular scales on the exterior to linear or narrowly oblanceolate, acute inner segments, the longest c 15 mm long and 4 mm wide, ± entire, yellowish-green, brownish or shades of rusty-red to light beetroot red, paler at base giving the flower a lighter throat. *Stamen filaments* c 6 mm long, green to pinkish; anthers yellow, 1-1.3 mm long. *Style* 10-12 mm long, 1 mm in diameter; stigmas 8-12, to 6 mm long, light to dark green. *Ovary locule* shortly ovoid, c 3.5 mm long at anthesis. *Fruit* nearly spherical, 9-12 mm long, very spiny, greenish. *Seeds* black, 1-1.2 mm long, intercellular testa-cell pits present.

DISTRIBUTION. Cent N Mexico: Chihuahua; USA: W Texas and S New Mexico; mostly in or near the margins of the Chihuahuan Desert, at 900-1830 m altitude.

Echinocereus chloranthus (Engelm.) Hort. F. A. Haage, Cacteen-Verzeichniss, 19 (1859); Britton & Rose, Cact. 3: 16, t. 2, fig. 3 (1922); Weniger in Cact. Succ. J. (US) 41: 38-39 (1969) and Cacti of the Southwest, 16-17, t. 2 (1970); L. Benson, Cacti US & Can. 677-678, 948, fig. 714 (1982).

Cereus chloranthus Engelm., Syn. Cact. US. 22-23 (1856) and Cact. Mex. Bound. 29-30, tt. 37 & 38 (1859). Lectotype (Benson, tom. cit.): USA, Texas, 'El Paso' and 'Stony Hills near the Rio Grande at Frontera', 2 April 1852, *C. Wright* (MO).

22a. var. **russanthus** (Weniger) Lamb ex G. Rowley in Repert. Pl. Succ. 23: 7 (1974). (PLATE 7).

Echinocereus russanthus Weniger in loc. cit. 41, fig. 5 (1969) and tom. cit. 18-20, t. 3 (1970); Schreier in Kakt. and. Sukk. 33: 187 (1982); Leuck & J. M. Miller in Amer. J. Bot. 69: 1670-1671, figs. 3 & 4 (1982). Type: USA, Texas, SW. Brewster Co., 1968, *Weniger* 712 (UNM).

Stem often branching at the base. *Radial spines* 30-45; centrals 7-12. *Perianth-segments* light beetroot-red or bright red.

DISTRIBUTION. Chihuahua, valley of the Rio Santa Clara, and W Texas, in the Big Bend. The plant figured is *Hunt* 9576A (Texas, Big Bend area).

22b. var. **cylindricus** (Engelm.) N. P. Taylor in Kew Mag. 1: 169 (1984).

Cereus viridiflorus (Engelm.) Engelm. var. *cylindricus* Engelm., Syn. Cact. US. 22 (1856) and Cact. Mex. Bound. 28-29, t. 36 tantum quoad figs. 1-3 & 16 (1859). Type: USA, Texas, 'east of El Paso'. Lectotype (Benson, tom. cit.): Texas, Jeff Davis Co., Davis Mountains, 'Valley of the Limpia', etc., 11 June 1851, *C. Wright* (MO?).

Echinocereus viridiflorus Engelm. var. *cylindricus* (Engelm.) Ruempler in C. F. Foerster, Handb. Cacteenk. ed. 2, 812, fig. 106 (1885); E. & B. Lamb, Ill. Ref. Cact. Succ. 3: 610-611, colour pl. 114 (1963); Weniger in loc. cit. 36 (1969); L. Benson, tom. cit. 677, 672 (map), 947, figs. 711 & 712 (1982); Leuck & J. M. Miller, loc. cit. (1982).

Stem usually solitary. *Radial spines* 14-24; centrals 0-3. *Perianth-segments* brownish-green to reddish.

DISTRIBUTION. W Texas, in the Big Bend, to Cent S New Mexico, 1200-1830 m altitude.

22c. var. **chloranthus**

Stem solitary, rarely 1-2-branched. *Radial spines* 12-23; centrals 3-6. *Perianth-segments* yellowish-green to brown.

DISTRIBUTION. S New Mexico and adjacent W Texas, 900-1350 m altitude.

22d. var. **neocapillus** Weniger in loc. cit. 39-40, fig. 4 (1969) and tom. cit. 17-18, t. 2 (1970); L. Benson, tom. cit. 677 (map), 678, 948, fig. 715 (1982). Type: USA, Texas, 5-10 miles S of Marathon, 1968, *Weniger* '711' (UNM). It appears that the labels or numbering of Weniger's collections are somewhat confused (*Weniger* 711 is *E. viridiflorus* var. *correllii* L. Benson) and so Benson (l.c. 948) has designated a different collection of *Weniger* (UNM 43582) as 'lectotype'.

Juvenile (seedling) spination long and hair-like, persisting at the base of mature stems. *Radial spines* 30-40; centrals 5-10. Otherwise like var. *chloranthus*.

DISTRIBUTION. W Texas (Brewster Co., S of Marathon), c 1350 m altitude.

23. ECHINOCEREUS VIRIDIFLORUS

This is a very successful dwarf species, having spread further north than any other member of the genus, into the cooler regions of the Great Plains grasslands, as far as S South Dakota, and into the mountainous areas of New Mexico and central Colorado. Not surprisingly it is a very cold resistant plant and has even been tried out-of-doors in NW Europe, on well-drained rockeries, where it will survive for a while, especially if protected from excessive winter damp. It can certainly been grown successfully in an unheated greenhouse or frame, and is popular, as it produces it greenish, lemon-scented flowers freely, and without special treatment. The species was discovered by Wislizenus in New Mexico in 1846 and described by Engelmann two years later. It is one of the commonest members of the genus in cultivation.

Of greater interest for the connoisseur are its rarer southern varieties, from the desert grasslands of W Texas, of which var. *davisii* is perhaps the most remarkable plant in the entire genus. Among the dwarf echinocerei this is undoubtedly the smallest, the adult plant in habitat normally having a stem only 1.2-2 cm long and 0.9-1.2 cm in diameter. It is found on a very unusual, rather infertile rock type, known as Caballos Novaculite, in a small area of Brewster County, Texas, where it grows half buried in moss and is almost impossible to see unless in flower. In the same general area grow various other extraordinary, dwarf cacti, including two choice species of *Escobaria* and a beautiful variety of *Thelocactus bicolor*. In cultivation var. *davisii* is often grafted, when its atypical branching allows for easy propagation.

Another *Echinocereus* found growing near this dwarf variety is the much larger growing *E. viridiflorus* var. *correllii*, with ovoid to cylindric stems up to 12.5 cm high. Its spines are arranged in greenish-yellow and ashy white horizontal bands and give it a very attractive appearance.

Both these southern varieties agree with typical *E. viridiflorus* in their floral characters, as noted under the preceding species, except that their perianth-segments have more pointed apices (cf. *E. chloranthus*). They should be watered more carefully in keeping with the warmer and drier habitat they occupy in the field. In general the species is propagated by seed, and both rarer varieties are becoming increasingly common in cultivation through this method of increase.

DESCRIPTION. Like the preceding species, but stem globose, ovoid or cylindric, 1.2-12.5 cm long, 0.9-5 cm in diameter, epidermis not or partly obscured by the spines. *Ribs* 6-14. *Radial spines* 8-24; central spines 0-3(-4). *Flowers* mostly opening widely, lemon-scented. *Perianth-segments* rounded to emarginate or acute at apex, green to yellowish-green or outermost with reddish midribs, not conspicuously paler in the throat or at base. *Stamen anthers* 0.7-1 mm long. *Stigmas* 5-8, c. 3 mm long. *Fruit* 6-9 mm long. *Seeds* 1-1.5 mm long, intercellular testa-cell pits absent (where known).

DISTRIBUTION. Central-S USA: SW South Dakota, SE Wyoming, cent. & E Colorado, SW Kansas, cent. & E New Mexico, W Oklahoma and W & N Texas; open montane woodlands and Great Plains and desert grasslands, 900-2700 m altitude.

Echinocereus viridiflorus Engelm. in Wislizenus, Mem. Tour North. Mex. 91, in adnot. (1848); Boissev. & Davidson, Colorado Cacti, 49-51, figs. 34 & 35 (1940); Weniger, Cacti of the Southwest, 13-14, t. 1 (1970); L. Benson, Cacti US & Can. 671, 672 (map), 673-675, 947, figs. 708-710, 712.1-4 (1982); Leuck & J.M. Miller in Amer. J. Bot. 69: 1670-1672, figs. 1-2 (1982); W. Cullmann et al., Kakteen, ed. 5, 158-159, with superb pl. (1984). Syntypes: New Mexico, on Wolf Creek [*Wislizenus*], Santa Fe, *Fendler*. Lectotype (Benson, 1982): 'Near Wolf Creek on Santa Fe Road', 24 June 1846 (MO).

23a. var. **viridiflorus**
Stem ovoid to elongate-ovoid, 2.5-5(-12.5) cm long, 2.5-3.8 cm in diameter (becoming larger in cultivation), 10-14-ribbed. *Spines* red, brownish, white or pale grey, the radials to 4.5 mm long.

DISTRIBUTION. As for species (except Pecos & Brewster Cos., Texas); 1500-2700 m altitude (highest in the S).

23b. var. **correllii** L. Benson in Cact. Succ. J. (US) 41: 128 (1969) et tom. cit. (1982); Leuck & J.M. Miller, loc. cit. 1670 (1982). Type: Texas, Brewster Co., S of Marathon, hills at 1200 m, 4 April 1965, *D. & H. Correll & E. & L. Benson* 16485 (POM 317079).
Stem elongate-ovoid to cylindric, 7.5-12.5 cm long, 3.8-5 cm in diameter, 10-14-ribbed. *Spines* greenish-yellow and ashy-white in horizontal bands, the radials to 9 mm long.

DISTRIBUTION. W Texas, in Pecos Co. (vicinity of Ft. Stockton) and Brewster Co. (ca Marathon); desert grassland on caballos novaculite chert at 900-1350 m altitude.

23c. var. **davisii** (A.D. Houghton) W.T. Marsh. in Marshall & Bock, Cactaceae, 119 (1941); L. Benson, tom. cit. (1982); Leuck & J.M. Miller, loc. cit. 1670 (1982); E. Haustein, Der Kosmos-Kakteenführer, 230, with pl. (1983).
E. davisii A.D. Houghton in Cact. Succ. J. (US) 2: 466, with fig. (1931); Weniger, tom. cit. 15-16, t. 2 (1970); Rauh, Kakt. an ihren Standorten, Farbt. 4, figs. 2 & 3 (1979). Type: Texas, Brewster Co., nr Marathon, *A.R. Davis* in *Houghton* 700 (US 1566585).
Stem globose to ovoid, 1.2-2(-2.5) cm long, 0.9-1.2 cm in diameter (larger in cultivation especially if grafted), 6-9-ribbed. *Spines* (all radial) black then grey to white or with red tips, 6-15 mm long.

DISTRIBUTION. Texas, Brewster Co. (S of Marathon); desert grassland on caballos novaculite chert amongst moss, 1200-1350 m altitude.

Section V. Reichenbachii

Echinocereus sect. **Reichenbachii** N.P. Taylor, **sect. nov.** *Flores late infundibulares magni, receptaculi tubo areolis et spinis dense dispositis vel valde lanatis, perianthii segmentis pernumerosis in receptaculi tubo dense insertis teneris et delicatis, puniceis usque magenteis vel luteis (raro albis), numquam aurantiaco-rubris vel coccineis. Caro fructuum maturorum exsucca fraga non olens, seminibus numerosis. Spinae in areolis caulinis breves paucae usque numerosissimae; caules erecti saepe cylindrici costis usque 26. Typus: Echinocereus reichenbachii* (Terscheck ex Walp.) Hort. F.A. Haage.

This newly recognized section is the largest in the genus with a total of 13 species. They are characterized by medium-sized or, more often, rather large flowers, usually borne near the stem apex. The receptacle-tube is well developed above the ovary and densely covered in numerous areoles bearing either abundant short spines or slender bristles and much wool. The perianth-segments are very numerous, thin and delicate, not particularly fleshy at the base, and densely inserted at the tube apex. The fruits are not juicy but have white pulp and do not smell of strawberries when ripe. In most species the flower-buds appear to develop at the stem areoles rather than bursting through the epidermis above them. Three species groups can be defined:

The E. SUBINERMIS GROUP (species 24-26) is the least specialized with stems averaging only 8-13 ribs, the epidermis often visible between the spines, which have a maximum length of 2-4 cm. The seeds are the smallest in the genus, averaging c. 1 mm long. It includes three well-defined, early to late summer-flowering species, from the west side of the Sierra Madre Occidental of Mexico (NW Jalisco to W Chihuahua).

The E.RIGIDISSIMUS GROUP (species 27-32) comprises six rather similar, mid to late summer-flowering species, mostly from the Mexican part of the Sonoran Desert and desert grasslands around its periphery (incl. SE Arizona & SW New Mexico). They have a more specialized vegetative morphology, the epidermis of the 12-26-ribbed stems being more or less obscured by numerous short spines, to a maximum of c. 1.5 cm long. The seeds are mostly rather small, ranging between c. 1-1.5 mm in length. The receptacle-tube is covered in densely-spined areoles and sometimes also loose wool.

The E. REICHENBACHII GROUP (species 33-36) includes four, spring to early summer-flowering species, found east of the Sierra Madre Occidental, in and around the Chihuahuan Desert in Mexico, one extending to the E coast and northwards into Texas, New Mexico, Oklahoma and S Colorado. They are highly specialized, ranging from plants with dwarf, depressed, weakly-spined stems supported by tuberous rootstocks, to those with many-ribbed, densely-spined stems fully protected from the desert environment. The seeds are mostly larger than in the two previous groups (c. 1.5 mm long) and have very prominent, almost pointed testa tubercles. The receptacle-tube areoles produce long, fine bristles and abundant dense wool.

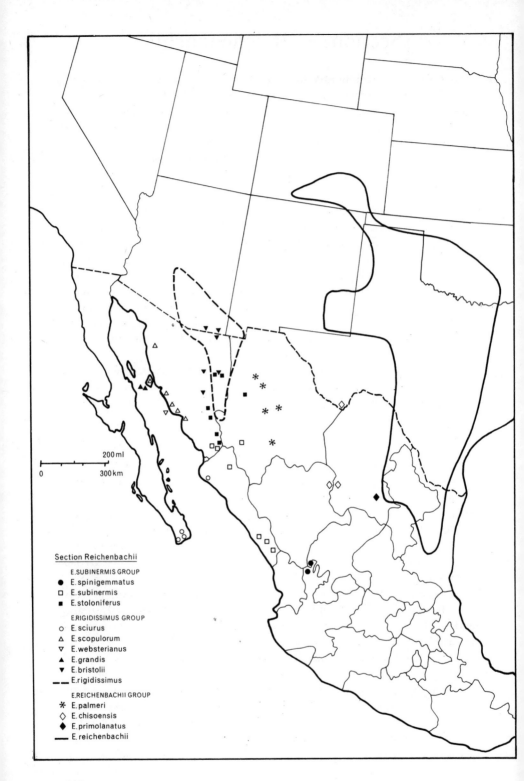

Section Reichenbachii

E.SUBINERMIS GROUP
● E.spinigemmatus
□ E.subinermis
■ E.stoloniferus

E.RIGIDISSIMUS GROUP
○ E.sciurus
△ E.scopulorum
▽ E.websterianus
▲ E.grandis
▼ E.bristolii
--- E.rigidissimus

E.REICHENBACHII GROUP
✳ E.palmeri
◇ E.chisoensis
◆ E.primolanatus
— E.reichenbachii

200 ml
0   300 km

24. ECHINOCEREUS SPINIGEMMATUS

Although this very distinctive, yellow-spined species was described as recently as November 1984, it was in fact discovered in the year 1900. In May of that year Leon Diguet collected in the Sierra de Nayarit of NW Jalisco and three sheets of herbarium material, representing his collection, are conserved at Paris (P). One of these sheets corresponds to *Cereus huitcholensis* Weber, here referred to *E. polyacanthus*, but the other two comprise a mixture of flowers from Weber's species and a double-stemmed plant (cut in half) with flower-buds and a mature flower of *E. spinigemmatus* A. Lau (1984). The holotype collection of *E. spinigemmatus* bears Lau's number 1246 and is conserved in the herbarium of the municipal succulent collection of Zurich (ZSS). However, it is to be regretted that this all-important type material is represented by a sterile stem and seeds only, and so it is necessary to rely on Diguet's earlier collection for details of the flower of this interesting plant. Lau's published description of his species is also a cause for concern, there being serious inaccuracies and important omissions of detail (e.g. the type plant has up to 14 ribs, not 12-13; the nectar chamber and stamen filaments cannot be as large as stated; and the receptacle-tube can sometimes bear abundant wool in addition to the conspicuous spines described).

The position of *E. spinigemmatus* within *Echinocereus* was at first a difficult question to answer. Its placement in section *Reichenbachii* is based on interpretation of pressed flower material and colour photographs, rather than from a knowledge of fresh or liquid-preserved material, but despite this the writer is convinced of its affinity. Viewed from above the flowers and buds are similar to those of *E. sciurus* and *E. bristolii* var. *pseudopectinatus,* and the very densely spiny receptacle-tube is typical of the E. RIGIDISSIMUS GROUP. Furthermore, the flowers develop very near the stem apex and the very spiny fruits contain rather small seeds. Vegetatively, however, *E. spinigemmatus* has more in common with the E. SUBINERMIS GROUP, its spination and elongate stem being somewhat reminiscent of *E. stoloniferus,* whose flowers agree very closely too (colour excepted). Such a relationship is also more probable on geographical grounds, since *E. subinermis* and *E. stoloniferus* likewise inhabit the western flanks of the Sierra Madre Occidental. Certainly, its affinity with *E. viereckii* and *E. fendleri* var. *ledingii,* as suggested by Dr G.R.W. Frank (Kakt. and. Sukk. 36: 116. 1985), is hard to accept when its subapical flowers, basally-tapered young fruits, unusually small seeds and wild provenance are taken into account.

The cultivation of *E. spinigemmatus* appears to be easy, although experience is currently limited to seedlings. Lau says the plant is found in full exposure in the wild so plenty of sunlight would seem desirable. Its willingness to produce its seemingly attractive, pinkish-lilac flowers is as yet unknown, but if this proves to be no problem it is sure to become a sought-after plant.

DESCRIPTION. *Stems* branching to form loose clumps of 7-10 heads, cylindric but gradually tapered towards apex, to 30 cm long, 4-7 cm in diameter, green. *Ribs* 10-14, slightly tuberculate, 2-4 mm high, to 1.2 cm apart. *Areoles* oval, 3 mm long, c. 1 cm apart, with yellowish wool at first. *Spines* yellow, later brownish, slender; radials 10-13, 3-23 mm long; centrals (2-)4, 5-30(-40) mm long, porrect to deflexed, difficult to distinguish from radials. *Flowers* funnelform, 5 cm long, 6 cm in diameter, arising very near stem apex. *Receptacle-tube* 3.5 cm long, 2.3 cm wide at apex, exterior with areoles bearing up to 15, to 1.5 cm long, whitish-yellow spines and wool. *Nectar chamber* 'c. 1.2 cm long, 1 cm in diameter' (*fide* Lau) [1.2 × 1.0 mm?]. *Perianth-segments* oblanceolate, to 3 cm long and 1.2 cm wide, apex rounded, fimbriate, pinkish-lilac to pale violet with darker midstripes, whitish near base. *Stamen filaments* 2 cm long [?], white. *Style* 3 cm long, white; stigmas 10-14, 6 mm long, slender, bright green. *Fruit* ovoid, 3.5 cm long, 2.5 cm in diameter, green, very spiny. *Seeds* (see Glaetzle in Lau, loc. cit., 250) broadly ovoid, 0.9-1.2 mm long, with relatively low tubercles, black.

DISTRIBUTION. W Mexico: W Zacatecas and NW Jalisco; drainage of Rio Huaynamota & Rio Bolanos, conglomerate rocks at 1000-1800 m altitude.

Echinocereus spinigemmatus A.Lau in Kakt. and. Sukk. 35: 248-250, 281, with figs. (1984). Type: Mexico, NW Jalisco, nr San Andres Cohamiata, 1600 m, 25 April 1974, *Lau* 1246 (ZSS AA18-48, sterile stem only at date of valid publ.).

25. ECHINOCEREUS SUBINERMIS

This species, long known for its exceptionally fine yellow flowers, has now been in cultivation for 140 years, following its discovery by one of the Potts brothers, probably near the Chihuahua-Sonora border, in about 1845 (see notes on *E. scheeri*). The type collection (the form which is commonly associated with the name today) was practically spineless, although in notes following the original description Scheer (1856) clearly mentions the existence of long-spined variants. As pointed out by George Lindsay (1944) the presence or absence of spines, like differences in rib number, is a feature of little taxonomic significance, spiny and spineless forms occurring together in the field. He has shown how the naming of the synonymous *E. luteus* by Britton & Rose (1913) was due to ignorance of the true provenance of *E. subinermis* and to inadequate knowledge of its variability in habitat. Similarly, the recent description of *E. subinermis* var. *aculeatus* G. Unger (1984), for a spiny form from the vicinity of La Bufa (Chihuahua), is of doubtful value and is not really an extension of range for the species either, Lindsay having already traced it well into SW Chihuahua in 1938. As noted under *E. viereckii* the occurrence of spineless few-ribbed variations in this genus is associated with wooded or shady cliff habitats, but in the case of *E. subinermis* the naked ecotype seems less stable and certainly not worthy of botanical separation from its spine-bearing forms, *luteus* and *aculeatus*. However, these later names are perhaps worth retaining at cultivar rank, since the plants they represent seem distinctive in a horticultural context.

The southern limits of geographical range of the variable plant just discussed are not certain. Lindsay and Lau (no. 622) both record it from NE Sinaloa, but it is also noted from La Noria, much further south near Mazatlan by Ortega (1929, as *E. luteus*). This locality is close to the type station of *E. ochoterenae* J.G. Ortega, a southern vicariant of *E. subinermis*, which Unger appropriately treats as a variety.

In contrast to the minor variants not accepted above, var. *ochoterenae* (J.G.

Ortega) G. Unger is a distinct and ecologically interesting taxon. Its stems generally have more ribs than in var. *subinermis* (8-11 vs. 5-9) and are quicker to offset. Some forms have up to 4 conspicuous, blackish central spines in each stem areole (0-1 in var. *subinermis*), and the smaller flowers have very woolly receptacle-tubes. Ortega (1929) particularly notes its occurrence on rocks of copper carbonate devoid of other vegetation, which suggests that it may have tolerance to high levels of copper, a valuable biological asset if competition with other species is to be avoided. It is in cultivation from recent collections made in S Sinaloa by Lau (nos. 624, 624a & 771), but the ecological details of these have not been made known.

DESCRIPTION. *Stem* solitary or branched at base and forming clumps of up to 10 stems, depressed-globose to cylindric, 4-25(-32.5) cm high, 4-15 cm in diameter, grey- to dark bluish-green, sometimes reddish to purplish in full exposure, in winter or in drought. *Ribs* 5-11, to 1.5 cm high, acute, tuberculate or even-edged. *Areoles* orbicular to elliptic, minute or to 3 mm long, 6-20 mm apart. *Radial spines* 0-9(-10), 1-20(-30) mm long, slender, pale yellow to grey, dark-tipped; centrals 0-4, 1-20 mm long, like the radials or blackish, porrect or the lowermost deflexed. *Flowers* funnelform, sweet-scented, 7-10 cm long, 5-13 cm in diameter, arising towards stem apex; buds rather woolly, brown. *Receptacle-tube* to 5 cm long, ovary occupying basal 1-2 cm but locule base to 6 mm above base of receptacle, to 1 cm in diameter, contracted above to 6-8 mm then flared to 2 cm in diameter at apex, tube exterior green with prominent tubercles each bearing an areole with up to c. 15, 2-10 mm long, fine, pale to brown spines and often much loose, white to brown wool. *Nectar chamber* to 6 mm long, and 3 mm in diameter, half-filled by style base. *Perianth-segments* cuneate-oblanceolate, to 6 cm long and 2 cm wide, apex acuminate, nearly entire, outer segments

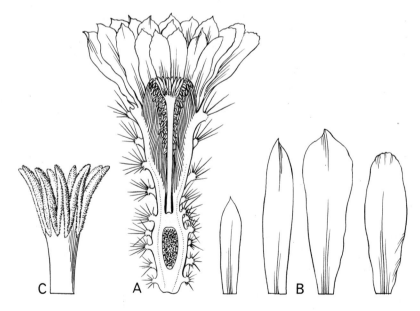

Echinocereus subinermis var. **subinermis**. A, half-flower, × 1; B, outer (l) to inner (r) perianth-segments, × 1½; C, top of style with stigmas, × 4 (ex Hort. G. E. Cheetham).

reddish-brown to yellow streaked with red, inner bright yellow. *Stamen filaments* to c. 1 cm long, pale yellow; anthers oblong, 1.5 mm long. *Style* 2.5-3 cm long, 1.5 mm in diameter at base but thickened to 3 mm at apex, greenish-white; stigmas 8-11, to 6 mm long, dark green. *Ovary locule* elongate-ovoid, to 11 mm long, 4 mm in diameter. *Fruit* obovoid, 1.8-4 cm long, 1.3-2.2 cm in diameter, grey-green, spiny, dehiscent by a longitudinal split, pulp white. *Seeds* broadly ovoid, 0.8-1.2 mm long, strongly tuberculate.

DISTRIBUTION. NW Mexico: Sinaloa, SW Chihuahua and S Sonora; Pacific drainage of the Sierra Madre Occidental, at or above 200 m altitude.

Echinocereus subinermis Salm-Dyck ex Scheer in Seemann, Bot. HMS Herald, 291 (1856); G. Lindsay in Cact. Succ. J. (US) 16: 134-136, fig. 122 (1944); G. Unger in Kakt. and. Sukk. 35: 164-165 (1984). Type: a plant sent to F. Scheer from NW Mexico [nr Chihuahua-Sonora border], 1845-1850, by *Potts* (not preserved). Neotype (designated here): Schumann in Bluehende Kakt. 1: t. 4 ('3') (1900), illustration of a flowering plant at Berlin, originally received shortly after 1845.

E. luteus Britton & Rose in Contrib. US. Nat. Herb. 16: 239, t. 67 (1913). Type: Sonora, mts above Alamos, 19 March 1910, *Rose et al.* 15207 (US).

E. subinermis var. *aculeatus* G. Unger, loc. cit., with figs. (1984). Type: SW Chihuahua, Rio Batopilas, vicinity of La Bufa, 700 m, 1980, *Unger* (ZSS AA50-70).

25a. var. **subinermis**

Stems often solitary, or 1-2-branched, to 15 cm in diameter, sometimes spineless. *Ribs* 5-9(-10). *Central spines* 0-1. *Flowers* to 10 cm long and 13 cm in diameter. *Receptacle-tube* only slightly woolly at anthesis.

DISTRIBUTION. N & (?) S Sinaloa, S Sonora & SW Chihuahua; canyon walls and rocky cliffs, often in partial shade, above 500 m altitude.

25b. var. **ochoterenae** (J.G. Ortega) G. Unger, loc. cit., with fig. (1984).

E. ochoterenae J.G. Ortega in Mexico Forestal 6: 88-90, with figs. (1928) et Apuntes para la Flora Indigena de Sinaloa, unpaged (1929) et in An. Inst. Biol. Mex. 1: 177-180, with figs. (1930). Type: Sinaloa, Municipalidad Concordia, Cerro de la Cobriza, 24 May 1927, *J.G. Ortega* (MEXU?).

Stems usually branched and forming small clumps, to 7 cm in diameter, always spiny. *Ribs* 8-11. *Central spines* 1-4. *Flowers* c. 7 cm long, 5-6.5 cm in diameter. *Receptacle-tube* conspicuously woolly at anthesis.

DISTRIBUTION. S Sinaloa; on bare rocks containing copper, c. 200 m altitude.

26. ECHINOCEREUS STOLONIFERUS

Of the five species of *Echinocereus* with bright yellow flowers only two are closely related: *E. subinermis* and *E. stoloniferus*. Both emanate from the west side of Mexico's Sierra Madre Occidental, from S Sinaloa northwards to E Sonora and adjacent Chihuahua. Their ranges could be termed allopatric, since *E. stoloniferus* replaces *E. subinermis* north of Alamos (S Sonora). While closely related, they are clearly not to be considered geographical races of one variable species—the vegetative and, more especially, the floral differences are too great to permit such a classification.

In the field *E. stoloniferus* and its variety *tayopensis* adopt the unusual habit, for a cactus, of branching by means of slender underground rhizomes (or stolons), the aerial stems appearing as if unconnected until the whole plant is uprooted. This specialized habit, the greater rib count, and the denser spination should enable *E. stoloniferus (sens. lat.)* to be readily distinguished from *E. subinermis* when not in flower. However, in cultivation var. *tayopensis* often branches atypically to form a compact clump and this, together with its broader ribs, can make it appear similar to the caespitose *E. subinermis* var. *ochoterenae*. Fortunately, any doubts about the differences between these two are quickly dispelled once flowers are produced. Flower size varies considerably in both species but the proportions and differences in the shape of the tube and perianth-segments remain fairly constant. Firstly, the receptacle-tube of *E. stoloniferus* is relatively short, the nectar chamber only 1.5-2 mm long; secondly, the perianth-segments are remarkably broad for their length (to 2.5 × 3.9 cm, resp.). In *E. subinermis* the long-tubed flowers have nectar chambers to 6mm long and perianth-segments to 6 cm long, but to only 2 cm broad.

Echinocereus stoloniferus was discovered in SE Sonora by Radley *et al.* in 1934, and described by the American cactologist, William Taylor Marshall, in 1938. Eighteen years later Marshall described *E. tayopensis* from a collection of Dudley Gold and Hernando Sanchez-Mejorada, which they had obtained further north in central E Sonora. Subsequently both plants were studied in the field and reported on by Parrish (1963), who drew attention to their close relationship but maintained them as distinct species. However, they are so similar that their classification as geographically distinct varieties of one species seems more appropriate and is in keeping with the more conservative approach now favoured by taxonomists working with Cactaceae.

Cultivated stocks of both varieties of *E. stoloniferus* vary somewhat in their appearance and behaviour. Some forms of var. *stoloniferus* seem to remain solitary and refuse to produce subterranean stolons even when bedded-out. The plant figured here, from the collection of Mr G.E. Cheetham, appears to be one of these. Others freely produce them and require a wide pan in which to grow properly. When taking such a plant to a competitive show one sincerely hopes that the judge will realise that all the stems interconnect beneath the compost and not be tempted to disqualify the entry for having more than one plant in the pot! Judges and growers should also note that a form of var. *stoloniferus* in cultivation is among various plants to which Backeberg's invalid name, '*E. subterraneus*' has been misapplied. Furthermore, not every plant labelled as *E. stoloniferus* is the pure species. At Holly Gate Nurseries, Sussex, there is a plant whose vegetative appearance answers to the species, but has a flower with a longer tube and red perianth-segments. The specimen in question is of wild origin and its flowers strongly suggest the hybrid influence of *E. scheeri* (sect. *Triglochidiatus*), which is also recorded from SE Sonora and at similar altitudes to var. *stoloniferus*.

E. stoloniferus var. *tayopensis*, as represented in living collections, appears very different to var. *stoloniferus*. This is because it usually fares better in cultivation, flowering freely and developing more robust stems than in the wild (where similarities between the two varieties far outweigh their differences). Its mode of branching, as already noted, appears to be atypical of the species in the field, where the rhizomatous habit seems to be the rule.

Vegetative propagation of *E. stoloniferus* should present little difficulty, unless one of the non-branching forms has been acquired. Otherwise, assuming that generous root-room has been provided, plants will have clustered and the underground rhizomes to be divided may already have developed their own roots. In var. *tayopensis* the branches, which originate near or at the surface of the compost, should be severed and treated as cuttings once any cut surfaces have healed.

DESCRIPTION. *Stems* usually branching by means of underground stolons, forming colonies (in cultivated specimens of var. *tayopensis* often branching at stem base and sides), ovoid to cylindric, 9-30 cm high, 3-6(-8) cm in diameter, deep olive-green, not or only partly obscured by the spines. *Ribs* 11-16, low, 2-6 mm high, 7-15 mm apart, at most only slightly tuberculate. *Areoles* ± circular, small, to 2 mm in diameter, 3-9 mm apart, with a little wool at first. *Radial* spines (8-)10-13, to 15 mm long, finely acicular, ± adpressed, grey or whitish with brownish tips, darker when young; centrals 1-5, to 25 mm long, slightly stouter, the longest one pointing downwards, brownish to grey. *Flowers* shortly funnel-shaped, to 7.5 cm long and 8(-10) cm in diameter, arising near stem apex. *Receptacle-tube* to 4 cm long, the ± spherical ovary occupying about half this length, contracting slightly to c. 1.1 cm wide above ovary, expanding to c. 3 cm wide at apex, rather thick, exterior green to purplish-brown, bearing areoles with up to 12 spines and conspicuous white wool, the spines whitish and to c. 5 mm long on the part enclosing the ovary, but brown and up to 15 mm long near apex of tube. *Nectar chamber* only 1.5-2 mm long, mostly filled by base of style. *Outer perianth-segments* small, triangular to elliptic, tinged reddish, the acute tip often dying and turning brown; inner segments in 2 rows, broadly obovate-oblanceolate, 2.5-3.9 cm long and 1-2.5 cm wide, base cuneate, apex rounded then shortly acuminate, margins entire or slightly irregular, bright yellow, midrib on underside sometimes greenish. *Stamen filaments* 8-13 mm long, pale yellow; anthers darker, oblong, c. 1 mm long. *Style* 1.8-3 cm long, 1.5-2 mm in diameter, pale yellow; stigmas 9-10,

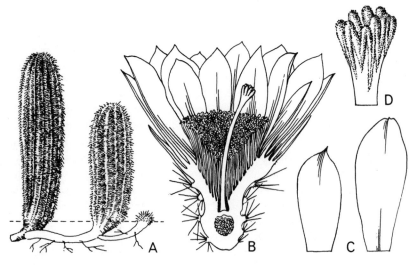

Echinocereus stoloniferus. A, habit sketch from photograph taken in the field, × ⅓; B, half-flower, × 1; C, outer (left) and inner (right) perianth-segments, × 1; D, top of style with stigmas, × 3 (ex Hort. G. E. Cheetham).

3-5 mm long, deep green. *Ovary locule* nearly spherical, c. 5 mm in diameter at anthesis. *Fruit* described as 'reddish, very spiny' (Marshall, 1938). *Seeds* broadly ovoid, c. 1 mm long, strongly tuberculate, black.

DISTRIBUTION. NW Mexico: W slopes of Sierra Madre Occidental in E Sonora and adjacent Chihuahua; open forest (mainly oak) on volcanic and conglomerate substrates, 650-1550 m altitude.

Echinocereus stoloniferus W.T. Marsh. in Cact. Succ. J. (US) 9: 159-160, with fig. (1938); H. Gentry, Rio Mayo Plants, 193 (1942); Backeb., Die Cact. 4: 2018, Abb. 1920a & b (1960); G. Lindsay ('stoloniferous') in Cact. Succ. J. (US) 34: 119, fig. 80 (centre right) (1962); C. Parrish in ibid. 35: 22-25, figs. 22 (map) & 24 (1963). Type: Mexico, Sonora, 30 miles E of Alamos, mountain facing Rancho Guirocoba, 5000 ft., 19 March 1935, *B. Bristol & W.T. Marshall* (DS 251176).

26a. var. **stoloniferus** (PLATE 8)

Stems cylindric, to 30 cm high and 5 cm in diameter, branching only by means of underground stolons. *Ribs* 12-16. *Areoles* 3-5 mm apart. *Radial spines* to 6 mm long; centrals to 10(-25) mm long.

DISTRIBUTION. SE Sonora (Guirocoba and in the Sierra Saguaribo at Bacachaca).

26b. var. **tayopensis** (W.T. Marsh.) N.P. Taylor in Kew Mag. 2: 258 (1985).

Echinocereus tayopensis W.T. Marsh. in Saguaroland Bull. 10: 78, 80, with figs. (1956); C. Parrish, loc. cit., figs. 22-24 (1963). Type: Mexico, NE Sonora, between Bacadehuachi and Nacori Chico, Rancho Saucito, 29°42'N, 109°04'W, 3500 ft., 1956, *D. Gold & H. Sanchez-Mejorada* (DES).

Stems ovoid to shortly cylindric, to 15 cm high and 6(-8) cm in diameter, at least in cultivation branching from the stem base and sides (stoloniferous in habitat). *Ribs* 11-13. *Areoles* 5-9 mm apart. *Radial spines* to 15 mm long; centrals to 20 mm long.

DISTRIBUTION. E Sonora and W Chihuahua (Rio Yaqui drainage W to the vicinity of Temosachic).

27. ECHINOCEREUS SCIURUS

With the exception of the easily recognized *E. rigidissimus*, the species of this chiefly Sonoran Desert group are all much alike and are best compared with *E. sciurus*, the earliest among them to be described. None are particularly common in cultivation, nor are they well-studied in the field, where their ranges seem to be quite restricted. This geographical isolation from one another presumably accounts for their apparent differences and justifies their recognition at specific rank, though it is always possible that detailed field investigation will uncover intermediates in the future. However, their wholesale removal to the synonymy of *E. pectinatus*, as begun by Benson (1968) and further hinted at in Benson (1982: 602), is not only premature, but also seems ill-conceived when judged on floral morphology, their vegetative likeness to that species (here referred to a different section) representing the product of convergent evolution.

Echinocereus sciurus was discovered by Townshend Brandegee in 1897 on hills at the southern tip of Baja California, and described by his daughter, Katherine, seven years later. The epithet records the plant's resemblance to a squirrel's tail, its stem being covered in numerous, often porrect, bristle-like spines. Its range has hitherto been thought of as limited to the southern Cape region of the Baja peninsula, but Backeberg's *E. floresii*, described from the opposite side of the Gulf of California, on the coast of N Sinaloa, in 1949, differs in few respects and is scarcely even worthy of varietal status. Both have the somewhat thickened rootstock and widely-opening pinkish-magenta flowers of exceptional beauty that characterize the species. The plants are caespitose and benefit from plenty of root room in cultivation, where a warm position in full sun is required for successful flowering.

In habitat the restricted range of *E. sciurus* may be cause for concern. The typical variety, from the Cape region of Baja California, mainly occurs on coastal hills, including those near the growing tourist resorts of Cabo San Lucas and San José del Cabo. There, it is now difficult to find the large caespitose individuals mentioned in early reports of the species (this perhaps being due to their removal by collectors) and the crumbling granite, on which the plant is found, does not withstand the passage of numerous feet and makes the plant easy to lift from its chosen place. The conservation status of *E. sciurus* var. *floresii*, known only from the region of Topolobampo in N Sinaloa, is not known. It is in cultivation from *Lau* 71.

A poorly known plant to be mentioned here is the invalidly published '*E. subterraneus*' Backeb. (1960: 2012). Backeberg's description and photograph of a flowering specimen agree quite well with *E. sciurus*, except that the stated flower size is rather small. Unfortunately we are not told where in the field the plant was obtained and, since the name is invalid (for lack of a type specimen), further speculation about its affinity seems pointless. It should be noted that '*E. subterraneus*' has been used by field collectors in various senses, especially for forms of *E. scheeri* and *E. stoloniferus*, and all sorts of plants can be found in cultivation so labelled. However, Backeberg's taxon does not seem to be among these.

DESCRIPTION. *Plant* caespitose, sometimes forming clumps of many stems to 60 cm broad. *Stems* cylindric or tapered towards apex, to 20 cm long, 3-5 cm in diameter, ± obscured by spines; rootstock somewhat tuberous. *Ribs* 12-17, 3-5 mm high, finely tuberculate. *Areoles* circular, soon losing their wool, to 7 mm apart. *Spines* to c. 22, 3-16 mm long, slender, brownish to nearly white with darker tips, adpressed or the majority somewhat porrect, not differentiated into radials and centrals or the latter (0-)2-6. *Flowers* funnelform, to c. 8 cm long, 7-10 cm or more in diameter, arising near stem apex or from lower down; buds slightly woolly. *Receptacle-tube* to 4 cm long, ovary occupying basal 1.5-2.2 cm but base of locule c. 7 mm above receptacle base, to 1.7 cm in diameter, tube contracted above to 1.2 cm then flared to c. 2 cm or more in diameter at apex, densely covered in areoles with up to 15-20, to 1.5 cm long, white, brown-tipped spines. *Nectar chamber* 4 mm long, 3 mm in diameter, mostly filled by style base. *Perianth-segments* in 2-4 rows, cuneate-oblanceolate, to 5 cm or more long and 1.2 cm wide, apex acuminate, entire, outer segments with a brownish midline, inner segments bright pinkish-magenta with a darker midstripe, fading to whitish-green at base. *Stamen filaments* 7-11 mm long, greenish. *Style* c. 2.5 cm long, 2.5 mm in diameter, pale greenish; stigmas 8-15 or more, to 7 mm long, deep green. *Ovary locule* nearly spherical, 6-7 mm long an anthesis, ovules very numerous. *Fruit* subglobose, 2 cm long, 2.5 cm in diameter, reddish-green, flesh white. *Seeds* nearly globose, c. 1 mm long, tuberculate, black.

DISTRIBUTION. NW Mexico: NW Sinaloa and S Baja California Sur; Sonoran Desert (Central Gulf Coast phase) and arid subtropical regions, mostly near the coast on hills at low elevations.

Echinocereus sciurus (K. Brandegee) Dams in Monatsschr. Kakteenk. 14: 130 (1904); Britton & Rose, Cact. 3: 22-23, t. 4.1 (1922); Borg, Cacti, ed. 2, t. 26a (1951); Backeb., Die Cact. 4: 2024, Abb. 1924 & 1925 (1960); G. Lindsay in Cact. Suc. Mex. 12: 72, 86, figs. 32-34 (1967); E. Kleiner in Kakt. and. Sukk. 26 (8) front cover (1975).
Cereus sciurus K. Brandegee in Zoe 5: 192-193 (1904). Type: Mexico, Baja California Sur, hills nr San Jose del Cabo, April 1897, *T.S. Brandegee* (UC).

27a. var. **sciurus**
Spines scarcely or not differentiated into radials and centrals, adpressed or mostly porrect. *Flowers* to 8 cm long and at least 8-10 cm in diameter, usually from stem apex.
DISTRIBUTION. Baja California Sur (S Cape region); on slopes of decomposed granite.

27b. var. **floresii** (Backeb.) N.P. Taylor, stat. nov.
Echinocereus floresii Backeb. in Blaetter f. Sukkulentenk. 1: 5 (1949) et tom. cit. 2023, Abb. 1923 (1960). Type: Mexico, Sinaloa, Topolobampo, *R. Flores & F. Schwarz* (not preserved).
[*E. scopulorum* Britton & Rose, Cact. 3: 30-31 (1922) pro parte (*Rose et al.* 13349 et fig. 34) excl. typ.]
[*E. pectinatus* var. *minor* (Engelm.) L. Benson in Cact. Succ. J. (US) 40: 125-127 (1968) pro parte, non *Cereus dasyacanthus* var. *minor* Engelm.]
Spines differentiated into c. 18 ± adpressed radials and (0-)2-4 porrect centrals. *Flowers* c. 5 cm long and 7 cm in diameter, often arising well below stem apex.
DISTRIBUTION. NW Sinaloa (Vicinity of Topolobampo).

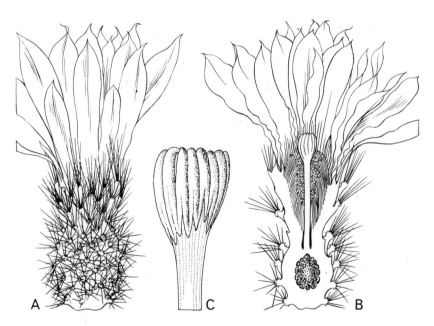

Echinocereus sciurus. A, flower, × 1; B, half-flower, × 1; C, top of style with stigmas, × 3 (ex Hort. A. J. Ward).

28. ECHINOCEREUS SCOPULORUM

Although this species is something of a rarity in cultivation, those specimens seen by the author (mostly ex *Lau* 601) seem to be correctly identified, having very similar flowers to *E. sciurus*, but with perianth-segments deeply coloured only near apex, the rest fading to white, then green at base. Unless grafted the stems remain solitary, the condition in the wild, and the spines are much stiffer and more dense than in the caespitose *E. sciurus*.

The true *E. scopulorum* appears to have only once been illustrated in the literature*, and even then the photograph was poorly reproduced (Lindsay, 1967). Britton & Rose's fig. 34, accompanying the original description of the species (1922) depicts a plant collected at Topolobampo, Sinaloa, which is referable to *E. sciurus* var. *floresii*, while Backeberg's Abb. 1928 (1960) is a misidentification of *E. reichenbachii* var. *reichenbachii*.

Although of limited range *E. scopulorum* is not of concern for conservationists. It is found on a seldom visited part of the dry Sonoran coast and on the almost uninhabited desert island of Tiburon. In cultivation it forms a fine partner to the equally attractive *E. rigidissimus*, which it resembles in habit.

DESCRIPTION. *Stem* normally solitary, cylindric, 10-40 cm high, to 10 cm in diameter, obscured by spines. *Ribs* 13-15, to 1.5 cm apart, 5 mm high. *Areoles* circular, soon glabrous. *Spines* brown, pink or whitish, darker tipped; radials c. 20, adpressed, to 8-14 mm long; centrals (3-)6-10, shorter than radials and ± porrect. *Flowers* funnelform, fragrant, to 8.5 cm long and 10 cm in diameter, arising very near stem apex. *Receptacle-tube* c. 4 cm long, ovary occupying basal half but base of locule c. 8 mm above receptacle base, oblong, 1.5 cm in diameter, tube slightly contracted above then flared to 2.7 cm in diameter at apex, exterior densely covered in areoles with up to 15, to 1.3 cm long, white, brown-tipped spines. *Nectar chamber* 2.5 mm long, 2 mm in diameter, filled by base of style. *Perianth-segments* in c. 2 rows, oblanceolate-spathulate, to 4.5 cm long and 1.5 cm wide, base tapered into a long narrow claw, apex rounded to acute, serrate, mucronate, pale to deep pink with a darker midstripe on the outer segments, white in the throat, green at base. *Stamen filaments* to 14 mm long; anthers oblong, 1.5 mm long. *Style* c. 3 cm long, 2.5 mm in diameter, white; stigmas 10-13, 5 mm long, dark green. *Ovary locule* oblong, 1.2 cm long at anthesis. *Fruit* not described. *Seeds* nearly globose, to 1 mm long, strongly tuberculate.

DISTRIBUTION. Sonora: Isla Tiburon and adjacent coast N of the Rio Yaqui; Sierra del Viejo (*fide* Zimmerman in Yatskievych & Fischer, 1983); Sonoran Desert (Central Gulf Coast phase).

Echinocereus scopulorum Britton & Rose, Cact. 3: 30-31 (1922), excl. fig. 34 et *Rose et al.* 13349; G. Lindsay in Cact. Suc. Mex. 12: 75-76, 86-87, figs. 34 & 37 (1967); Yatskievych & Fischer in Desert Pl. 5(4): 182 (1983). Type: Mexico, Sonora, nr Guaymas, 10 March 1910, *Rose et al.* 12570 (US).

[*E. pectinatus* var. *minor* (Engelm.) L. Benson in Cact. Succ. J. (US) 40: 125 (1968) pro parte, non *Cereus dasyacanthus* var. *minor* Engelm.]

---

* Not counted here is an excellent and correctly identified colour photograph published in the calendar for September, 1980 by *Kakteen und andere Sukkulenten*.

29. ECHINOCEREUS WEBSTERIANUS

The precise identity of this sought-after plant presents no difficulty if one is able to visit the small, rocky island of San Pedro Nolasco, in the Gulf of California, due west of Guaymas, Sonora, where it is endemic. However, few of us are fortunate enough to enjoy a visit to this natural cactus garden and must be content instead with attempting to grow the plant at home in a greenhouse. Unfortunately, here there is a problem, for while *E. websterianus* is not particularly difficult to grow, the true species is seldom offered for sale, various flowering plants shown to the author being either of doubtful identity or obvious hybrids (see p.154). According to the original description and subsequent notes by Lindsay (1947, 1967) the flowers are very like those of its mainland neighbour, *E. scopulorum*, especially in being tricoloured, differing primarily in their small size.

Echinocereus websterianus is undoubtedly an island ally of *E. scopulorum*, here maintained as a separate species with some reservation, its differences being more conspicuous than significant. However, as in *E. sciurus*, the plants are freely caespitose, the erect stems growing to a height of 60 cm, this being the tallest self-supporting member of the genus. To complete the imposing effect they are densely clothed in attractive golden spines, making *E. websterianus* one of the choicest species as well as one of the rarest.

DESCRIPTION. *Plant* caespitose forming a clump of up to 60 cm in diameter and 50 stems. *Stems* cylindric, to 60 cm high and 8 cm in diameter. *Ribs* 18-24, to 5 mm high. *Areoles* circular, to 6-9 mm apart. *Spines* golden yellow, brown in age, to c. 1 cm long; radials 14-18, spreading; centrals 6-8, ± porrect. *Flowers* like those of the preceding, but smaller (described as 6 cm long and 3-4 cm in diameter), receptacle exterior with a little, white wool. *Perianth-segments* only 3 cm long and 8 mm wide, apex acuminate. *Fruit* not described. *Seeds* nearly globose, c. 1 mm long, strongly tuberculate, black.

DISTRIBUTION. Sonora, Gulf of California: endemic to Isla San Pedro Nolasco; Sonoran Desert (Central Gulf Coast phase).

Echinocereus websterianus G. Lindsay in Cact. Succ. J. (US) 19: 153-154, figs. 102 & 103 (1947) et in Cact. Suc. Mex. 12: 74-75, 86, figs. 34 & 36 (1967); Backeb., Die Cact. 4: 2033, Abb. 1935 & 1936 (1960); P Stacey in Nat. Cact. Succ. J. (GB) 33: 61, with fig. (1978). Type: Mexico, Gulf of California, San Pedro Nolasco Island, 24 Feb. 1947, *Lindsay & Bool* 498 (DS 314191).
[*E. grandis* Britton & Rose, Cact. 3: 18 (1922) pro parte (*I.M. Johnston* 3137 tantum).]

30. ECHINOCEREUS GRANDIS

Like the preceding this is a giant island species, whose closest geographical neighbour is also *E. scopulorum*. A direct relationship with its nearest congener is not apparent, however, and *E. grandis* seems in no immediate danger of being synonymized with any other member of the E. RIGIDISSIMUS GROUP. Its stems, clothed in creamy white spines, are solitary or sparingly branched, reaching a maximum height of 50 cm and as much as 12 cm thick! The flowers are quite unmistakable, having an elongate receptacle-tube, protected by unusually long, slender spines, and with very narrow, pale-coloured perianth-segments (see illustrations cited below).

On its own roots this slow-growing species will make some progress, but much more slowly than if it is grafted and kept in a very sunny position. Grafting also encourages the formation of branches, which are useful for propagation as cuttings or further scions, particularly if reliable seed is not available. This is especially important with documented field-collected specimens, whose availability is limited by the inaccessible nature of the islands in the Gulf of California where *E. grandis* grows.

DESCRIPTION. *Stem* solitary or sparingly caespitose with up to 15 branches, cylindric, to 50 cm high and 12 cm in diameter. *Ribs* 18-25, low, to c. 8 mm high. *Areoles* large, elliptic, c. 1 cm apart. *Spines* dull white to cream; radials 15-25, 5-10 mm long, adpressed; centrals 8-12, 3-6 mm long, in 1-2 porrect rows. *Flowers* narrowly funnelform, 5-7 cm long and c. 5-8 cm in diameter when fully open, arising near stem apex. *Receptacle-tube* 3-4 cm long, densely clothed in areoles bearing numerous, long, slender, bristly, pale yellow, porrect spines and white wool. *Perianth-segments* in c. 2 rows, narrowly cuneate-oblanceolate, 2 cm or more long, c. 6 mm wide, apex long acuminate, serrate, white, pale yellow or pale pink, green towards base. *Style* white; stigmas 10-11, dark green. *Fruit* globular, densely spiny. *Seeds* ± globular, 1 mm long, strongly tuberculate.

DISTRIBUTION. Baja California (Mexico), Gulf of California: endemic to Islas San Esteban, San Lorenzo Sur and San Lorenzo Norte (Isla de las Animas); Sonoran Desert (Central Gulf Coast phase) at low elevations.

Echinocereus grandis Britton & Rose, Cact. 3: 18, t. 3.3, fig. 18 (1922), excl. *I.M. Johnston* 3137; G. Lindsay in Cact. Suc. Mex. 12: 72-73, 86, figs. 34 & 35 (1967); E. & B. Lamb, Ill. Ref. Cact. Succ. 5: t. 304 (1978). Type: Mexico, Gulf of California, Isla San Esteban, 13 April 1911, *J.N. Rose* 16823 (US).

31. ECHINOCEREUS BRISTOLII

This is a poorly understood species deserving careful investigation at its type locality of Soyopa, Sonora, and throughout its range to the north, which extends into the United States in SE Arizona. The plant cultivated as *E. bristolii* at present (from Alfred Lau's field numbers 96, 607, 607a and 609) is not typical of the taxon originally described by W.T. Marshall (1938), having much broader perianth-segments and fewer radial spines. Here it is recognised as a new variety, var. *pseudopectinatus*, a name which refers to its confusion with the unrelated *E. pectinatus* by botanists from the United States (see synonymy below). Its occurrence there is restricted to the southern part of Cochise County, Arizona, an area where new and interestng species of cacti and other plants are frequently turning up, e.g. *Escobaria robbinsorum* in 1976 (see A.D. Zimmermann in Cact. Succ. J. (US) 50: 293. 1978). To the south var. *pseudopectinatus* ranges at least as far as Moctezuma, Sonora, where Lau has obtained the living collection chosen, and now preserved, for the type (*Lau* 607).

No living plant corresponding to *E. bristolii* var. *bristolii* has been seen by the writer, and its exact relationships with other species of this Sonoran group are difficult to determine. Its easily grown variety, however, is a more familiar taxon, which seems to connect, both geographically and morphologically, the caespitose, slender-spined *E. sciurus* with the solitary-stemmed stoutly-spined *E. rigidissimus*. The zoning of colour in the rather large flowers is similar to that in *E. sciurus*, while their somewhat woolly receptacles more nearly match those of *E. rigidissimus*.

DESCRIPTION. *Stem* solitary or sparingly branched at base or above, cylindric, tapered towards apex, to 20 cm long and 5 cm in diameter, light green, partially obscured by spines. *Ribs* 15-16, somewhat tuberculate, 5-10 mm apart, low but acute-edged. *Areoles* elliptic, 2-3 mm long, very woolly at first, 5-7 mm apart. *Radial spines* adpressed. 12-20, to 9(-12) mm long, white to pale brown, dark tipped, the uppermost short and slender, white; centrals 1-3(-5), to 5(-15) mm long, one deflexed, the other(s) ascending. *Flowers* funnelform, to 11 cm long and 13 cm in diameter, slightly fragrant, arising near stem apex; buds rather woolly. *Receptacle-tube* to 4.5 cm long, ovary occupying most of basal half but base of locule to 1 cm above receptacle base, globose to oblong, 1.5 cm in diameter, tube contracted above to 8 mm, then flared to 2.5 cm in diameter at apex, exterior green near base, brownish above, bearing areoles with loose wool and up to 20 brown spines to nearly

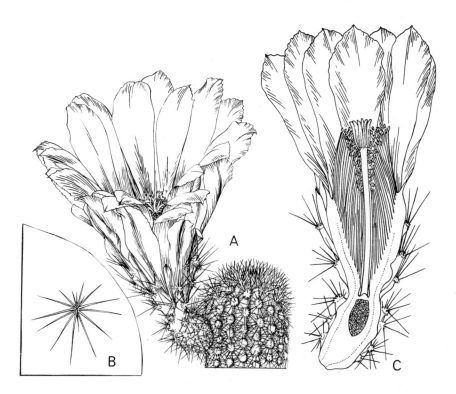

Echinocereus bristolii var. **pseudopectinatus**. A, stem apex with flower, × ⅔; B, stem areole, × 1 ½; C, half-flower, × 1 (from the holotype).

2 cm long near tube apex. *Nectar chamber* 4 mm long, 2 mm wide, almost filled by style base. *Perianth-segments* very thin, of diverse shape, inner segments 4.5-6 cm long, 6-22 mm wide, base cuneate, apex long acuminate to apiculate, margins entire or serrate, light magenta with a darker midstripe, greenish-white near base. *Stamen filaments* to 15 mm long, pale green. *Style* 29-33 mm long, to 2.5 mm thick, white; stigmas 9-11, to 7 mm long, dark green. *Ovary locule* oblong, to c. 1 cm long at anthesis. *Fruit* globose, red, spiny (*fide* Marshall). *Seeds* broadly ovoid, c. 1 mm long, strongly tuberculate.

DISTRIBUTION. Central E Sonora to SE Arizona, drainage of the Rio Yaqui and its northern tributaries; Sonoran Desert (foothills of Sonora) and desert grassland, low elevations to c. 1350 m altitude.

Echinocereus bristolii W.T. Marsh. in Cact. Succ. J. (US) 9: 160-161, with figs. (1938). Type: Mexico, Sonora, Soyapa [Soyopa], steep banks of the city reservoir, 'about 5000 feet'[?], 1934, *B. Bristol & W.T. Marshall* (DS 251175).

[*E. pectinatus* var. *minor* (Engelm.) L. Benson in Cact. Succ. J. (US) 40: 125-127 (1968) pro parte, non *Cereus dasyacanthus* var. *minor* Engelm.]

31a. var. **bristolii**
    Radial spines c.20. *Inner perianth-segments* narrowly lanceolate, 6 mm wide, entire.
    DISTRIBUTION. Central E Sonora (known certainly only from the type locality); Sonoran Desert, low elevations.

31b. var. **pseudopectinatus** N.P. Taylor, **var. nov.** *a var. bristolii differt perianthii segmentis multo (usque ter saltem) latioribus et spinis radiantibus paucioribus (12-15) in areolis caulinis.* *Holotypus*: Sonora, Moctezuma, c. 1973, *Lau 607*, cultivated by N.P. Taylor, 21 June 1984 (K, spirit coll.).

[*E. pectinatus* var. *pectinatus* sensu Kearney & Peebles, Ariz. Fl. 571, t. 28 (1951) et L. Benson, Cacti of Arizona, ed. 3, 146, figs. 3.21 & 3.22 (1969) et Cacti US & Can. 658 (map), 945 (1982), tantum quoad specim. ex Ariz., non *Echinocactus pectinatus* Scheidw.]
    Radial spines 12-15. *Inner perianth-segments* cuneate-oblanceolate, to 22 mm wide, irregularly serrate towards apex.
    DISTRIBUTION. NE Sonora and border region of adjacent SE Arizona (S Cochise Co.); Sonoran Desert and desert grassland, to 1350 m altitude.

32. ECHINOCEREUS RIGIDISSIMUS

Echinocereus connoisseurs should be pleased to find one of their favourite plants restored to specific rank. *E. rigidissimus* (Engelm.) Hort. F.A. Haage is easily one of the most distinct species in the genus, but has been unjustly treated as a variety of *E. pectinatus* (Scheidw.) Engelm. by many authors. It seems that previous students of this genus have placed too much emphasis on vegetative similarities, no doubt because characters of the stem, such as spination, can be observed at any time of year, and also without difficulty in herbarium material. In contrast, the flowers are available only briefly *in vivo* and cannot be studied satisfactorily in the herbarium unless preserved in spirit. Nevertheless, there is really no excuse for the lack of observation and the shortsightedness, which seem to have caused the rejection of *E. rigidissimus* as a species. Its flowers differ in a number of important respects from those of *E. pectinatus* and deserve more attention than that accorded by many writers (e.g. Weniger, 1970).

The flowers of *E. rigidissimus* are typical of section *Reichenbachii* in that the perianth-segments are thin and delicate, not fleshy at the base, and densely inserted at the apex of the elongate receptacle-tube, which is protected by numerous closely packed, many-spined areoles. This description cannot apply to *E. pectinatus* (q.v.) with which it has so often been synonymized. Two additional though minor differences also set it apart from its true Sonoran Desert allies (spp. nos. 27-31 in this treatment). First there is the colour of its perianth-segments, which in the centre of the flower are white right to the base (not green) and, secondly, its stem areoles without central spines. In these particular features and also in its very tuberculate seeds it actually comes closer to the eastern ranging E. REICHENBACHII GROUP., especially *E. primolanatus* and the neotype form of *E. reichenbachii*. However, they have characteristically fewer, long and slender receptacle-tube bristles (rather than numerous short spines) and are not confusable with *E. rigidissimus* if examined carefully when in flower. Nevertheless, *E. rigidissimus* would seem to be the taxon which links these eastern and western groups together, both morphologically and geographically.

Echinocereus rigidissimus occurs at generally higher altitudes, further north and east than the other members of its group, as it is found on the Pacific slope of the Sierra Madre Occidental, in W Chihuahua and NE Sonora, and the northern extension of these highlands in SE Arizona and SW New Mexico.

The type was collected in the 'Sierras of Pimeria Alta' in southern-most Arizona, near the Sonoran border by Mr Arthur Schott in 1855, and was described by Engelmann the following year. He chose the epithet *rigidissimus* because of the very stiff radial spines, which are arranged in a comb-like row down each side of the elongate areoles. As they emerge from the growing point so their colour varies through paler to darker shades of brown, red or yellowish-white, giving the stem an attractive banded effect. This has earned the species its common name of 'rainbow cactus'.

In Chihuahua, near the western edge of the state in the Sierra Oscura, the typical form of the species (var. *rigidissimus*) is replaced by a dwarfer plant with more numerous crimson-coloured spines and flowers with brownish-green stigmas. This has recently been distinguished as *E. pectinatus* var. *rubispinus* G. R. W. Frank (1982) and is now transferred to varietal status under *E. rigidissimus*. The type was collected by Alfred Lau in 1972 and bears his number, *Lau* 88. It is becoming freely available in cultivation and is well worth acquiring, since it flowers without difficulty when quite small.

Though Alfred Lau deserves the credit for introducing this dwarf variety to cultivation, he may not have been the first to collect it. Engelmann, in his famous *Cactaceae of the Boundary* (1859), mentions a 'small specimen, with only 15 ribs, smaller areolae and smaller and more numerous spines (30-35, only 1-1½ line long)'. Unfortunately we are not told where this plant was found, but its description is very suggestive of var. *rubispinus*.

DESCRIPTION. *Stem* solitary, rarely branched, globose to cylindrical 6-18(-30) cm long, 4-9(-11) cm in diameter, ± obscured by spines. *Ribs* (15-)18-23(-26), low, with flattened tubercles. *Areoles* approximate, linear-elliptic, 2.5-7 mm long, with wool at first. *Spines* (15-) 18-35, all adpressed, pectinately arranged into two closely set rows, interlaced, to 5-10 mm long, stout, red, white, yellowish or brownish, often forming coloured bands around the stem; centrals 0. *Flowers* from the side of the stem or its 'shoulder', 6-7 cm long, 6-9 cm in diameter; young flower-buds very woolly. *Receptacle-tube* c 3.0 cm long, lower 1.3 cm swollen, enclosing the ovary, 1.3-1.5 cm in diameter, contracting to 0.8 cm above ovary, covered in numerous, closely set, 1-2 mm long tubercles, each bearing an areole with c 20 or more 3-5 mm long, white, brown-tipped, ± porrect spines and loose, floccose wool, upper 1.7 cm of tube funnel-shaped, expanding to c. 2.3 cm in diameter, areoles more widely spaced, with spines to 6 mm long; sometimes apex of tube subtending linear scales to c 12 mm long and 1.5 mm wide, each tipped by an areole with 6-7 spines, to 9 mm long. *Nectar chamber* c 4 mm long, very narrow, filled by the base of the style. *Perianth-segments* in about 2 rows, obovate-oblanceolate, acute to 4 cm long and c 1.0 cm wide, margins ± entire or lacerate, inner segments abruptly contracted into a narrow claw near base, brilliant pinkish-red to magenta in upper half, white in the throat. *Stamens* tightly packed around style, c 2.5 cm long. *Style* to 4.5 cm long, 2 mm in diameter, part exceeding stamens pinkish-red; stigmas 12-15, to 9 mm long, green to brownish. *Fruit* ovoid, 2.5-5 cm long, 1.5-3 cm in diameter, described as greenish, brownish or red, fleshy, exterior very spiny. *Seeds* ovoid, 1-1.5 mm long, black.

DISTRIBUTION. NW Mexico: W Chihuahua & NE Sonora; SW USA: SW New Mexico & SE Arizona; mostly in desert grassland or on rocks, usually above 1000 m altitude.

Echinocereus rigidissimus (Engelm.) Hort. F.A. Haage, Special offer [catalogue], 13 (1897); Britton & Rose, Cact. 3: 27-28, figs. 28-31 (1922); H. Bravo-H. in An. Inst. Biol. Mex. 21: 466, fig. 13 (1951); E. & B. Lamb, Colourful Cacti, 187, tt. 56-59 (1974).

Cereus pectinatus (Scheidw.) Engelm. var. *rigidissimus* Engelm., Syn. Cact. US. 23-24 (1856) and Cact. Mex. Bound. 31-32 (1859). Lectotype (cf. Benson, loc. cit. infra): USA, Arizona, near the border with Sonora, 'Sierra del Pajarito and farther west in similar localities', 1855, *A. Schott* (MO).

Echinocereus pectinatus (Scheidw.) Engelm. var. *rigidissimus* (Engelm.) Ruempler in C. F. Foerster, Handb. Cacteenk., ed. 2, 818 (1885); R. Carlson (Ed.), The Flowering Cactus, 27 (1954) (superb colour plate); Weniger, Cacti of the Southwest, t. 7 (1970); L. Benson, Cacti US & Can. 659, 944-945, figs. 695-696, colour plate 107 (1982), excl. fig. 694.

32a. var. **rigidissimus**

Stem to 9(-11) cm in diameter. *Areoles* 5-7 mm long. *Radial spines* 15-23, 6-10 mm long. *Stigmas* mid-green. *Fruit* c 3 cm in diameter.

DISTRIBUTION. N & E Sonora, SW New Mexico (S Hidalgo Co.) and SE Arizona (formerly as far as Phoenix in the Sonoran Desert); to 1550 m altitude.

32b. var. **rubispinus** (G. R. W. Frank & A. Lau) N. P. Taylor in Kew Mag. 1: 175 (1984). (PLATE 2, PRO PARTE) (Text figure, p.54)

E. pectinatus var. *rubispinus* G. R. W. Frank & A. Lau in Kakt. and. Sukk. 33(2): 35, with figs. (1982). Type: Mexico, W. Chihuahua, Sierra Oscura, nr. Campito, Canyon de Barbarocas, 1972, *Lau* 88(ZSS).

Stem 4-6 cm in diameter. *Areoles* c 2.5 mm long. *Radial spines* 30-35, to 5 mm long. *Stigmas* brownish-green. *Fruit* c. 1.5 cm in diameter.

DISTRIBUTION. W Chihuahua, Sierra Oscura; 1600-2000 m altitude.

33. ECHINOCEREUS PALMERI

The dwarf *Echinocereus palmeri* is at the peak of specialization within section *Reichenbachii*, its few-ribbed stems being reduced to a minimum, the business of water storage taken over by a much larger tuberous taproot. Here is a clear parallel with the E. PULCHELLUS GROUP of sect. *Pulchellus* and also with sect. *Wilcoxia* (especially *E. schmollii*). In habit *E. palmeri* is somewhat intermediate between these divergent tuberous-rooted taxa, having stems more cereoid than the former, but much shorter than those of the latter. In terms of relationship, however, it cannot be ranged with either, its flowers and their mode of origin clearly placing it in the E. REICHENBACHII GROUP, its circular areoles and open spination specifically relating it to *E. chisoensis*. Its affinity with *E. adustus*, as judged by Frank (1983), seems ill-conceived.

The botanical history of *E. palmeri* is relatively brief. It was named by Britton & Rose in 1922 for its discoverer, Dr Edward Palmer (1831-1911), the famous North American field botanist. Palmer came upon three plants, one of which was in flower, on a small hill near the city of Chihuahua in April 1908. Britton & Rose's original description was very poor and they provided no illustration either. Apparently the first published photograph of this distinctive plant was in Backeberg's monograph in 1960 (Abb. 1933), which was accompanied by a second illustration (Abb. 1934) purporting to be a form of *E. palmeri*, but actually depicting its close relative, *E. chisoensis* var. *fobeanus*.

In the last two decades fieldwork by Glass & Foster, Alfred Lau, and others has resulted in the species becoming better known in the literature and in cultivation. In spite of its inconspicuous nature it is now recorded from at least five localities besides that of Palmer, and proves to be both widespread (in Chihuahua) and somewhat variable, especially in flower size, colour and perianth-segment shape.

It is not difficult to grow so long as the tuberous taproot (which needs a much larger pot than the aerial part of the plant would suggest) is surrounded by very open compost containing plenty of coarse grit or similar material. Alternatively, the risk of rot starting in the roots can be avoided if the stem is grafted, but this, at least for the writer, seems to take away some of the interest in the plant. Propagation by seed is easy, or appears to be with fresh seed produced in cultivation, which requires that two non-clonal specimens are cross-pollinated. The young plants start to flower when very small, the 4-5 cm long and wide, lavender perianths dwarfing the tiny dark green stems. Accordingly, *E. palmeri* is to be rated highly and ranked alongside other choice miniatures like *E. pulchellus* var. *pulchellus*, *E. knippelianus* var. *kruegeri* and *E. viridiflorus* var. *davisii*.

DESCRIPTION. *Stem* solitary or with one or more branches, 3-8 cm long (eventually larger in cultivation), 2-3 cm in diameter, ovoid to cylindric, tapered towards apex, annually constricted, rather dark green, not obscured by spines, forming a neck with the tuberous, greatly swollen taproot. *Ribs* 6-10 low, scarcely tuberculate. *Areoles* circular, 1.5 mm in diameter, retaining their white wool for some time, 3-4 mm apart. *Radial spines* 9-15, to c. 4 mm long, adpressed, white, dark-tipped; central(s) 1(-2), 1-2 cm long, slender, ascending, or porrect in areoles which have borne flowers, dark brown to blackish near apex. *Flowers* funnelform, fragrant, to 5.5 cm long and 5 cm in diameter*, arising near stem apex, buds not bursting through the stem epidermis nor leaving a scar after fruit production. *Receptacle-tube* to c. 3 cm long, ovary occupying lower half but base of locule 6-7 mm above base of receptacle, 8-9 mm in diameter in ovary region, narrowing to 7-8 mm above before expanding to 1.6 cm at apex, exterior green, clothed in woolly areoles with up to 10, to 1.3 cm long, bristle- to hair-like, black and white spines. *Nectar chamber* minute, c. 0.7 mm long, filled by style base. *Perianth-segments* in 3 rows, the largest oblanceolate, to 2.5 cm long and 1.1 cm broad (variable in shape and size), apex apiculate or acuminate, adjacent margins irregularly fimbriate-serrate, base tapered into a narrow claw, outer segments brownish, inner pinkish-lavender to purple with a darker midstripe, paler to greenish near base. *Stamen filaments* c. 1.3 cm long, whitish; anthers with golden yellow pollen. *Style* 2.3 cm long, greenish-white; stigmas 7-10, c. 5-6 mm long, light green. *Ovary locule* obovoid, to 8 mm long at anthesis. *Fruit* ovoid, to 1.5 cm long, green splitting to reveal the white pulp. *Seeds* (see Frank, loc. cit.) broadly ovoid, c. 1.5 mm long, strongly tuberculate.

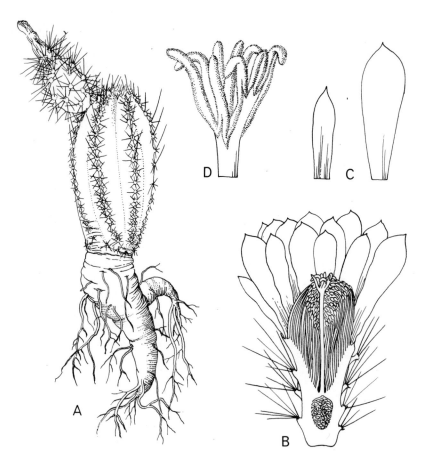

Echinocereus palmeri. A, plant with fruit, × 1; B, half-flower, × 1½; C, outer (l) to inner (r) perianth-segments, × 2; D, top of style with stigmas, × 6 (ex Hort. N. P. Taylor).

DISTRIBUTION. N Mexico: Cent. & S Chihuahua (nr Buenaventura, Santa Clara, Cusihuiriachic, Cd. Chihuahua, Rio Florido & Pelayo); grassy E slopes of the Sierra Madre Occidental foothills to edge of Chihuahuan Desert, 1400-1900 m altitude.

Echinocereus palmeri Britton & Rose, Cact. 3: 34 (1922); Backeb., Die Cact. 4: 2032, Abb. 1933 tantum (1960); C. Glass & R. Foster in Cact. Succ. J. (US) 46: 9-10, figs. 3 & 4 (1974); H. Hirao, Colour Encycl. Cacti, fig. 617 (1979); G.R.W. Frank in Kakt. and. Sukk. 34: 179-182 Abb. 8 & ll, 219-221 Abb. D1-3 (1983); A. Lau in J. Nat. Cact. Succ. Soc. India 3: 48-49, with figs. (1983). Type: Mexico, Chihuahua, small hill nr Chihuahua City, April 1908, *E. Palmer* 121 (US).

* Riha in Chrudimsky Kaktusar 1982: 5 (1982) claims flower diameters in habitat of 15 cm!

34. ECHINOCEREUS CHISOENSIS

Echinocereus chisoensis W.T. Marshall is a little-known, but very interesting Chihuahuan Desert species, referred by Benson (1969, 1982) to *E. reichenbachii* as a variety, but more nearly related to *E. palmeri*. Its non-pectinate, hair-like spines and minute areoles immediately distinguish it from *E. reichenbachii*. The plants originally described by Marshall (1940) came from the southernmost part of the Big Bend in Texas, where they occupy a relatively small area in the Chisos Mts, mostly under desert shrubs. This, the type variety, is particularly vulnerable to the depredations of ruthless collectors, but fortunately it occurs entirely within the Big Bend National Park where it is theoretically protected. It is still quite rare in cultivation, the only material seen by the author having originated from propagations made by the International Succulent Institute and distributed in 1980 (ISI 1168). The flowers are very beautiful, but seldom open fully to reveal the perianth-segments to their best effect. Inside, these are zoned from shocking pink, near their tips, to white in the throat, then a contrasting rich crimson at the very base.

Marshall's plants were discovered in 1939 by Radley, but a different variety of the species was grown in Europe as early as 1924. Only months after Marshall's description of 1940 was published, Oehme named it *E. fobeanus* from plants cultivated in Germany. The wild provenance of these was not revealed by Gasser, the importer, though Oehme suggested Arizona. However, in recent years plants matching the original description and illustration of *E. fobeanus* have been collected in Mexico, in SW Coahuila and adjacent NE Durango, about 400 kilometers due south of the Big Bend region. From these it is clear that *E. fobeanus* is con-specific with *E. chisoensis*, differing chiefly in its branching stems and larger flowers, which open fully. Here it is treated as a disjunct variety, though the disjunction may be more apparent than real, the area between the two taxa being one of the wildest and least explored parts of Mexico.

Two forms of var. *fobeanus* are currently in cultivation, of which *H. Kuenzler* 303 seems to be that most often encountered. It is interesting for its tendency

to produce a thickened or tuberous rootstock*, though this is not so pronounced as in the closely related *E. palmeri*. The flowers are exceptionally large
for the size of the plant, but in good weather rarely last more than two days. In
cultivation the stems of this variety become constricted and somewhat ugly,
this probably being due to the abrupt return of growth which follows
flowering. The form figured here, from the collection of Mr D. Parker, has
been distributed as 'sp. de Coahuila', without further locality. It is very
similar to *HK* 303, but appears to lack the tuberous rootstock (unless this is
due to vegetative propagation) and has somewhat smaller flowers with longer
and finer spines on the receptacle-tube. Both forms are easy to grow, except
that like var. *chisoensis* they seem to fare better when the winter temperature is
not allowed to fall below 5-7°C.

Propagation of *E. chisoensis* var. *chisoensis* is by seed, or grafting followed by
decapitation of the scion to induce offsetting. Since it is normally caespitose,
var. *fobeanus* can be increased by removal of its branches as cuttings, but if two
flowering plants are available for cross-pollination, abundant seed can be
produced and sown instead. Flowering often seems to take place in spring and
again in late summer, the flower buds produced in late spring remaining only
half-developed while the plant makes vegetative growth before its second
flowering.

DESCRIPTION. *Stem* solitary or branched, 5-20(-25) cm long, c. 3-5 cm in diameter,
cylindric or tapering towards apex, sometimes constricted between annual sections, pale
grey-green to yellowish- or blue-green, rootstock sometimes thickened or tuberous. *Ribs*

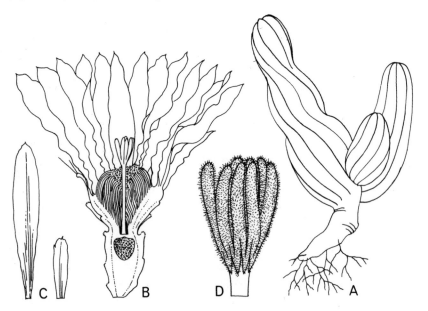

Echinocereus chisoensis var. **fobeanus**. A, habit, areoles and spines omitted, × ⅑; B, half-flower,
× 1; C, outer (left) and inner (right) perianth-segments, × 1; D, top of style with stigmas, × 4 (ex
Hort. D. Parker).

126

(10-)11-16, strongly tuberculate, vertical or somewhat spiralled, 7-9 mm apart. *Areoles* very small, but with much diffuse wool at first, later naked or some wool persistent, especially on the enlarged flower-bearing areoles, 6-8 mm apart, circular. *Radial spines* 11-16, uppermost short or minute, laterals to 1 cm, lowermost 1-3 to 1.2-2 cm long, finely acicular, adpressed to somewhat porrect, white to pinkish-grey with brown tips, not obscuring stem; centrals (1-)2-6, very slender, dark brown, the lowermost longest, to 1.7 cm, porrect, others ascending and diverging. *Flowers* funnel-shaped, 6-9.5 cm long, 5-12 cm in diameter, sometimes not opening widely (var. *chisoensis*). *Receptacle-tube* to 4.5 cm long, 2-2.5 cm wide at apex, base of ovary locule c. 1 cm, its apex c. 1.4 cm, from base of tube, exterior green, to dark brownish-red near apex, ribbed-tuberculate, bearing evenly spaced areoles with 7-14, 9-21 mm long, bristle-like to hair-like, white, brown-tipped spines and much wool. *Nectar chamber* only 1-2 mm long, ± filled by base of style. *Perianth-segments* in 2 rows, very thin and delicate, the largest oblong-oblanceolate, to 5 cm long and 1.6 cm wide, light pinkish-magenta with a darker midstripe, white in the throat, abruptly contracted into a claw at the greenish, brownish or deep-crimson base, apex long acuminate, serrate. *Stamen filaments* to c. 1.3 cm long, white to pink; anthers oblong, 1.5 mm, yellow. *Style* c. 2.5 cm long, stout, to 3 mm in diameter at apex, white, exserted 4-5 mm above stamens; stigmas 10, 3-6 mm long, to 1.5 mm thick, dark green. *Ovary locule* rounded-obconic, 5-6 mm in diameter at anthesis. *Fruit* clavate, 2.5-3.5 cm long and 1.3 cm wide, drying red or brownish-green, with wool and bristle-like spines, often splitting open, pulp white, somewhat viscid or almost dry. *Seeds* ovoid, c. 1.2 mm long, black, strongly tuberculate.

DISTRIBUTION. W Texas (Big Bend) to SW Coahuila and adjacent Durango; Chihuahuan Desert, on limestone, at or above 600 m altitude.

Echinocereus chisoensis W.T. Marsh. in Cact. Succ. J. (US) 12: 15, 1 (cover illustration) (Jan. 1940); Weniger, Cacti of the Southwest, 29, t. 7 (1970). Type: U.S.A., Texas, Big Bend National Park, Chisos Mts, 10 April 1939, *F. Radley* (DS 263216).
E. reichenbachii var. *chisoensis* (W.T. Marsh.) L. Benson ('chisosensis') in Cact. Succ. J. (US) 41: 127 (1969) and Cacti US & Can. 666, 670, 667 (map), colour pl. 113 (1982).

34a. var. **fobeanus** (Oehme) N.P. Taylor in Kew Mag. 2: 261 (1985). (PLATE 9).
E. fobeanus Oehme in Beitr. Sukkulentenkunde u. -pflege Lfg 3: 49-50, with fig. (1940, after Jan.); L. Germer in Kakt. and. Sukk. 33: 151, with fig. (1982). Type: a living specimen derived from a plant imported in 1924 (assumed not to have been preserved). Lectotype (Taylor, loc. cit.): Oehme, l.c., fig., p. 49.

Stem branched, often constricted into annual sections. *Flower* 6-9.5 cm long, 7-12 cm in diameter; base of inner perianth-segments pale greenish or brownish.
DISTRIBUTION. Mexico: border region of SW Coahuila and E Durango (vicinity of San Pedro de las Colonias & N of Gomez Palacio), at or above 1100 m altitude.

34b. var. **chisoensis**
Stem solitary, not annually constricted. *Flower* c 6 cm long, 5 cm in diameter; base of inner perianth-segments deep crimson.
DISTRIBUTION. Texas, in the southernmost part of the Big Bend, Chisos Mts, 600-900 m altitude.

---

* Unidentified plants with thickened rootstocks found near San Pedro de las Colonias by R.E. Flores in 1943/44 may be referable here (see Cact. Succ. J. (US) 16: 98, fig. 92/1. 1944).

35. ECHINOCEREUS PRIMOLANATUS

It is a pleasure to be able to validate the botanical name of this interesting and very choice Chihuahuan Desert species. *E. primolanatus* is a remarkable little plant: as a seedling it is covered in very fine, hair-like central spines but, as the stem begins to fatten-out and mature, their development ceases and the very densely set pectinate radial spines are revealed. These completely obscure the green stem surface in field-collected specimens, representing a formidable barrier to the transpiration of the plants valuable moisture. As soon as the 'hairy' juvenile phase has passed the small plants start to flower, sometimes producing large woolly buds on stems scarcely 2.5 cm in diameter. The flowers are a very beautiful bright pink with a white throat and leave no doubt as to the plant's close affinity with *E. chisoensis* and *E. reichenbachii*.

Echinocereus primolanatus is geographically and morphologically intermediate between its two closest allies. At present it is known only from the southern reaches of the Sierra de la Paila, in S Coahuila, which is to the east of the habitats of *E. chisoensis* var. *fobeanus* and west of the neotype locality of *E. reichenbachii* near Saltillo. Its juvenile stems resemble the former in their long slender central spines and, at maturity, in their tendency to form a tuberous rootstock. At first sight its adult stems can hardly be distinguished from those of the similarly pectinate-spined *E. reichenbachii* var. *reichenbachii*, though they are usually smaller. However, at maturity the stems have a higher rib count than either of its relatives, i.e. (21-)25-26 vs. 10-19.

The history of *E. primolanatus* is not well documented. According to Backeberg (1960) it was discovered and christened by Friedrich Schwarz, a commerical field collector who invariably left others to validate his species names and guess at where his material had been gathered. The name presumably refers to the hair-like central spines developed at first on immature stems, but could also describe the very woolly young growth seen in cultivated specimens. Backeberg's attempt at validating Schwarz's binomial characteristically failed, because he neither cited nor preserved a type specimen, as required by the International Code since 1958. The wild origin of the plant, as publicized here, is already well-known to some field collectors (who are almost certainly operating illegally) and raises the question of how secure the species is in habitat. Until its range is better understood, the purchase of habitat-collected specimens (even if legally obtained) must be discouraged, lest their continued removal should lead to it becoming endangered. Its propagation by field- or home-produced seed is, however, to be applauded and seems easy so long as extra winter warmth is provided.

The ecology of *E. primolanatus* is yet to be reported on, our only knowledge being that it emanates from the Chihuahuan Desert region and seems to grow in fine silty soil (no doubt overlying limestone). The purpose of its hair-like juvenile spination can only be speculated at. Perhaps it helps imprison a greater layer of insulating air around the seedling, reducing the desiccating effects of sun and wind or protecting against severe cold. Or do the fine spine points assist in the collection of night-time dews, increasing the amount which drips down around

Plate 9

Echinocereus chisoensis var. *fobeanus*

Plate 10

Echinocereus poselgeri

the plant? Whatever its purpose, other Chihuahuan Desert echinocerei seem to have developed similar structures, e.g. *E. delaetii* var. *delaetii* and *E. chloranthus* var. *neocapillus*.

Echinocereus primolanatus is clearly adapted to withstand considerable drought and is thus sensitive to excess moisture. Some growers recommend a clay pot, rather than plastic, but with either type quick-draining compost with a high inorganic content is essential. Warmer conditions in winter (5°C min.) are beneficial and give a greater margin for error if, for example, the plant was watered a bit late in the season or unfortunately gets dripped on while resting. Propagation by seed is usual, but there is also a cristate (fasciated) form, admired by some, whose normal reversions can be removed, grafted until mature, then (if desired) separated from the stock and rooted.

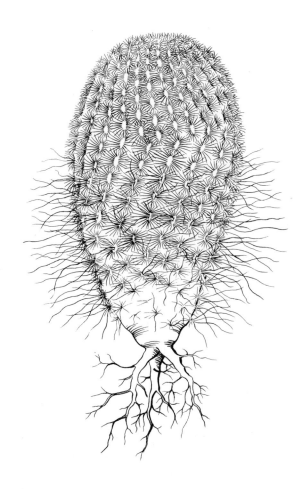

Echinocereus primolanatus. Plant, × 2 (ex Hort. A. Forno).

DESCRIPTION. *Stem* normally solitary, at maturity 4-12 cm long, 2.5-5.5 cm in diameter, globose to cylindric, sometimes irregularly constricted, in field-collected specimens completely obscured by dense adpressed spination, tapering towards the woody spineless, subterranean base (rootstock), which is sometimes swollen and tuberous. *Ribs* (21-)25-26, low, very slightly tuberculate. *Areoles* linear to elliptic, c. 2 mm long, approximate, very woolly at first (in cultivated specimens the wool covering stem apex). *Spines* of mature stems all radial, c. 20-28, to 4 mm long, adpressed in 2 comb-like rows on either side of areole, dirty white; seedlings and juvenile stems with 1-3, to 15 mm long, finely hair-like, brownish central spines per areole. *Flowers* broadly funnelform, to at least 6 cm long and 10.5 cm in diameter; flower buds very woolly. *Receptacle-tube* variable in degree of elongation, at least 3.5 cm long, exterior green but sometimes almost obscured by closely-spaced areoles with dense, long wool and fine hair-like white to blackish-brown bristles, to c. 15 mm long. *Outer perianth-segments* narrowly linear, brownish; inner segments in c. 2 rows, cuneate-oblanceolate, to c. 5 cm long and 1 cm broad, margins somewhat irregularly serrate near the long acuminate apex, bright pink (with a slightly darker midstripe) in upper half, lower half white turning to green or faintly reddish-brown at base. *Style* not exceeding stamens; stigmas c. 10, dark green. *Fruit* ovoid, nearly dry, densely woolly and bristly. *Seeds* broadly ovoid, 1.5 mm long, strongly tuberculate, black.

DISTRIBUTION. Mexico: S Coahuila, nr S edge of Sierra de la Paila; Chihuahuan Desert.

Echinocereus primolanatus F. Schwarz ex N.P. Taylor, **sp. nov.**, E. reichenbachii *arcte affinis sed caulibus maturis costis numerosioribus (21-26) praeditis, caulibus junioribus spinis centralibus longis capilliformibus gracillimis instructis. Holotypus:* Mexico, S Coahuila, Sierra de la Paila, N of Estacion Marte (collector?); cultivated at Bordesley Green East, Birmingham, UK, by D. Parker, 1985 (K, spirit coll.).

'*E. primolanatus*' F. Schwarz ex Backeb., Die Cact. 4: 2043, Abb. 1939a,b,c (1960); ibid. 6: 3852, Abb. 3493 (1962), nom. inval. (Arts. 37 & 9.5).

36. ECHINOCEREUS REICHENBACHII

Unlike the preceding species in this group, *E. reichenbachii* has a long botanical history. Its name was first validly published, so far as can be determined, by Walpers in 1843, who described it under the heading '*Echinocactus reichenbachii* Terscheck, l.c.' [Suppl. Cact. 2], and merely stated 'Habitat in Mexico' for the type. Little or nothing is known of Terscheck and his publications, but the contemporary author Fennel cited his epithet as the adjectival '*reichenbachianus*' (in Allg. Gartenz. 11: 281-282. 1843). Similarly, Salm-Dyck (1845) and Foerster (1846), when referring the plant to the genus *Echinopsis*, employed the epithet '*reichenbachiana*'. This is also true of the F.A. Haage nursery catalogue for 1859, in which the combination *Echinocereus reichenbachianus* was given. However, there is no reason to suppose that these different forms of Terscheck's epithet referred to different plants and the writer is inclined to treat the adjectival form as an error for the genitive form, the latter being the first to be validated and now in universal use. Apart from Walpers, the authors referred to above all regarded Terscheck's binomial as a synonym or variety of *Echinopsis pectinata* (i.e. *Echinocereus pectinatus*), which was itself being misapplied at that time to another form of the species under discussion here*. Their descriptions of its flowers, which were first observed independently by Fennel and Salm-Dyck in June 1843, supplement the vegetative details published by Walpers in the same year and leave no doubts about the identity of the name *E. reichenbachii*. This needs to be explained, since Weniger (1970) has cast doubt on its identity and would substitute the later *Cereus caespitosus* Engelm. (1845) for our well-known plant. More recently, however, the application of the epithet *reichenbachii* has been fixed in a more certain way with Benson's provision of a neotype from the vicinity of Saltillo, Coahuila (Benson, 1982).

The Mexican form of the species from the region of the neotype is in cultivation and is an exceptionally fine plant. It has numerous, adpressed, pectinate radial spines, but no centrals, and produces bright pink flowers contrasted with white in the throat. Specimens from further north, in Texas and Oklahoma, often have differently coloured flowers, with purplish-magenta pigments which darken in the throat (as in the synonymous *E. purpureus* Lahman). This the type variety, *reichenbachii*, is wide-ranging and intergrades with the much longer-spined var. *baileyi* in Oklahoma and with var. *perbellus* in central and northern Texas. Both of these have less elongate areoles with fewer radials and sometimes one or more minute central spines. The former is a very popular plant in cultivation, where various spine colour forms are encountered (mostly under invalid varietal names of Backeberg).

More distinctive than either of these are the varieties *armatus* and *fitchii*, both with the capacity to produce quite conspicuous central spines. The first-named has been regarded as a separate species by recent authors (e.g. Frank, 1983) but closely agrees with *E. reichenbachii* in its floral morphology. The flowers are often very large and green in the throat, but its most obvious difference lies in the irregularly developed, dark central spines, to 2 cm long. The occasional forms which completely lack these look very like var. *reichenbachii*. It seems to be known only from Huasteca Canyon, a few miles west of Monterrey, Nuevo Leon.

Echinocereus reichenbachii var. *fitchii* is an old favourite of many cactus enthusiasts. It emanates from the lowland plain of the Rio Grande, in S Texas and adjacent NE Mexico. The flowers are particularly beautiful and distinctive, the rich pink perianth-segments contrasted with deep crimson in the throat. The stigmas are an unusual dark grey-green. The typical form has up to seven divergent central spines per stem areole, but other forms, known as '*E. melanocentrus*' (nom. inval.) and var. *albertii* L. Benson, have fewer but longer centrals. These come from the same lowland habitat type as typical var. *fitchii* and have similar if not identical flowers. They are synonymized with it here.

It is doubtful whether there are any species of *Echinocereus* more popular than *E. reichenbachii* and its varieties. Not only is it an attractively-spined plant, but the freely produced flowers, with many, satin-like perianth-segments, are of remarkable beauty. It can even be grown and flowered on a sufficiently sunny

* The true *Echinocereus pectinatus* was evidently an ephemeral plant in European living collections and soon became supplanted by its more easily grown look-alike, *E. reichenbachii* (cf. Engelmann in Wislizenus, 1848).

window-sill and is often seen on sale in florists' shops and supermarkets. While the *Echinocereus* connoisseur may regard it as a common plant, it is still worth growing and propagating (by seed), being an excellent species by which to encourage a beginner, in the form of a gift.

DESCRIPTION. *Stems* solitary or with 12 or more branches, to 30(-40) cm high and 10 cm in diameter, erect, globose to cylindric or tapered towards apex, often constricted, epidermis light to dark green but ± obscured by spines. *Ribs* (10-)11-19, narrow, with low tubercles. *Areoles* elliptic to linear, to 4 mm long, very woolly at first, mostly 2-4.5 mm apart. *Radial spines* 12-36, 3-12(-25) mm long, adpressed and pectinately arranged in a row on each side of the areole, in some forms considerably interlaced with those of the adjacent ribs; central spines 0-7, 1-20 mm long, variously coloured, slender. *Flowers* funnelform, 5-12 cm long and to 12 cm in diameter, fragrant, arising near stem apex. *Receptacle-tube* to 5 cm long, ovary occupying basal 2 cm, to 2 cm in diameter, base of locule to 8 mm above receptacle base, tube above ovary scarcely contracted, but flared to 3 cm in diameter at apex, exterior ± obscured by the very numerous areoles bearing up to 15 or more, to 14 mm long, fine blackish to whitish bristle-like spines and much diffuse wool, the uppermost areoles often elevated on narrow scales. *Nectar chamber* to 4 mm long, ± filled by base of style. *Perianth-segments* in 2-4 rows, very numerous, oblanceolate, to 4.5 cm long and 7.5-15 mm wide, long apiculate-acuminate and entire to lacerate at apex, shades of pink to magenta, darker or white in the throat, crimson to greenish at base. *Stamen-filaments* to 2 cm long; anthers oblong, 1.5 mm long. *Style* to 3.5 cm long and 3 mm in diameter; stigmas 8-22, to 6 mm long, dark to grey-green. *Ovary locule* ovoid, to 1.1 cm long at anthesis. *Fruits* globose to ovoid to 1.5(-3) cm long, green, splitting down longitudinally to reveal fleshy white pulp, or nearly dry. *Seeds* ovoid, 1.5 mm long, strongly tuberculate (see Frank, loc. cit.).

DISTRIBUTION. NE Mexico (E flanks of the Sierra Madre Oriental and Rio Grande plain) and SW USA (Texas, W Oklahoma, E New Mexico & S Colorado); sea-level to c. 1500 m altitude.

Echinocereus reichenbachii (Terscheck ex Walp.) Hort. F.A. Haage ('reichen-bachianus'), Cacteen-Verzeichniss, 20 (1859); Britton & Rose, Cact. 3: 25–26, fig. 25 (1922); E. & B. Lamb, Ill. Ref. Cact. Succ. 4: t. 209 (1966); L. Benson, Cacti US & Can. 666, 667 (map), 668, 946, figs. 703-705, colour pl. 110 & 111 (1982).

Echinocactus reichenbachii Terscheck ex Walp., Repert. Bot. 2: 320 (1843). Type: cultivated plants ex Mexico (not preserved). Neotype (Benson, 1982): Mexico, Coahuila, vicinity of Saltillo, 10 April 1905, *E. Palmer* 511 (US 570013).

Echinopsis pectinata [var.] *reichenbachii* (Terscheck ex Walp.) Salm-Dyck ('reichen-bachiana'), Cact. Hort. Dyck. 1844, 26 (1845); C.F. Foerster ('reichenbachiana'), Handb. Cacteenk. 365 (1846).

Cereus caespitosus Engelm. in Boston J. Nat. Hist. 5: 247, in adnot. (1845). Type: U.S.A., Texas, Austin Co., W of San Felipe, gravelly soil near Cat-Spring, *Lindheimer*. Lectotype (Benson 1982): 'about 15 miles from Cat-Spring', *Lindheimer*, cultivated at St. Louis, June 1845 (MO).

Echinocereus caespitosus (Engelm.) Engelm. in Wislizenus, Mem. Tour North. Mex. 110, in adnot. (1848); Weniger, Cacti of the Southwest, 19-22, t. 3 (1970).

E. purpureus Lahman in Cact. Succ. J. (US) 6: 141, with fig. (1935). Type: Oklahoma, near Medicine Park (MO).

36a. var. **reichenbachii**

Areoles almost linear, 3 mm or more long. *Radial spines* 18-30 or more, to c. 6 mm long; central spines 0. *Perianth-segments* pink to magenta in upper half, darker or white below, pale brownish to crimson at base.

DISTRIBUTION. N, Cent. & S Texas (except in extreme S), adjacent Oklahoma (except in NW) and NE Mexico, E flanks of the Sierra Madre Oriental in E Coahuila, Nuevo Leon & W Tamaulipas; (?) San Luis Potosi (*fide* Benson, 1982); Great Plains grassland, Edwards Plateau (Texas) and E edge of Chihuahuan Desert, near sea-level to c. 1500 m altitude.

36b. var. **armatus** (Poselger) N.P. Taylor, comb. nov.

Cereus pectinatus (Scheidw.) Engelm. [var.] *armatus* Poselger in Allg. Gartenz. 21: 134 (1853). Type: Mexico, Nuevo Leon, mountains near Monterrey, 1849-1852, *Poselger* (presumed not to have been preserved).

Echinocereus armatus (Poselger) A. Berger, Kakteen, 179 (1929); G.R.W. Frank in Kakt. and. Sukk. 34: 179 Abb. 1 & 2, 198 Abb. 2 & 4, 219-221 Abb. A1-A3 (1983); P. Bourdoux in Cactus (Belgium) 9: 11, with superb colour pl. (1985).

Areoles linear-elliptic, at least 3 mm long. *Radial spines* up to 23, to 8 mm long; central spines (0-)1-2, to 20 mm long. *Perianth-segments* pinkish-magenta, paler in the throat, green at base.

DISTRIBUTION. NE Mexico: Nuevo Leon, Sierra Madre Oriental W of Monterrey (Cañon de Huasteca), at c. 550-1500 m altitude.

36c. var. **fitchii** (Britton & Rose) L. Benson in Cact. Succ. J. (US) 41: 127 (1969) et tom. cit. 666, 670 (1982).

E. fitchii Britton & Rose, tom. cit., 30, t. 3, fig. 2 (1922); Weniger, tom. cit. t. 5 (1970). Type: U.S.A., Texas, nr Laredo, 1913, *Rose* 18037 (US).

E. reichenbachii var. *albertii* L. Benson, loc. cit. (1969) et tom. cit., fig. 707, colour pl. 114 (1982). Type: U.S.A., Texas, Jim Wells Co., nr Alice, 25 May 1965, *R.O. Albert & L. Benson* 16550 (POM 317080).

'*E. melanocentrus*' Lowry in Desert Pl. Life 2: 20 (1936), nom. inval. (Art. 36); Backeb., Die Cact. 4: 2030 (1960), nom. inval. (Arts. 37 & 9.5); Weniger, tom. cit. 24, t. 5 (1970). Based on plants from the same region as var. *albertii*.

Areoles elliptic, 1.5-2 mm long. *Radial spines* up to 22, to 7.5 mm long; central spines (0-)1-7, to 9 mm long. *Perianth-segments* deep pink contrasted with deep crimson at base.

DISTRIBUTION. Southernmost Texas (Webb, Jim Wells, Kleberg, Zapata & Starr Cos.) and adjacent NE Mexico (N Nuevo Leon & N Tamaulipas); Rio Grande plain brush-lands, near sea-level to 300 m altitude.

36d. var. **perbellus** (Britton & Rose) L. Benson, loc. cit. (1969) et tom. cit. 666, 670, fig. 706, colour pl. 112 (1982).

E. perbellus Britton & Rose, tom. cit., 24-25, fig. 24 (1922). Type: Texas, Big Springs, 23 Feb. 1910, *Rose & Standley* 12215 (US).

Areoles elliptic, 1.5 mm long. *Radial spines* up to 16(-20), to 6 mm long; central spines 0-1, 1 mm long. *Perianth-segments* pinkish-magenta, crimson at base.

DISTRIBUTION. S Colorado, E New Mexico and N & cent. Texas; Great Plains grassland at 600-1200 m altitude.

36e. var. **baileyi** (Rose) N.P. Taylor, stat. nov.

Echinocereus baileyi Rose in Contrib. US. Nat. Herb. 12: 403, tt. 56 & 57 (1909); Stapf in Bot. Mag. 148: t. 8971 (1922); Weniger, tom. cit., t. 6 (1970). Type: Oklahoma, Wichita Mountains, Aug. 1906, *V. Bailey* (US 53167).

E. baileyi var. *albispinus* (Lahman) Backeb. in Kakteenkunde 1941: 4 (1941).

E. reichenbachii var. *albispinus* (Lahman) L. Benson, loc. cit. (1969) et tom. cit., 666, 670, 671, 947 (1982); W. Cullmann et al., Kakteen, ed. 5, 157 (1984) (superb colour illustration).

For additional synonymy see Benson (1982).

Areoles narrowly elliptic, 2 mm long. *Radial spines* up to 14, to 12(-25) mm long; central spines 1-3, to 3 mm long. *Perianth-segments* as for var. *reichenbachii*.

DISTRIBUTION. S Oklahoma and adjacent Texas (in Childress Co.); Great Plains grassland at c. 400-600 m altitude.

Section VI. Wilcoxia

Echinocereus sect. **Wilcoxia** (Britton & Rose) N.P. Taylor, stat. nov.
Wilcoxia Britton & Rose in Contrib. US. Nat. Herb. 12: 434 (1909). Type: *E. poselgeri* Lemaire.

The decision to include in *Echinocereus* the three species discussed and described below was an easy one. Despite having very slender scandent stems arising from tuberous roots, the evidence for their close relationship with the genus is overwhelming. In respect of flower, fruit, seed, pollen, spine and epidermal morphology there is general agreement between these three species and the remainder of *Echinocereus*. Other species referred to *Wilcoxia* by Britton & Rose (1909, 1920) or subsequent authors are all more closely allied with *Peniocereus* Britton & Rose (1909), having slender tubular flowers (with pale coloured, not green, stigmas), elongate pointed fruits, much larger seeds, different pollen (cf. Leuenberger, 1976), distinct spination and, most importantly, a conspicuously papillose-pubescent stem epidermis, which appears to be unique within the cereoid cacti. With the exception of *Wilcoxia papillosa* Britton & Rose (1920), whose status as a species (though not its generic affinity) is somewhat uncertain, all of these excluded species now have name combinations in *Peniocereus* where they clearly belong (some under different species names of which they are synonyms). Taking a wider view of the situation, it seems likely that *Echinocereus* and *Peniocereus* are sister taxa, which have probably diverged from a *Nyctocereus*-like ancestor. In this light *Echinocereus* sect. *Wilcoxia* and *Peniocereus* must be seen as convergent, their differences being too fundamental for the suggestion that the former represent a connecting link between the remainder of *Echinocereus* and the latter.

The slender, 8-10-ribbed stems of this section are not particularly specialized, but their tuberous-rooted habit is, and their relatively small, non-fleshy flowers with narrow perianth-segments seem more derived than those of most species in the first four sections of the genus. When habit and flowers are taken together they seem to be most readily compared with sections V & VII, and hybrids with the latter have been raised. Furthermore, Buxbaum (1975) has noted interesting similarities between the wilcoxias and *E. pulchellus*.

The geographical distribution of the section is markedly disjunct, suggesting that it has been more successful in earlier times, but the ranges of its species have since contracted. The occurrence of *E. leucanthus* in S Sonora and N Sinaloa is within the W Mexican area from which other groups in the genus seem to have radiated.

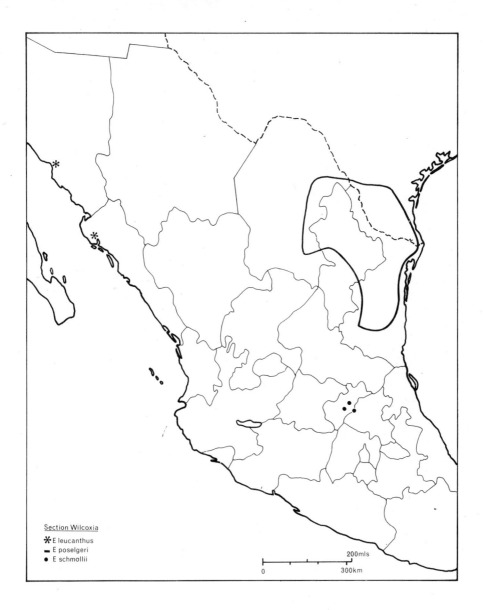

Section Wilcoxia
✳ E leucanthus
▬ E poselgeri
● E schmollii

200mls

0   300km

37. ECHINOCEREUS LEUCANTHUS

The above name is required when *Wilcoxia albiflora* Backeb. (1952) is transferred
to *Echinocereus*, owing to the prior existence of *E. albiflorus* Weingart, a validly
published name now treated as a synonym of *E. fendleri*. This is unfortunate but
unavoidable; however, the epithet chosen is etymologically identical to that of
Backeberg, but from Greek rather than Latin. If the blame for this change of
epithet lies anywhere, it should be with Britton & Rose, whose generic splitting of

hairs led to the creation of *Wilcoxia* in 1909, previous authors having placed *E. poselgeri* (the only slender-stemmed species then known) in *Echinocereus* or within that taxon when treated as a subgenus or section of *Cereus*.

White-flowered echinocerei are not as few as might at first be thought, although *E. leucanthus* is the only species where this is the norm. *Echinocereus fendleri, E. grandis, E. pulchellus* and *E. knippelianus* all have forms or varieties with white flowers and they occur more rarely in *E. pectinatus, E. pentalophus, E. enneacanthus* and perhaps other species also. The stems of *E. leucanthus* are the most slender in the genus being about half the thickness of its close, though geographically remote, ally *E. poselgeri*, of NE Mexico and adjacent Texas.

Echinocereus leucanthus is known from only two or three localities, in SW Sonora south of Guaymas, and further south in NW Sinaloa, near Los Mochis. It was discovered and introduced to cultivation by Friedrich Schwarz, who kept his field localities secret. However, thirteen years after its first description was published by Backeberg, Myron Kimnach (1965) reported its rediscovery in the field and provided an amplified description. Since then it has become quite common in cultivation as a grafted plant and has been repeatedly figured in the popular literature. When grown in this way it seems to flower profusely and tends to produce flowers terminating the vegetative axes, which is not normally the case in habitat. Grafting has also ensured its rapid vegetative propagation and has removed potential pressure on the limited wild populations, although its apparent infrequency in the field may be due to the difficulty of finding its slender stems among other vegetation. It can also be grown on its own roots and cuttings root without difficulty.

Coming from subtropical lowlands, *E. leucanthus* is probably less hardy than most echinocerei and should, at least, be protected from frost.

DESCRIPTION. *Stems* branched mostly near base, light to dark or purplish-green, very slender, cylindric, 3-6 mm thick, supported by surrounding vegetation to a height of 30 cm, branches tapering at base and stems becoming woody above the tuberous, *Dahlia*-like rootstock (see H. Bravo-H., loc. cit. fig. 240). *Ribs* 8, very low, 2 mm wide and 0.5 mm high. *Areoles* minute, orbicular, 3-5 mm apart. *Radial spines* 9-18, c. 1 mm long, white; centrals 2-3 or more, less than 1 mm long, blackish. *Flowers* funnelform, 2-4 cm long, to 4 cm in diameter, terminating the stem or borne laterally near its apex. *Receptacle-tube* 1.3-2.4 cm long, ovary occupying basal half, c. 5 mm in diameter, tube exterior green, bearing numerous areoles with 12-18, to 3-5 mm long, whitish, dark-tipped acicular spines and short white wool. *Nectar chamber* 4 mm long. *Perianth-segments* in c. 2 rows, outermost linear, dark-coloured, recurved, remainder long-acuminate, entire, white, sometimes with faint pink midstripes, to brownish in the throat. *Stamen filaments* 7 mm long, cream below, purplish above; anthers oblong, to 0.5 mm long. *Style* 2 cm long, 1 mm in diameter, white or greenish-yellow; stigmas 6-8, 1-2 mm long, green. *Ovary locule* to 7 mm long, 2 mm in diameter at anthesis. *Fruit* ovoid, 1.5 cm long, 8 mm in diameter, olive-green, flesh sweet-smelling; *seeds* c. 1 mm, red to blackish-brown.

DISTRIBUTION. NW Mexico: SW Sonora (S of Guaymas) and NW Sinaloa (nr Los Mochis) at low altitude.

Echinocereus leucanthus N.P. Taylor, **nom. nov.**

Wilcoxia albiflora Backeb. in Cactus (Paris) 7(33) Suppl. 2: 16, with fig. (1952); Krainz, Die

Kakteen, Lfg. 13, with fig. (1960); Kimn. in Cact. Suc. Mex. 10: 98-100, 107, figs. 66 & 67 (1965); H. Bravo-H., Las Cactaceas de Mexico, ed. 2, 407-411, figs. 240 & 241 (1978); E. Haustein, Der Kosmos-Kakteenfuhrer, 226, with colour pl. (1983); W. Cullmann et al., Kakteen, ed. 5, 313 (1984) (excellent colour pl.), non *Echinocereus albiflorus* Weingart in Kakteenk. 1933: 156-157 (1933) (= *E. fendleri*). Type (cf. Backeb., loc. cit. 9): cultivated material from the Marnier-Lapostolle collection at Les Cedres (P).

38. ECHINOCEREUS POSELGERI

The botanical name of the 'sacasil', its Mexican vernacular, commemorates the German cactus collector, Dr. H. Poselger, who made a valuable journey through the southwestern United States and adjacent Mexico in search of cacti between 1849 and 1852. Among the species he described upon his return was *Cereus tuberosus* Poselger (1853), an apt name for the plant figured here. Unfortunately the same name had already been used by Pfeiffer (1837) for a different plant, and so in 1868 Lemaire appropriately renamed Poselger's species in his honour. Regrettably not all subsequent authors have adopted Lemaire's epithet *poselgeri*, which is the earliest legitimate available, but have used the illegitimate *tuberosus* instead (as *Echinocereus tuberosus* Ruempler 1885 or *Wilcoxia tuberosa* Kreuzinger 1935, both with the same type as the earlier published *E. poselgeri* – see the International Code of Botanical Nomenclature, Art. 63).

In habitat *E. poselgeri* favours bushy places, where it prefers to clamber through woody vegetation for support of its slender, drab stems. These are rather difficult to see and its frequency, especially in the low altitude brushlands of NE Mexico, may well be greater than the few scattered records suggest. At the western limit of its known range in SE Coahuila, it is found in the Chihuahuan Desert, at greater altitudes and has there been christened *Wilcoxia kroenleinii* A. Cartier (1980). However, this form differs from the norm in no important respects and clearly does not deserve specific rank. An even less justified additional name for the species, presently encountered in cultivation, is '*Wilcoxia australis*' (*nom. nud.*), the provenance of which has not been published. There is also Werdermann's *W. tamaulipensis*, described in 1938, to be considered as yet another synonym. Here the original description and illustration differ in some details from *E. poselgeri* (in particular the more numerous spines, including 5-10 centrals per areole), but until plants matching these requirements are relocated in the field its status will remain uncertain. (The stems illustrated as Werdermann's species by Backeberg (1960) are of typical *E. poselgeri* only.)

The exceptionally beautiful flowers of *E. poselgeri* contrast sharply with its inconspicuous stems and immediately proclaim its horticultural value. However, they are freely produced only by plants that have grown vigorously the previous season. To this end growers are advised to give this species plenty of root-room and to replace the plants with cuttings every four or five years. Alternatively, an older specimen can be 'pruned' to induce the development of new stems, which should then flower the following spring. Healthy plants make rapid growth and need supporting with a strong cane, since their aerial branches can make them rather top-heavy. If strong growth is successfully encouraged, many flowers can be expected, after which it is a good time to take cuttings, especially if fellow cactophiles have seen the plant in flower! Unfortunately, all too often, poor, non-flowering, pot-bound specimens growing in spent compost are seen, which have tended to deny this species the fine reputation it deserves. However, the young plant figured here, from the collection of Mr David Parker, clearly shows the rewards of good cultivation.

DESCRIPTION. *Stems* slender, cylindric, to c. 1(-2) cm thick, often clambering through vegetation in thickets to a height of 60-120 cm, dark blue-green, branched above, apex pointed when in growth, thinner and becoming woody near base, arising from a tuberous, *Dahlia*-like rootstock; *root tubers* to 5-7.5 (-10) cm long, 2.5-5 cm in diameter. *Ribs* 8-10, low and inconspicuous, scarcely tuberculate. *Areoles* 2-4.5 mm apart, circular, quite woolly at first. *Spines* adpressed, except at stem apex, roughened, subulate; radials 8-16, 2-4.5 mm long, the lowermost and laterals longest, whitish or grey, darker tipped; central spines 1, to 9 mm long, pointing towards stem apex, somewhat flattened, dark brown to black, lighter near base. *Flowers* funnel-shaped, to 6 cm long and 7 cm in diameter, sweet-scented, sometimes terminating the stem but usually lateral near its apex, on growth of the previous year. *Receptacle-tube* to 2.7 cm long, above ovary only 7 mm, at apex 14 mm wide, ovary occupying basal 9 mm, exterior dark green, bearing areoles with abundant loose wool and 1-10, to 2 cm long, hair-like, dark brown spines. *Nectar chamber* 2 mm long and 2.5 mm wide, half-filled by base of style. *Perianth-segments* in 2 rows, cuneate-oblanceolate, to 3.5 cm long, very variable in width (4-12 mm), margins somewhat irregular near the long attenuate to acuminate apex, outer segments dark brownish, inner pinkish-magenta, with darker midstripes, especially near base, margins sometimes rather pale. *Stamen filaments* to c. 12 mm long, white; anthers oblong, 2 mm long, yellow. *Style* to 2.5 cm long and 1.3 mm thick,

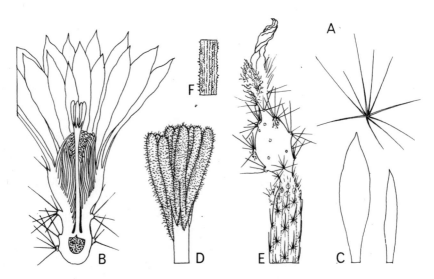

Echinocereus poselgeri. A, areole from receptacle-tube, × 2; B, half-flower, × 1; C, outer (right) and inner (left) perianth-segments, × 1; D, top of style with stigmas, × 3; E, fruit developed from a terminal flower, × 1; F, portion of spine from A, × 32 (ex Hort. D. Parker).

white; stigmas 7-12, to 9 mm long, bright to deep green. *Ovary locule* oblong, 7 mm long and 4 mm wide at anthesis, ovules very numerous. *Fruit* ovoid, fleshy and juicy, to 2 cm long and 1 cm in diameter, dark green to brownish, wool and spines often persistent, apparently indehiscent. *Seeds* ovoid, 1-1.5 mm long, tuberculate, black.

DISTRIBUTION. S Texas, E Coahuila, N Nuevo Leon and N & SW Tamaulipas; on sandy soils, in brushlands at low elevations and Chihuahuan Desert to c. 1150 m altitude.

Echinocereus poselgeri Lemaire, Cactees, 57 (1868) (*nom. nov.*). (PLATE 10).
Cereus tuberosus Poselger in Allg. Gartenz. 21: 135 (1853), *nom. illegit.* (Art. 64), *non* Pfeiffer (1837). Type: U.S.A., Texas, nr. the Rio Grande, *Poselger* (living plants only?). Lectotype (Benson, 1982): 'Rio Grande above Belleville, Dr Poselger coll 1850' (MO).
Cereus poselgeri (Lemaire) J. Coulter in Contrib. US. Nat. Herb. 3: 398 (1896); L. Benson, Cacti US. & Can. 595-597, 936, figs. 632 & 633, colour pl. 78 (1982).
Wilcoxia poselgeri (Lemaire) Britton & Rose in Contrib. US. Nat. Herb. 12: 434 (1909) and Cact. 2: 111, figs. 164 & 165 (1920); E. & B. Lamb, Colourful Cacti, t. 13 (1974).
W. tuberosa Kreuzinger, Verzeichniss, 18 (1935); H. Bravo-H., Las Cactaceas de Mexico, ed. 2, 1: 405-406, fig. 236 (1978); E. Haustein, Der Kosmos-Kakteenführer, 226, with excellent colour fig. (1983), *nom. illegit.* (Art. 63.1).
W. kroenleinii A. Cartier in Succulentes 2(2): 2-3 (1980) and in Cact. Suc. Mex. 27: 67-69, figs. 28-31 (1982).

39. ECHINOCEREUS SCHMOLLII

This species is more specialized than the other members of section *Wilcoxia*, having more compact stems clothed in fine hair-like spines and with a large napiform root buried underground (see H. Bravo-H., fig. 238). The turnip-like, rather than dahlia-like, rootstock in *E. schmollii* represents one of the parallels with the genus *Peniocereus*, in which both root types also occur. It seems that long, thin, well-branched, wiry stems, as in *P. striata* and *E. leucanthus*, and thicker, fewer stems, as in *P. greggii* and *E. schmollii*, correlate with dahlia-like and napiform roots, respectively. There is also a correlation with habitat and altitude—no doubt the major reason for this parallel development having occurred.

Echinocereus (Wilcoxia) schmollii is a choice free-flowering species, whose requirements in cultivation are similar to those of *E. poselgeri* (q.v.). It is of restricted occurrence in the field, in Querétaro, where it occupies a southern phase of the Chihuahuan Desert at considerably greater altitudes than its immediate allies. Only three, or perhaps four, localities for it are currently known, and in view of its vulnerability to commercial exploitation it has been placed on Appendix 1 of the Convention on International Trade in Endangered Species of Fauna and Flora (CITES). This will hopefully reduce the risks of its extermination in the field by ruthless collectors, since under Appendix 1 trade in habitat-collected specimens is prohibited. However, for *Echinocereus* enthusiasts this should not prove a hindrance to obtaining a specimen, for it is not rare in cultivation, being of easy propagation by cuttings or grafting. The flowers are a very beautiful shade of deep pink and make up for the sometimes rather tatty appearance of the stems.

DESCRIPTION. *Stem* solitary, or sparingly branched (more so in cultivation), cylindric, to 15(-25) cm long and 1.1 cm in diameter (to 2 cm in cultivation) purplish to blackish-green, tapered above the napiform, 7 cm long and 3 cm in diameter, swollen, blackish-grey rootstock. *Ribs* 9-10, tuberculate, rounded. *Areoles* 0.5 mm in diameter, 1.5-2 mm apart. *Spines* finely hair-like, c. 35, to 7 mm long, at first pinkish but soon white, grey or blackish, giving the stem a soft woolly appearance. *Flowers* funnelform, 3.5(-4) cm long, to 5 cm in diameter, mostly arising near stem apex, occasionally terminal. *Receptacle-tube* 2 cm long, exterior brownish to purplish-green, bearing areoles with fine hair-like spines as on the stem. *Nectar chamber* only 1.5 mm long, 2mm wide. *Perianth-segments* in 2-3 rows, narrowly elliptic-oblanceolate, c. 2 cm long and 3-6 mm wide, long acuminate, bright pink. *Style* to 2 cm long; stigmas 7-11, bright green. *Fruit* ovoid to spherical, c. 1.8 cm in diameter, juicy, purplish-green. *Seeds* nearly globular, c. 1 mm, tuberculate.

DISTRIBUTION. Central E Mexico: SE Querétaro (nr El Infiernillo*, NE of Cadereyta & N of Vizarrón); Chihuahuan Desert type vegetation, at or above (1200-)1800 m altitude.

Echinocereus schmollii (Weingart) N.P. Taylor, comb. nov.
Cereus schmollii Weingart in Monatsschr. Deutsch. Kakt.-Gesells. 3: 251-252, with fig. (1931). Type: field-collected material from *F. Schmoll* of Querétaro (not preserved). Lectotype (designated here): Weingart, loc. cit. 252 (illustration).
Wilcoxia schmollii (Weingart) Backeb. in Blaetter Kakteenforsch. 1935, 11, with fig. (1935); E. & B. Lamb, Pocket Encycl. Cacti, t. 191 (1969) (excellent colour pl.); F. Buxb. in Krainz, Die Kakteen, Lfg. 55-56, Abb. 1, 5 & 6 (1973); Krainz, loc. cit., with colour fig. (1973); H. Bravo-H., Las Cactaceas de Mexico, ed. 2, 407, figs. 238 & 239 (1978).

* El Infiernillo, nr the Rio Moctezuma, is marked on some maps on the east bank of the river in Hidalgo (cf. H. Bravo-H., tom. cit. fig. 238. 1978).

Section VII. Pulchellus

Echinocereus sect. **Pulchellus** N.P. Taylor, **sect. nov.** *sectioni Reichenbachii similis sed floribus graciliter infundibuliformibus vel minusculis, areolis in receptaculi tubo paucis vel late dissitis, perianthii segmentis saepe anguste lineari-oblanceolatis; fructus carne exigua fere exsucca, seminibus paucis magnis; caulibus saepe depressis vel quasi in solum retractis. Typus: Echinocereus pulchellus* (C. Martius) Schumann.

The five species included in this newly recognized section are characterized by narrow perianth-segments, few or widely spaced, very woolly receptacular areoles and scarcely fleshy to dry fruits with relatively few, large seeds. They inhabit montane or high plateau environments in Mexico and most nearly resemble species of section *Reichenbachii*, but are even more specialized, with generally smaller flowers and less fleshy fruits, representing a trend towards greater economy. The flower-buds mostly burst through the stem epidermis above the areole with which they are associated–another specialized feature. Two spring-flowering species groups can be defined:

The E. ADUSTUS GROUP (species 40-42) is characterized by a well-developed, slender receptacle-tube enclosing an elongate nectar chamber. The stems are

Section Pulchellus

E.ADUSTUS GROUP
■ E.pamanesiorum
▲ E.adustus
▼ E.laui

E.PULCHELLUS GROUP
✳ E.pulchellus
● E.knippelianus

200 ml

0   300 km

rather spiny and eventually become ovoid or cylindric. They emanate from the Sierra Madre Occidental at altitudes of 1000 m or more.

The E. PULCHELLUS GROUP (species 43 & 44) is more specialized with a semi-geophytic habit, the weakly spined stem being more or less buried in the ground with only the depressed, green apex exposed. The flowers are very short-tubed and the nectar chamber and ovary are minute. They range from S Mexico (N Oaxaca), across the central plateau, west and north to the Sierra Madre Occidental of Zacatecas and the S.M. Oriental of SE Coahuila, mostly above 2000 m altitude, where the climate is more temperate in aspect.

This is the most recently described species belonging in section *Pulchellus* and promises to be one of the highest horticultural merit. Its flowers are the largest in the section, and exceptionally beautiful, and limited experience of its culture suggests that it is also easy to grow and propagate.

Its history is very brief. Alfred Lau first noticed it in 1974, while travelling the Fresnillo (Zacatecas) to Tepic (Nayarit) highway, then under construction, which crosses the Sierra Madre Occidental. He initially found a plant near the bridge over the Rio Huaynamota, between Huejuquilla and San Juan Capistrano and, although later visits were rewarded by more specimens, the range of the species remains limited to a small part of this valley in westernmost Zacatecas. In his brief discussion of the plant, which follows its validating description, Lau (1981) correctly identifies its immediate allies as *E. adustus (E. schwarzii)* and *E. laui*, noting their fruit and flower structure and colour. More recently Frank (1983) has suggested that there is a closer relationship with the geographically remote *E. armatus*, from the Sierra Madre Oriental. However, their similarities, if any, are only superficial, little attention having been paid to their floral anatomy. Furthermore, the seeds of *E. armatus* (as illustrated by Frank), with their rather pointed testa tubercles, clearly show its affinity with *E. reichenbachii*, of which it is only a variety.

In its habit and less reduced flowers *E. pamanesiorum* represents the least specialized species in section *Pulchellus*, and its geographical location, near to members of both E. ADUSTUS and E. PULCHELLUS GROUPS, is surely significant. It could be interpreted as the taxon closest to the ancestor of the section and this would also be supported by its occurrence in the same general area, west of the

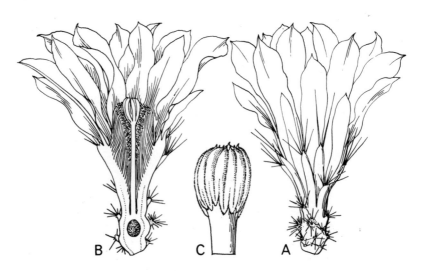

Echinocereus pamanesiorum. A, flower, × 1; B, half-flower, × 1; C, top of style with stigmas, × 3 (ex Hort. D. Parker).

Sierra Madre Occidental, where the least specialized species belonging to other sections of the genus are found.

DESCRIPTION. *Stem* solitary or sparingly branched, cylindric, to 35 cm high and 8 cm in diameter, dark green. *Ribs* 12-19, to 1.5 cm apart, 5 mm high. *Areoles* oval, to 4 mm long, 1.0-2 cm apart, woolly only in the first season. *Radial spines* 9-12, to 1 cm long, adpressed, yellowish to white with dark tips; centrals 0-2, to 1.7 cm long, porrect to deflexed, brownish, darker-tipped. *Flowers* funnelform, to 9 cm long and in diameter. *Receptacle-tube* slender, 3 cm long, ovary occupying basal 1 cm, 1.2 cm in diameter, tube contracted above to 1 cm then flared to 2 cm in diameter at apex, exterior with widely spaced areoles bearing 8-10, to 11 mm long, slender, brown, white-based spines. *Nectar chamber* 6 mm long, 2 mm in diameter. *Perianth-segments* in c. 2 rows, oblanceolate, to 3.5 cm long and 1 cm wide, serrate near the acuminate apex, deep pink with darker midstripes, white in the throat. *Stamen filaments* to c. 9 mm long, light yellowish-green. *Style* to 2.4 cm long, 2mm in diameter, white; stigmas 9-13, to 6 mm long, dark green. *Ovary locule* broadly ovoid, c. 4.5 mm long at anthesis. *Fruit* ovoid, 2.2 cm long, 1.3 cm in diameter, brownish-green, woolly and spiny. *Seeds* (see Frank, loc. cit.) broadly ovoid, 1.5 mm long, strongly tuberculate, black.

DISTRIBUTION. W Zacatecas: Rio Huaynamota valley at 1000 m altitude.

Echinocereus pamanesiorum A. Lau in Cact. Suc. Mex. 26: 38-41, figs. 11, 19-21 (1981); G.R.W. Frank in Kakt. and. Sukk. 34: 179 Abb. 3, 182 Abb. 1, 198 Abb. 1 & 3, 219-221 Abb. B1-3 (1983). Type: Mexico, W Zacatecas, Rio Huaynamota, nr bridge between Huejuquilla and San Juan Capistrano, 1000 m, *Lau* 1247 (MEXU).

41. ECHINOCEREUS ADUSTUS

This species was discovered by Dr A. Wislizenus at Cusihuiriachic (or Santa Rosa de Cosihuiriachi), Chihuahua, in the autumn of 1846. Wislizenus had not made plans to visit this remote mining settlement, but arrived there as a prisoner of the Mexican authorities after war had broken out with the United States. His six-month exile, though very inconvenient, was not entirely wasted, for he was permitted to roam the environs of Cusihuiriachic, which lies on the eastern flank of the Sierra Madre Occidental, and collect botanical and other specimens. As Engelmann, who described his plant collections, subsequently noted 'he could not have selected a more favourable field for botanical researches . . . in fact almost everything collected there appears to be new' (Engelmann in Wislizenus, 1848).

Engelmann received living specimens from Wislizenus and, in 1848, named four species of *Echinocereus* from Cusihuiriachic. Two of these, *E. radians* and *E. rufispinus*, have proved to be forms of the variable *E. adustus*, whose spination is remarkably diverse. The type of *E. adustus* had only short radiating spines, white with brown tips (hence Engelmann's epithet '*adustus*', meaning scorched). In *E. radians*, however, these radials were supplemented by much longer and stouter, porrect, blackish central spines, which were also present in *E. rufispinus*, whose radial spines were longer too. The distinctive flowers of the species were first described in 1856, when Engelmann reported them for the form he called *E.*

rufispinus. He drew attention to the long receptacle-tube and the whitish stigmas, the latter being rather unusual in *Echinocereus*. The tube accommodates a well-developed nectar chamber, which is like that found in the sympatric *E. polyacanthus*, presumed to be hummingbird-pollinated, though it seems less likely that these vectors visit *E. adustus* in view of its flower colour.

The true *Echinocereus adustus* was rarely seen in cultivation until a few years ago, when C. Glass & R. Foster visited the type locality and reintroduced it via the International Succulent Institute. Earlier, the name of one of its synonyms, *E. radians*, became linked with another plant, introduced without provenance data by F. Schwarz, and figured in colour by Backeberg (1960). This misidentification survived until Alfred Lau rediscovered Schwarz's taxon at two sites in Durango and named it *E. schwarzii* A. Lau (1982). Here *E. schwarzii* is reduced to a variety of *E. adustus*, from which it differs primarily in stem size, spination and in the somewhat larger, though otherwise very similar flowers. However, were *E. schwarzii* deemed worthy of species rank, it is doubtful whether Lau's epithet would have priority. As long ago as 1910, the Mexican botanist Patoni described *E. madrensis* in an obscure and very rare journal. Patoni reported his *Echinocereus* from 3000 metres elevation in the Sierra Madre of Durango. At first his description does not seem to compare very well with that of *E. schwarzii* A. Lau, but careful examination of the plant in question suggests that Lau's data is not fully representative of the taxon he collected. The only discrepancies that remain to be checked in the field are the number of ribs (16-17 vs 11-14 in Lau's plant) and the altitudinal range (3000 vs 1800-2100 m).

Echinocereus adustus with its variety *schwarzii* represents an obvious link between the large-flowered *E. pamanesiorum* from W Zacatecas and the small-flowered *E. laui* from E Sonora. All three have slender-tubed flowers with well-developed nectar chambers, the receptacle-tube exterior bearing rather few areoles but much wool. In these floral characters members of the E. ADUSTUS GROUP are clearly not closely related to *E. palmeri* and *E. armatus* (= *E. reichenbachii*), contrary to the opinion of Frank (1983).

DESCRIPTION. *Stem* mostly solitary, depressed-globose to short cylindric, to 19 cm high and 5-8(-12) cm in diameter, light to dark green, rootstock fibrous. *Ribs* 11-16 (or more?), slightly tuberculate, sinuses 2-10 mm deep; *areoles* with abundant whitish wool the first year, later naked, 5-7 mm apart, oval-elliptic, c. 2 mm long. *Radial spines* 15-23(-31), uppermost very short, laterals longest, to 18 mm, straight or somewhat curved, subulate to acicular, white, brown-tipped or brown; centrals 0-5, uppermost when present often very short, lowermost porrect to deflexed, to 3.2 cm long, dark brown to blackish. *Flowers* slender funnel-form, (3-)4.7-8 cm long, 4-7 cm in diameter. *Receptacle-tube* 2.5-4(-5) cm long, narrowed to 7-10 mm in region of nectar chamber, to 13 mm wide at apex, ovary occupying basal 8 mm, exterior ribbed, green to brown, bearing very woolly areoles, widely spaced on narrowest part of tube, denser in ovary region and near apex, spines 2-11, to 9 mm long, slender, white to brown. *Nectar chamber* to 12 mm long, 2 mm wide, not completely filled by style. *Perianth-segments* in about 2 rows, linear-oblanceolate, to 3.5 cm long and 5-7(-10) mm in diameter, pink, with a darker midstripe, apex gradually tapering to a sharp point, margins entire to finely serrate, paler, outermost segments brownish. *Stamens* with filaments to 1.5-2.0 cm long, white; anthers oblong, 1 mm long, pale yellow.

144

Plate 11

Echinocereus adustus var. *schwarzii*

Plate 12

Echinocereus pulchellus var. *weinbergii* (top)   *E. p.* var. *pulchellus* (bottom)

Style to 3.2 cm long, white; *stigmas* 6-9, 3-4 mm long, white or very pale green. *Ovary locule* ± globose, 4-6 mm long at anthesis. *Fruit* ovoid, to 2 cm long, with deciduous spines and wool, rather dry at maturity, splitting down in one or more places to reveal the seeds. *Seeds* large, oblong, 1.5-2 mm long, ± tuberculate, black (see Frank, loc. cit.).

DISTRIBUTION. Chihuahua and Durango, E slopes of the Sierra Madre Occidental, open pine/oak forest, at or above 1800 m altitude.

Echinocereus adustus Engelm. in Wislizenus, Mem. Tour North. Mex. 104, in adnot. (1848); Britton & Rose, Cact. 3: 23, fig. 22 (1922); Glass & Foster in Cact. Succ. J. (US) 46: 8-11, figs. 1 & 6-8 (1974); G.R.W. Frank in Kakt. and. Sukk. 34: 179 Abb. 6 & 7, 182 Abb. 6-8, 219-221 Abb. F1-3 & G1-3 (1983). Type: Mexico, Chihuahua, Cusihuiriachic [Cosihuiriachi], c. 1900m, 1846, *Wislizenus* (living plants only?).

41a. var. **schwarzii** (A. Lau) N.P.Taylor in Kew Mag. 2: 268 (1985). (PLATE 11).
Echinocereus schwarzii A. Lau in Cact. Succ. J. (US) 54: 27-28, figs. 1 & 2 (1982); G.R.W. Frank, loc. cit. 179 Abb. 4, 219-221 Abb. E1-3 (1983). Type: Mexico, Durango, ca Guanacevi, 1800-2100 m, *Lau* 1305 (POM).
? *E. madrensis* Patoni in Bol. Alianza Cient. Univ. Durango 1: 42 (1910).
[*E. radians* sensu Backeb., Die Cact. 4: Abb. 1931 & 1932 (1960) non Engelm. 1848 (= var. *adustus*).]
Stem 6-12 cm in diameter. *Radial spines* to 15(-17) mm long; centrals 1-5. *Flowers* to 7 cm in diameter.
DISTRIBUTION. Durango, vicinity of Guanacevi & Canatlan.

41b. var. **adustus**
Stem to 6(-7) cm in diameter. *Radial spines* to 8(-18) mm long; centrals 0-1. *Flowers* to 5 cm in diameter.
DISTRIBUTION. Chihuahua, vicinity of Cusihuiriachic.

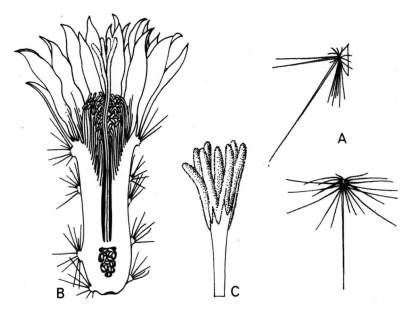

Echinocereus adustus var. **schwarzii**. A, stem areole, two views, × 1; B, half-flower, × 1½; C, top of style with stigmas, × 4 (ex Hort. D. Minnion).

42. ECHINOCEREUS LAUI

It is very appropriate that this attractive, recently described species is named in honour of its discoverer, Dr Alfred B. Lau. For the past 15 years he has done more than anyone else towards a better knowledge of *Echinocereus* in the field, his collections and various new finds having helped stimulate horticultural interest in the genus, without which this account would probably not have been written.

Echinocereus laui is the most specialized member of the E. ADUSTUS GROUP, with clusters of dwarf, low-ribbed stems clothed in very dense spination, and small, bright pink flowers helping economize on the plant's precious resources. It has already proved itself easy of cultivation, its propagation by seeds or cuttings being straightforward. Plenty of sunlight is essential for regular flower production, but in the dry conditions of a sunny, well ventilated greenhouse a watch must be kept for red spider mite and mealy bugs, both of which like the delicate epidermis concealed beneath its spiny exterior.

DESCRIPTION. *Stems* branching at base and forming clumps of up to 20 heads, cylindric, to 10 cm long and 4 cm in diameter, epidermis obscured by dense spines. *Ribs* 14-16, straight or somewhat spiralled, low, narrow, 6 mm apart, finely tuberculate. *Areoles* oval, to 3 mm long, 4-5 mm apart. *Radial spines* 18-21, 5-10 mm long, bristle-like, white; centrals 4, to 30 mm long, reddish-brown, porrect to deflexed. *Flowers* narrowly funnelform, 3-5 cm long and in diameter, arising away from stem apex. *Receptacle-tube* 2-2.5 cm long, ovary occupying basal 5 mm, 6 mm in diameter, exterior brownish, with few areoles bearing 12-16, c. 5 mm long, white, bristle-like spines and much wool. *Nectar chamber* 8 mm long. *Perianth-segments* in c. 3 rows, narrowly linear-oblanceolate, c. 1.5 cm long and c. 6 mm wide, acuminate, outer segments brownish, inner pink with a pronounced darker midstripe. *Stamen filaments* white. *Style* 2 cm long, white; stigmas 8-9, greenish-white to bright green. *Fruit* spherical, 8-12 mm in diameter, brownish-green, with wool and thin brownish spines. *Seed* (see Frank, loc. cit.) ovoid, 1.5 mm long, strongly tuberculate, black.

DISTRIBUTION. E Sonora (nr Yecora): W side of Sierra Madre Occidental in oak woodland, c. 1800 m altitude.

Echinocereus laui G.R.W. Frank ('lauii') in Kakt. and. Sukk. 29: 74-77, with many figs. (1978) et ibid. 34: 179 Abb. 5, 182 Abb. 9 & 10, 219-221 Abb. C1-3 (1983); M. Haude & R. Kuendiger, Erfolg mit Kakteen, 80 (1983) (superb colour pl.). Type: Mexico, E Sonora, E of Yecora, nr El Trigo Ranch, oak woodland, 1800 m, Jan. 1974, *A. Lau* 780 (ZSS AA18-24).

43. ECHINOCEREUS PULCHELLUS

This species and the similar *E. knippelianus* are at the peak of specialization within *Echinocereus*. They behave almost like geophytes, retreating underground during the dry winter period for protection from the desiccating effects of sun and wind. The stem is reduced to a minimum, its shrunken base passing into a large tuberous taproot – the subterranean water store. The flowers, though eye-catching, are relatively small, in keeping with the plants' general economy, and the fruits, which contain rather few large seeds, are almost dry at maturity. Although there is no obvious long range dispersal strategy for its seeds, *E. pulchellus* is clearly a very successful species, with a remarkably wide distribution in the cooler highlands of Mexico. Unfortunately its preferred habitat, on grassy plains above 2000 metres altitude, is also favoured by man for agricultural purposes, and today *E. pulchellus* is a declining if not endangered species.

As treated here *E. pulchellus* comprises three varieties, of which var. *pulchellus* is the most unusual, having the smallest stem and least spines, both in number and size. It was discovered in Mexico about 1827-28 by Baron von Karwinsky (McVaugh, 1980), and Pfeiffer (1837) gives his locality as Pachuca (Hidalgo), near where it grows today. Martius published a description in 1832 and provided an excellent illustration, leaving no doubt as to the plant's identity. The specimen illustrated here (*Hunt* 8625) is from a second Hidalgo locality, near the Barranca of Tolantongo. Elsewhere it is known from near Vista Hermosa, Queretaro, and south through Puebla (two widely separated localities) to N Oaxaca, where its recent discovery at Tepelmeme de Morelos represents the most southerly occurrence of the genus. Its range and frequency may well be even greater than these records suggest, since it is very difficult to find when not in flower. The true plant is uncommon in cultivation and, unfortunately, it seems prone to losing its roots.

Connecting var. *pulchellus* to the largest variety, var. *weinbergii*, is var. *amoenus*. This is the commonest variety in cultivation (where it is frequently misidentified as var. *pulchellus*), but the least understood in the field. The type was collected by Carl Ehrenberg, probably about 1839-40, at a locality called San Mateo (Ehrenberg, 1846). The place in question is of uncertain position, although it is most likely in the state of Hidalgo or on one of the routes into the state, where Ehrenberg spent much of his time. Until its type locality is rediscovered and the plant restudied, the exact identity of var. *amoenus* will remain somewhat unclear, since there is only the brief original description of Dietrich (1844) to rely on. The plant so identified by Britton & Rose (1922) is the common form in cultivation, which is known from south-west of the city of San Luis Potosi, in the state of the same name (Glass & Foster, 1979). Plants identified by Lau (1983) as *E. pulchellus* from Aguascalientes may also be this form. A rather different dwarf form, with more tuberculate stems and white flowers, is known from near Ascension in SE Nuevo Leon. It has been propagated and distributed by the Californian nursery firm of Abbey Garden, presumably from the field collection of C. Glass & R. Foster (no. 3602). It probably merits a varietal name of its own.

The third variety, var. *weinbergii*, is from the high plain of the Sierra Madre Occidental in W Zacatecas. It reached cultivation in 1905, but its wild origin was not publicized until 1970 (Glass & Foster, loc. cit.). It is very closely related to var. *amoenus*, differing mainly in the greater size of all its parts. It seems to have undergone less reduction than the other taxa referable to the E. PULCHELLUS GROUP, and its geographical proximity to members of the less specialized, but allied, E. ADUSTUS GROUP seems significant. The latter occupy habitats in the Sierra Madre to the west and north of var. *weinbergii*, but lack tuberous roots and do not display the semi-geophytic habit characteristic of *E. pulchellus* and *E.*

knippelianus. The plant of var. *weinbergii* illustrated is a habitat-collected specimen from the collection of Mr G.E. Cheetham.

Echinocereus pulchellus is a choice, free-flowering species requiring a very well-drained compost and adequate room for its tuberous rootstock. The upper part of the rootstock and the stem base should be surrounded by coarse gravel to discourage rot, which can be a problem if damp compost comes into contact with the fleshy tissue for long periods. They stand a cold, dry winter rest without harm, but a careful watch for red spider mites must be kept. Propagation is usually by seed, the seedlings developing much longer and denser spination, quite unlike the adult plant.

DESCRIPTION. *Stem* normally solitary, but branching in cultivation, typically globose to hemispheric, 2.5-13 cm in diameter, the shrunken base merging into a thickened, carrot-like rootstock, bluish-green, retracting into the ground during drought. *Ribs* 9-15, slightly to conspicuously tuberculate to 15 mm apart, sinuses 1-5 mm deep. *Areoles* with whitish wool the first year, afterwards quite naked, 4-9 mm apart. *Spines* 3-11, 1-10 mm long, long and dense in seedlings and juvenile plants, uppermost 1-3 minute, others radiating, adpressed, yellow, whitish, or pink at first, later tipped brownish, or entirely brown; centrals 0. *Flowers* broadly funnel-shaped, 3-6 cm long, to 8 cm in diam. *Receptacle-tube* 0.8-2.5 cm long, to 2 cm wide distally, ovary occupying basal 3-5 mm, exterior green, bearing raised areoles with 1-10, 2-15 mm long acicular, white or brownish spines and usually abundant loose wool. *Nectar chamber* minute, less than 1 mm long, wide open. *Perianth-segments* in 2-3 rows, linear-oblanceolate, 1.5-3 cm long, 3-10 mm wide, tapering to an apiculate apex, outermost greenish, remainder pink to magenta or white, with pale or whitish, entire margins and darker midstripes. *Stamens* with filaments to c. 1.2 cm long, white; anthers oblong, less than 1 mm long, bright yellow. *Style* to 2.3 cm long, slender; stigmas (2-)3-10 filiform, to 4 mm long, light green, rarely white. *Ovary locule* obconic, to only 2 mm in diameter at anthesis, ovules rather few. *Fruit* ± globular, less than 1 cm long, smaller than the dried perianth remains, scarcely fleshy at maturity, few seeded to c. 50; *seeds* large, 1.5-2 mm, black (see Sterk, loc. cit.).

DISTRIBUTION. Mexico: N Oaxaca, Puebla, Hidalgo, Queretaro, SW San Luis Potosi, Aguascalientes, W Zacatecas & S Nuevo Leon; grassy highlands above 2000 m altitude.

Echinocereus pulchellus (C. Martius) Schumann in Engler & Prantl, Nat. Pflanzen-fam. 3, 6a: 185 (1894), Gesamtb. Kakt. 252-253 (1897) and Bluehende Kakt. 1: t. 33 (1903); A. Berger, Kakteen, Abb. 42 (1929); Backeb., Die Cact. 4: 1995, Abb. 1900 & 1904 (1960); F. Otero & J. Meyran in Cact. Suc. Mex. 11: 61-64, 74, figs. 22 & 30 (1966); J. Meyran in ibid. 14: 90, 96, fig. 41 (1969); Glass & Foster in Cact. Succ. J. (US) 51: 23-24, fig. 3 (1979); Riha in Chrudimsky Kaktusar 1982: 5 (1982); E. Haustein, Der Kosmos-Kakteenfuhrer, 226, with excellent colour fig. (1983); E. Hernandez & F. Otero in Cact. Suc. Mex. 29: 54 (1984).

Echinocactus pulchellus C. Martius in Nov. Act. Nat. Cur. 16: 342-344, tab. 23, fig. 2 (1832). Type (cf. McVaugh in Contrib. Univ. Mich. Herb. 14: 141-144. 1980): living plants sent from Mexico (Hidalgo, Pachuca, *fide* Pfeiffer, 1837), c. 1827-28, *Karwinsky*. Lectotype (Taylor, loc. cit.): C. Martius, loc. cit., tab. 23, fig. 2. (1832).

Cereus pulchellus (C. Martius) Pfeiffer, Enum. Cact. 74 (1837).

43a. var. **weinbergii** (Weingart) N. P. Taylor in Kew Mag. 2: 272 (1985). (PLATE 12, PRO PARTE)

Echinocereus weinbergii Weingart in Monatsschr. Kakteenk. 22: 83-84 (1912); H. Wagner in ibid. 24: 104, with fig. (1914); Britton & Rose, Cact. 3: 29, fig. 32 (1922); Glass & Foster in ibid. 42: 109-111, figs. 23-25 (1970); Hirao, Colour Encycl. Cacti, 157, fig. 618 (1979); A. Lau in J. Nat. Cact. Succ. Soc. India 3: 47-48, with figs. (1983). Type: living plants, originally received from North America in 1905; apparently discovered by *F. Weinberg* (locality not published). Neotype (Taylor, loc. cit.): Britton & Rose, tom. cit., fig. 32 (an illustration supplied by Weinberg).

Stem 6-13 cm in diameter. *Ribs* 14-15. *Spines* 8-11, to 10mm long, conspicuous.

DISTRIBUTION. W Zacatecas (between Sombrerete & Fresnillo, and NW of Jerez).

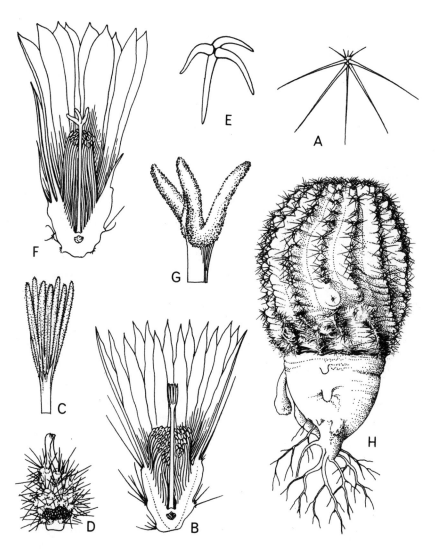

Echinocereus pulchellus var. **weinbergii**. A, stem areole, × 3; B, half-flower, × 2; C, top of style with stigmas, × 6; D, fruit × ⅔ (ex Hort. G. E. Cheetham). **E. pulchellus** var. **pulchellus**. E, stem areole, × 8; F, half-flower, × 2; G, top of style with stigmas, × 8, (*Hunt* 8625). **E. pulchellus** var. **amoenus**. H, habit, × ⅔ (white-flowered form from SE Nuevo Leon ex Hort. D. Parker).

43b. var. **amoenus** (A. Dietr.) Schumann, tom. cit. 253 (1897).
Echinopsis amoena A. Dietr. in Allg. Gartenz. 12: 187-188 (1844); C.A. Ehrenb. in Linnaea
  19: 358 (1846). Type (see Ehrenberg, loc. cit.): Mexico, [Hidalgo ?] 'nr San Mateo, 7500
  feet', c. 1839-40, *C.A. Ehrenberg* (probably not preserved).
Echinocereus amoenus (A. Dietr.) Schumann, tom. cit. (1894); Britton & Rose, Cact. 3: 33-34,
  fig. 40 (1922); Backeb., tom. cit. Abb. 1901 (1960); Glass & Foster, loc. cit. (1979).
[*E. pulchellus* sensu Hirao, tom. cit. 160, fig. 636 (1979) et W. Sterk in Succulenta (NL) 61:
  60-64, 61 (colour fig.) (1982) non (C. Martius) Schumann.]
  Stem 3-7.5 cm in diameter. *Ribs* (10-)11-14. *Spines* (6-)7-10, to 6(-10) mm long,
conspicuous.
  DISTRIBUTION. Hidalgo (?), SW San Luis Potosi & S Nuevo Leon (near Ascension &
Providencia); Aguascalientes (? - see Lau, 1983 *sub num.* 1084).

43c. var. **pulchellus** (PLATE 12, PRO PARTE)
  Stem 2.5-5 cm in diameter. *Ribs* 9-12. *Spines* 3-5(-7), to 4(-10) mm long, mostly
inconspicuous.
  DISTRIBUTION. N Oaxaca, Puebla, Hidalgo & SE Queretaro.

44. ECHINOCEREUS KNIPPELIANUS

Although the general features of *Echinocereus knippelianus* initially suggest that it is
directly related to the preceding species, careful examination of their characters
reveals no immediate or close connexion between them. In view of this it has to be
conceded that they may be the highly specialized products of quite different
evolutionary lines which have converged in many features adaptive to the
montane environment they inhabit. Vegetatively they differ markedly, *E. knippelianus* having only 5-7 ribs, and 1-4 very different spines per areole. Their seeds,
as seen under the Scanning Electron Microscope, are not particularly similar,
though they are rather large in both species. *Echinocereus pulchellus* is probably
related to the E. ADUSTUS GROUP, and so it is the plant discussed here that seems
the most isolated at present.
  Liebner described the species in 1895 and it soon became a sought-after plant,
as it remains today. Its exact wild provenance was not reported for more than 80
years, until the valuable paper by Glass & Foster (1978) was published. The
plant they regard as representative of that described by Liebner is found in the
Sierra Madre Oriental of SE Coahuila, where it grows among pines in open
forest, well above 2000 m altitude. Its normally solitary stems often branch in
cultivation and become quite atypical of the wild plant, which is in any case more
or less buried in the soil in habitat. It has pinkish-purple flowers from the stem
sides.
  Further east, at a locality in S Nuevo Leon, Glass & Foster were shown a
caespitose form, which they have named var. *kruegeri*, after its discoverer. This
has whitish flowers borne very near the stem apex and has smaller stems, mostly
with 3-4 spines per areole (often there is only 1 per areole in var. *knippelianus*).
Subsequently Lau (1980) has described another form from Nuevo Leon, as var.
reyesii, but apart from its larger, purplish-pink flowers it does not differ signifi-

cantly from Glass & Foster's variety and is here referred to synonymy. Lau records that the plants become more caespitose with increasing altitude, the upper limits of which are over 3000 m. Winter cold at this elevation must be quite severe, and if kept dry well before the onset of winter (or perhaps autumn), this species should be able to withstand considerable cold. However, it should not be

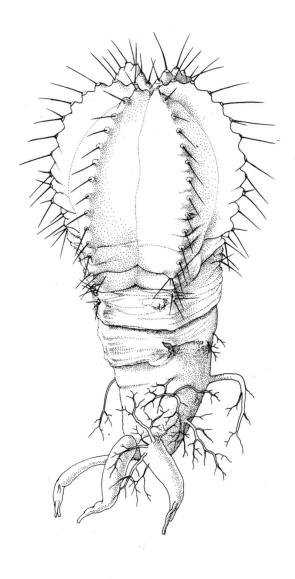

Echinocereus knippelianus var. **knippelianus**. Plant, × 1 (ex Hort. D. Parker).

forgotten that its habit may afford it some protection in the wild, whereas in cultivation it is grown with the fleshy part of the stem right out of the compost to discourage rot.

DESCRIPTION. *Stem* solitary, or branched and forming clumps of up to 50 stems, in habitat scarcely rising above the ground or quite subterranean during winter, the green part subglobose to shortly cylindric, 3-8 cm in diameter, dark to almost blackish-green, soft-textured, passing into the fleshy, wrinkled, contractile stem base/rootstock. *Ribs* 5-7, low and broad. *Areoles* circular, to 2 mm in diameter, 5-8 mm apart, with white or yellowish wool at first. *Spines* (0-)1-4, to 6 cm long, but very variable in size, mostly ± porrect, quite straight or tortuous, light yellow, acicular. *Flowers* shortly funnelform, 2.5-4 cm long, 4-6.5 cm in diameter, opening widely, arising at apex or on sides of stem. *Receptacle-tube* very short, green to brownish, bearing very few woolly areoles with 0-3, to 1 cm long, curved spines. *Nectar chamber* small, c. 1mm long, 1-1.5 mm in diameter. *Perianth-segments* in 1-2 rows, very narrowly linear-elliptic/oblanceolate, c. 6 mm wide, acuminate, outer segments deep purplish to brownish, inner segments pink to purplish or white, with darker midstripes. *Stamen filaments* white; anthers chrome-yellow. *Style* white, yellow above; stigmas 4-7, bright green, greenish-white or whitish, slender. *Fruit* very small, globose, dark purplish, bearing 1 or more spines and some wool, dehiscent by a longitudinal split. *Seeds* very few, globose to ovoid, large, 1.5-2 mm long, dark blackish-brown, tuberculate (see Glass & Foster, loc. cit. figs. 5 & 6).

DISTRIBUTION. NE Mexico: SE Coahuila and S Nuevo Leon; Sierra Madre Oriental in open grassy areas and edge of adjacent pine forest, 2200-3100 m altitude.

Echinocereus knippelianus Liebner in Monatsschr. Kakteenk. 5: 170 (1895); Schumann, Gesamtb. Kakt. 251-252, fig. 47 (1897) et Bluehende Kakt. 1: t. 12 (1901); C. Glass & R. Foster in Cact. Succ. J. (US) 50: 79-80, fig. 2 (1978); W. Cullmann et al., Kakteen, ed. 5, 155 (1984) (excellent colour pl.). Type: plants imported from Mexico (apparently none preserved). Lectotype (designated here): Liebner, loc. cit. (fig.).

44a. var. **knippelianus**

Stem usually solitary (often caespitose in cultivation), to 8 cm in diameter. *Spines* (0-)1-3 per areole, to c. 1.5 cm long. *Flowers* mostly arising on sides or 'shoulder' of stem, pinkish-lavender, rarely white.

DISTRIBUTION. SE Coahuila (nr Municipio La Victoria, S of General Cepeda), c. 2400 m altitude.

44b. var. **kruegeri** C. Glass & R. Foster, loc. cit., figs. 1, 3-6 (1978). Type: Nuevo Leon, N of Ascension, nr San Juanito, 1 March 1972, *Glass & Foster* 3902 (POM).
E. knippelianus var. *reyesii* A. Lau in Cact. Succ. J. (US) 52: 264-265, figs. 1-3 (1980). Type: Nuevo Leon, between Siberia and Encantada, 2800-3100 m, April 1977, *Lau* 1237A (POM).

Stem solitary, or branched to form a clump of up to 50 heads, to c. 5 cm in diameter. *Spines* 3-4 per areole, to 6 cm long. *Flowers* from stem apex, purplish-pink or white.

DISTRIBUTION. S Nuevo Leon, 2200-3100 m altitude.

Doubtful Species

Various plants of questionable affinity, or with names that are inadequately typified, have already been mentioned under the species to which they most nearly correspond and can be traced through the index. Of those that remain the following can be excluded from *Echinocereus* as they were stated or suspected to be of South American origin: *E. penicilliformis* A. Linke (1858), *E. persolutus* Foerster (1861) and *E. rigidispinus* Ruempler (1885) (*Cereus rigidispinus* Muehlenpfordt non Monv.). In addition, *E. princeps* Foerster (1861), *E. raphicephalus* Foerster (1861) and *E. uehrii* Hort. A. Blanc (1888), which were described without flowers or provenance details, are quite unidentifiable. *Echinocereus multicostatus* Cels ex Ruempler (1885) and *E. pleiogonus* Labouret ex Ruempler (1885) may be redescriptions of the equally poorly known *E. leeanus* (Hook.) Lemaire, which is discussed beneath *E. polyacanthus* Engelm. here.

Echinocereus octacanthus (Muehlenpfordt) Britton & Rose, Cact. 3: 13 (1922), based on *Echinopsis octacantha* Muehlenpfordt in Allg. Gartenz. 16: 19 (15 Jan. 1848), is discussed by Benson (1982) in relation to the *E. triglochidiatus* complex. If identifiable, this name would displace *E. triglochidiatus* Engelm. (Mar.-April 1848) and necessitate numerous new combinations at varietal rank. Muehlenpfordt's description of a plant brought from northern [central] Texas, by Dr Roemer, probably does refer to a member of this complex, despite Benson's doubts, but does not clearly fall within any of the infraspecific taxa defined by him. In view of its origin, the description implies that it may have been intermediate between *E. triglochidiatus* var. *melanacanthus* and *E. t.* var. *paucispinus*, but in the absence of any authentic preserved material this is speculation. For the sake of nomenclatural stability the name is best ignored.

'*Wilcoxia nerispina*' hort. ex Backeb., Die Cact. 4: 2078, Abb. 1960 & 1961 (1960) (*nom. inval.*) may be a species referable to *Echinocereus* section *Wilcoxia*, or perhaps a hybrid, possibly involving *E. schmollii* and a species from a different section of the genus. Its wild provenance is uncertain, although Backeberg suggests (*sub* Abb. 1960) that plants were distributed by Schmoll, a field collector based in the state of Querétaro, Mexico. Until it is either rediscovered in the wild, or resynthesized from its parents, its status will remain a matter for debate.

Hybrids

Almost without exception flowers of *Echinocereus* species appear to be self-incompatible, requiring pollen from a genetically different (non-clonal) individual to achieve fruit set. However, it is clear that in certain cases the pollen parent need not be of the same species and viable seeds and plants of hybrid origin can result. No satisfactorily proven natural hybrids can be reported at present, but there are strong suspicions that the following may occasionally interbreed in habitat: *E. pectinatus* var. *dasyacanthus* (sect. *Erecti*) and *E. triglochidiatus* (sect. *Triglochidiatus*), *E. scheeri* var. *scheeri* (sect. *Triglochidiatus*) and *E. stoloniferus* (sect.

Reichenbachii), and *E. enneacanthus* and *E. stramineus* (both sect. *Echinocereus*). The first of these suspected hybrid combinations has already been discussed beneath its respective parents, and may be represented by the names *E. roetteri* and *E. lloydii*. The second is known only from a single field collected plant, mentioned under *E. stoloniferus*, and the third has been collected and identified by Breckenridge & Miller (1982).

The bringing together in cultivation of species disjunct in the wild greatly increases the likelihood of hybrids and raises considerable problems for the grower-collector of *Echinocereus* species. Unfortunately, unscrupulous nurserymen or perhaps unknowing amateur growers may harvest seeds from their plants, following open pollination, raise them, and then distribute hybrid seedlings labelled the same as the mother plant. This is particularly a problem with rarer species such as *E. websterianus*. The writer has been supplied with colour transparencies depicting three different plants purporting to be this species, but in each case, although the vegetative details are not a bad match, the flowers in no way correspond to the description given by Lindsay (1947). It is difficult to be sure of the identity of the plants that have been crossed with *E. websterianus* to produce these presumed hybrids, but in respect of two of these the other parent can at least be guessed at. In one it was very likely a member of section *Triglochidiatus*, and in the other possibly *E. reichenbachii*. It is very frustrating, when trying to complete a collection of a genus such as this, to find that a plant obtained in good faith as a rare species is some nondescript hybrid. The only solution is to obtain wild-collected, documented seed or vegetative propagations from field-collected plants, all of which adds to the challenge of building up a representative collection of correctly named species. Having once obtained reliable documented material, its propagation and the keeping of proper records becomes an essential part of the hobby.

All this is not to suggest that hybrids have no place in a collection of echinocerei. Indeed some of those produced are very attractive plants and also indicate that there may be few genetic barriers to crossing within the genus. One of the widest crosses made involves *E. pentalophus* and *E. knippelianus*, the results of which are a plant more nearly resembling the latter, but with extraordinary elongated stems and much larger flowers. *Echinocereus (Wilcoxia) poselgeri* and *E. pulchellus* have also been crossed, and the former may be the other parent of a hybrid involving *E. palmeri*. No doubt various other hybrids are about, but either not recognized as such or still rare. Their production is to be encouraged, so long as they are carefully documented, for they may one day be of help in further assessment of relationships within the genus.

BIBLIOGRAPHY

Backeberg, C. (1960). Die Cactaceae 4: 1970-2072, Abb. 1895-1957, Taf. 211; 6: 3845-3856, Abb. 3482-3497 (1962).

—— (1963). Descriptiones Cactacearum Novarum 3: 6.

—— (1966). Das Kakteenlexicon, 119-129, Abb. 89-91.

Barthlott, W. (1979). Cacti, diagram on end papers. Stanley Thornes (Publ.) Ltd., Cheltenham, U.K.

Benson, L. (1969). The Cacti of Arizona, ed. 3, 21-23, 120-148, figs. 3.1-3.23.

—— (1982). The Cacti of the United States and Canada, 601-679, 936-948, figs. 638-715, colour pl. 78, 81-114.

Berger, A. (1926). Die Entwicklungslinien der Kakteen, 95-96. Fischer, Jena.

Bravo-Hollis, H. (1960). Una especies nueva del genero *Echinocereus*. *Echinocereus matudae* sp. nov. In An. Inst. Biol. Mex. 31: 119-121 (publ. 1961).

—— (1978). Las Cactaceas de Mexico, ed. 2, 1: 405-411, 442-444, figs. 236-241, 264-265.

Breckenridge, F.G. & Miller, J.M. (1982). Pollination Biology, Distribution, and Chemotaxonomy of the *Echinocereus enneacanthus* Complex (Cactaceae). In Syst. Bot. 7: 365-378.

Britton, N.L. & Rose, J.N. (1922). The Cactaceae 3: 3-44, figs. 1-55, tt. 2-5; 2: 110-111 (1920).

Buxbaum, F. (1958). The phylogenetic division of the subfamily Cereoideae, Cactaceae. In Madroño 14: 193-194.

—— (1974). See Endler (1974).

—— (1975). Gattung *Echinocereus*. In Krainz, Die Kakteen, Lfg. 60.

Cheetham, G.E. (1977). Choice Echinocerei. In Nat. Cact. Succ. J. 32(2): 43.

Clover, E.U. (1938). New species of cacti from Guatemala, Mexico and Texas. In Bull. Torrey Bot. Club 65: 565-568, figs. 1-4.

Endler, J. & Buxbaum, F. (1974). Die Pflanzenfamilie der Kakteen, ed. 3, 44-45, 103-105. Albrecht Philler Verlag, Minden.

Engelmann, G. (1848). See Wislizenus (1848).

—— (1849). In A. Gray, Plantae Fendlerianae Novi-Mexicanae. In Mem. Amer. Acad. ser. 2, 4: 50.

—— (1856). Synopsis of the Cactaceae of the United States and adjacent regions, 22-30 (reprinted with corrections in Proc. Amer. Acad. 3: 278-286, 314, 345-346. 1857).

—— (1859). Cactaceae of the Boundary, 28-39, tt. 36-59. (In Emory, W.H., United States and Mexican Boundary Survey.)

Frank, G.R.W. (1983a). In Kakt. and. Sukk. 34(8): inside front cover, cover illustration.

—— (1983b). *Echinocereus pamanesiorum* Lau. In Kakt. and. Sukk. 34: 178-182, 197-199, 218-222.

Hunt, D.R. (1967). In Hutchinson, J., The Genera of Flowering Plants 2: 443.

Lau, A.B. (1982). *Echinocereus schwarzii* resurrected. In Cact. Succ. J. (US) 54(1): 27-28.

—— (1983). Field Numbers of Dr Alfred B. Lau, Mexico and South America.

Leuck, E.E. & Miller, J.M. (1982). Pollination biology and chemotaxonomy of the *Echinocereus viridiflorus* Complex (Cactaceae). In Amer. J. Bot. 69: 1669-1672.

Leuenberger, B.E. (1976). Die Pollenmorphologie der Cactaceae, 88, 109, 122, 139 (Dissertationes Botanicae 31). J. Cramer, Vaduz.

Lindsay, G. (1944). *Echinocereus subinermis*. In Cact. Succ. J. (US) 16: 134-136.

Miller, J.M. & Bohm, B.A. (1982). Flavonol and dihydroflavonol glycosides of *Echinocereus triglochidiatus* var. *gurneyi*. In Phytochemistry 21: 951-952.

Ortega, J.G. (1929). Apuntes para la Flora Indigena de Sinaloa, unpaged. Mazatlan, Mexico.

Rowley, G.D. (1974). The unhappy medium: *Morangaya* – a new genus of Cactaceae. In Ashingtonia (GB) 1(4): 44-45, with colour pl.

Ruempler, T. (1885). Carl Friedrich Foerster's Handbuch der Cacteenkunde, ed. 2, 2: 773-834, figs. 97-110.

Salm-Dyck, J. (1850). Cacteae in Horto Dyckensi Cultae anno 1849, 41-43.

Scheer, F. (1856). Cactaceae. In Seemann, B., The Botany of the Voyage of HMS Herald, 285-286, 291.

Schumann, K. (1897). Gesamtbeschreibung der Kakteen, 245-290, figs. 47-49; Nachträge, 81-82 (1903).

Weniger, D. (1970). Cacti of the Southwest, 10-54, tt. 1-17. Univ. of Texas Press, Austin and London.

Wislizenus, A. (1848). Memoir of a tour to northern Mexico. United States Senate, Washington. (Pp. 87-115 are Botanical Appendix by G. Engelmann.)

Wooton, E.O. & Standley, P.C. (1915). Flora of New Mexico. In Contrib. US. Nat. Herb. 19: 457.

INDEX TO SPECIFIC AND INFRASPECIFIC EPITHETS

Numbers and letters given in parenthesis are those of the species and varieties recognized for *Echinocereus*. Accepted names are in bold type; synonyms are indicated by (=).

CEPHALOCEREUS
delaetii Guerke (= 20)

CEREUS
acifer Otto ex Salm-Dyck (= 10a)
aciniformis C.A. Ehrenb. (= 16a)
berlandieri Engelm. (= 14)
blanckii Poselger (see 13b)
caespitosus Engelm. (= 36a)
caespitosus var. *minor* Engelm. (= 36a).
chloranthus Engelm. (= 22)
cinerascens DC. (= 16)
coccineus Engelm. *non* DC. (= 11a)
coccineus var. *melanacanthus* Engelm. (= 11a)
dasyacanthus (Engelm.) Engelm. var. *minor* Engelm. (see 8 & 11)
deppei Salm-Dyck (= 16a)
dubius Engelm. (= 13a)
ehrenbergii Pfeiffer (= 16b)
engelmannii Parry ex Engelm. (= 4)
engelmannii var. *chrysocentrus* Engelm. & Bigelow (= 4f)
engelmannii var. *variegatus* Engelm. & Bigelow (= 4h)
fendleri Engelm. (= 7)
gonacanthus Engelm. & Bigelow (= 11g)
huitcholensis F.A.C. Weber (see 10a)
longisetus Engelm. (= 21)
macracanthus A. Linke (= 13a?)
mamillatus Engelm. (see 2)
maritimus M.E. Jones (= 5)
mojavensis Engelm. & Bigelow (= 11h)
munzii Parish (= 4c)
pectinatus (Scheidw.) Engelm. var. *armatus* Poselger (= 36b)
pectinatus var. *rigidissimus* Engelm. (= 32)
pensilis K. Brandegee (= 1)
pentalophus DC. (= 12)
phoeniceus Engelm. var. *pacificus* Engelm. (= 10c)
pleiogonus Labouret ex Ruempler see under Doubtful Species
propinquus Salm-Dyck ex Otto (= 12b, see 16b)
pulchellus (C. Martius) Pfeiffer (= 43c)
rigidispinus Muehlenpfordt *non* Monv. see under Doubtful Species
roemeri Engelm. (= 11a)
roemeri Muehlenpfordt (= 11a)
sanborgianus J. Coulter (= 2)
scheeri Salm-Dyck (= 9)

schmollii Weingart (= 39)
sciurus K. Brandegee (= 27)
stramineus Engelm. (= 17)
tuberosus Poselger *non* Pfeiffer (= 38)
viridiflorus (Engelm.) Engelm. var. *cylindricus* Engelm. (= 22b)

ECHINOCACTUS
pectinatus Scheidw. (= 8)
pectiniferus Lemaire (= 8a)
pulchellus C. Martius (= 43)
reichenbachii Terscheck ex Walp. (= 36)

ECHINOCEREUS
abbeae Parsons (= 7a)
acifer (Otto ex Salm-Dyck) Hort. F.A. Haage (= 10a)
acifer var. *durangensis* (Poselger ex Ruempler) Schumann (= 10b)
acifer var. *trichacanthus* Hildmann (= 10a)
adustus Engelm. (41)
adustus var. **adustus** (41b)
adustus var. **schwarzii** (A. Lau) N.P. Taylor (41a)
aggregatus Rydb., *nom. illegit.* (= 11a)
albatus Backeb., *nom. inval.* (= 19)
albiflorus Lowry ('albiflora') *non* Weingart (= 13b?)
albiflorus Weingart (= 7f)
albispinus Lahman (= 36e)
amoenus (A. Dietr.) Schumann (= 44b)
angusticeps Clover (= 15b)
arizonicus Rose ex Orcutt (= 11c)
armatus (Poselger) A. Berger (= 36b)
baileyi Rose (= 36e)
baileyi var. *albispinus* (Lahman) Backeb. (= 36e)
baileyi var. *brunispinus* Backeb., *nom. inval.* (= 36e)
baileyi var. *caespiticus* Backeb., *nom. inval.* (= 36e)
baileyi var. *flavispinus* Backeb., *nom. inval.* (= 36e)
baileyi var. *roseispinus* Backeb., *nom. inval.* (= 36e)
barcena Rebut ex A. Berger (see 21b)
barthelowanus Britton & Rose (3)
berlandieri (Engelm.) Hort. F.A. Haage (14)
berlandieri sensu Weniger (= 12b)
berlandieri var. *blanckii* (Poselger) P. Fournier (see 13b)
berlandieri var. *angusticeps* (Clover) L. Benson (= 15b)
berlandieri var. *papillosus* (Linke ex Ruempler) L. Benson (= 15a)

ECHINOCEREUS continued
bertinii (Cels) Schelle = Austrocactus bertinii (Cels) Britton & Rose
blanckii (Poselger) Ruempler (see 13b)
blan(c)kii sensu auctt. (= 14)
blanckii var. *berlandieri* (Engelm.) Backeb. (= 14)
blanckii var. *leonensis* (Mathsson) Backeb. (= 12a)
blanckii var. *poselgerianus* (A. Linke) Backeb. (= 14)
bonkerae Thornber & Bonker (= 7c)
boyce-thompsonii Orcutt (= 7b)
brandegeei (J. Coulter) Schumann (2)
bristolii W.T. Marsh. (31)
bristolii var. **bristolii** (31a)
bristolii var. **pseudopectinatus** N.P. Taylor (31b)
caespitosus (Engelm.) Engelm.(= 36a)
caespitosus var. *minor* (Engelm.) Weniger, *nom. inval.* (= 36a)
caespitosus var. *tamaulipensis* (Fric) Borg, *nom. inval.* (= 36a?)
candicans (Gillies ex Salm-Dyck) Lemaire = Echinopsis candicans (Gillies ex Salm-Dyck) G. Rowley
candicans Orcutt *non* (Gillies ex Salm-Dyck) Lemaire (= 32a)
canyonensis Clover & Jotter (= 11a)
carnosus Ruempler (see 13b)
castaneus (Engelm.) Hort. F.A. Haage (= 36a)
centralis (J. Coulter) Rose = Echinomastus intertextus (Engelm.) Britton & Rose
cereiformis W.v. Roeder, *nom. inval.* (= 14)
chiloensis (Colla) Console & Lemaire = Echinopsis chiloensis (Colla) H. Friedrich & G. Rowley
chisoensis W.T. Marsh. (34)
chisoensis var. **chisoensis** (34b)
chisoensis var. **fobeanus** (Oehme) N.P. Taylor (34a)
chloranthus (Engelm.) Hort. F.A. Haage (22)
chloranthus var. **chloranthus** (22c)
chloranthus var. **cylindricus** (Enge,m.) N.P. Taylor (22b)
chloranthus var. **neocapillus** Weniger (22d)
chloranthus var. **russanthus** (Weniger) Lamb ex G. Rowley (22a)
chlorophthalmus (Hook.) Britton & Rose (= 16a)
chrysocentrus (Engelm. & Bigelow) Orcutt (= 4f)
cinnabarinus (Hook.) Schumann = Echinopsis cinnabarina (Hook.) Labouret
cinerascens (DC.) Lemaire (16)
cinerascens var. **cinerascens** (16a)
cinerascens var. **ehrenbergii** (Pfeiffer) H. Bravo-H. (16b)
cirrhiferus (Labouret) Ruempler (= 16a)
clavatus Schumann = Erdisia spiniflora

ECHINOCEREUS continued
(Philippi) Britton & Rose
coccineus Engelm. (= 11a)
conglomeratus Foerster ex Schumann (= 17)
conoideus (Engelm. & Bigelow) Ruempler (= 11a)
ctenoides (Engelm.) Lemaire (= 8c)
cucumis Werderm. (= 9a)
dasyacanthus Engelm. (= 8c)
dasyacanthus var. *ctenoides* (Engelm.) Backeb. (= 8c)
dasyacanthus var. *steereae* (Clover) W.T. Marsh. (= 8c)
davisii A.D. Houghton (= 23c)
decumbens Clover & Jotter (= 11a?)
delaetii (Guerke) Guerke (20)
delaetii var. **delaetii** (20a)
delaetii var. **freudenbergeri** (G.R.W. Frank) N.P. Taylor (20b)
dubius (Engelm.) Ruempler (= 13a, see 12a)
durangensis Poselger ex Ruempler (= 10b)
ehrenbergii (Pfeiffer) Ruempler (= 16b)
emoryi (Engelm.) Ruempler = Bergerocactus emoryi (Engelm.) Britton & Rose
engelmannii (Parry ex Engelm.) Lemaire (4)
engelmannii var. **acicularis** L. Benson (4b)
engelmannii var. **armatus** L. Benson (4e)
engelmannii var. **chrysocentrus** (Engelm. & Bigelow) Ruempler (4f)
engelmannii var. **engelmannii** (4a)
engelmannii var. **howei** L. Benson (4g)
engelmannii var. **munzii** (Parish) Pierce & Fosberg (4c)
engelmannii var. **nicholii** L. Benson (4d)
engelmannii var. **purpureus** L. Benson (4i)
engelmannii var. **variegatus** (Engelm. & Bigelow) Ruempler (4h)
enneacanthus Engelm. (13)
enneacanthus f. *brevispinus* W.O. Moore (= 13b)
enneacanthus var. **brevispinus** (W.O. Moore) L. Benson (13b)
enneacanthus var. *carnosus* (Ruempler) Quehl (see 13b)
enneacanthus var. *conglomeratus* (Foerster ex Schumann) L. Benson (= 17)
enneacanthus var. *dubius* (Engelm.) L. Benson (= 13a)
enneacanthus var. **enneacanthus** (13a)
enneacanthus var. *stramineus* (Engelm.) L. Benson (= 17)
fasciculatus (Engelm. ex B.D. Jackson) L. Benson (= 7a)
fasciculatus var. *bonkerae* (Thornber & Bonker) L. Benson (= 7c)
fasciculatus var. *boyce-thompsonii* (Orcutt) L. Benson (= 7b)
fendleri (Engelm.) Ruempler (7)
fendleri var. *albiflorus* (= 7f, see also 7a & 7e)
fendleri var. **bonkerae** (Thornber & Bonker) L. Benson (7c)

fendleri var. **boyce-thompsonii** (Orcutt) L. Benson (7b)

fendleri var. **fasciculatus** (Engelm. ex B.D. Jackson) N.P. Taylor (7a)

fendleri var. **fendleri** (7f)

fendleri var. **kuenzleri** (Castetter *et al.*) L. Benson (7g)

fendleri var. **ledingii** (Peebles) N.P. Taylor (7d)

fendleri var. **rectispinus** (Peebles) L. Benson (7e)

fendleri var. *robustus* Fobe (= 7f ?)

fendleri var. *robustus* (Peebles) L. Benson *non* Fobe (= 7a)

ferreirianus H. Gates (6)

ferreirianus var. **ferreirianus** (6a)

ferreirianus var. **lindsayi** (Meyran) N.P. Taylor (6b)

finnii hort., *nom. nud.* (= 22a)

fitchii Britton & Rose (= 36c)

flavescens (Pfeiffer) Ruempler = Haageocereus sp.?

floresii Backeb. (= 27b)

fobeanus Oehme (= 34a)

freudenbergeri G.R.W. Frank (= 20b)

gentryi Clover (= 9a)

gladiatus (Lemaire) Ruempler = Echinopsis candicans (Gillies ex Salm-Dyck) G. Rowley

glycimorphus Ruempler (= 16a)

gonacanthus (Engelm. & Bigelow) Lemaire (= 11g)

grandis Britton & Rose (30, see 29)

hancockii E. Dawson (= 5b)

hempelii Fobe (= 7g)

hexaedrus (Engelm.) Ruempler (= 11a)

hildmannii Arendt (= 8c?)

huitcholensis (F.A.C. Weber) M. Guerke (see 10a)

hypogaeus (F.A.C. Weber ex Regel) Ruempler = Erdisia spiniflora (Philippi) Britton & Rose

intricatus (Salm-Dyck) Ruempler = Echinopsis strigosa (Salm-Dyck) H. Friedrich & G. Rowley

knippelianus Liebner (44)

knippelianus var. **knippelianus** (44a)

knippelianus var. **kruegeri** Glass & Foster (44b)

knippelianus var. *reyesii* A. Lau (= 44b)

koehresianus A. Lau, *nom. nud.* (= 9c)

krausei Smet ex Ruempler (= 11a)

kunzei Guerke (= 11a?)

kuenzleri Castetter *et al.* (= 7g)

lamprochlorus (Lemaire) Ruempler = Echinopsis lamprochlora (Lemaire) H. Friedrich & W. Glaetzle

laui G.R.W. Frank (42)

ledingii Peebles (= 7d)

leeanus (Hook.) Lemaire (see 10)

leeanus var. *multicostatus* (Ruempler) Schumann ('multicostata') see under Doubtful Species

leonensis Mathsson (= 12a)

leptacanthus (Salm-Dyck) Ruempler (= 12b)

leucanthus N.P. Taylor (37)

liebnerianus Schumann, *nom. illegit.* (= 44a)

limensis (Salm-Dyck) Ruempler = Haageocereus sp.?

lindsayi Meyran (= 6b)

lloydii Britton & Rose (see 8 & 11)

longisetus (Engelm.) Lemaire (21)

longisetus var. *albatus* W. Sterk, *nom. inval.* (= 19)

longispinus Lahman (= 36e)

lowryi Lowry (= 13b)

luteus Britton & Rose (= 25a)

madrensis Patoni (see 41a)

mamillatus (Engelm.) Britton & Rose (see 2)

mamillosus hort. ex Ruempler (= 16b?)

mariae Backeb., *nom. inval.* (cf. 36a/36e)

maritimus (M.E. Jones) Schumann (5)

maritimus var. **hancockii** (E. Dawson) N.P. Taylor (5b)

maritimus var. **maritimus** (5a)

marksianus F. Schwarz ex Backeb., *nom. inval.* (= 10a)

matthesianus Backeb., *nom. inval.* (see 10a)

matudae H. Bravo-H. (see 11b & 11c)

melanacanthus (Engelm.) W.H. Earle (= 11a)

melanocentrus Lowry, *nom. inval.* (= 36c)

merkeri Hildmann ex Schumann (= 13a)

mojavensis (Engelm. & Bigelow) Ruempler (= 11h)

mojavensis var. *zuniensis* (Engelm. & Bigelow) Ruempler (= 11a)

monacanthus Heese (= 11a)

morricalii Riha (= 18b)

multangularis (Willd.) Ruempler = Haageocereus sp.?

multicostatus Cels ex Ruempler see under Doubtful Species

munzii (Parish) L. Benson (= 4c)

neomexicanus Standley (= 11b)

nivosus Glass & Foster (19)

noctiflorus (*nocturniflorus*) hort., *nom. nud.* (= 9a)

ochoterenae J.G. Ortega (= 25b)

octacanthus (Muehlenpfordt) Britton & Rose see under Doubtful Species

oklahomensis Lahman (= 36e)

orcuttii Rose ex Orcutt (= 5a)

ortegae Rose ex J. G. Ortega (= 9b)

pacificus (Engelm.) Hort. F.A. Haage (= 10c)

palmeri Britton & Rose (33)

pamanesiorum A. Lau (40)

papillosus A. Linke ex Ruempler (15)

papillosus var. **angusticeps** (Clover) W.T. Marsh. (15b)

papillosus var. **papillosus** (15a)

paucispinus (Engelm.) Hort. F.A. Haage (= 11e)

pectinatus (Scheidw.) Engelm. (8)
pectinatus var. *castaneus* (Engelm.) Mathsson (= 36a)
pectinatus var. *ctenoides* (Engelm.) Weniger, *nom. inval.* (= 8c)
pectinatus var. **dasyacanthus** (Engelm.) N.P. Taylor (8c)
pectinatus var. *minor* (Engelm.) L. Benson (see 8, 27b, 28 & 31a)
pectinatus var. *neomexicanus* (J. Coulter) L. Benson (= 8c)
pectinatus var. **pectinatus** (8a, see 31b)
pectinatus var. *rigidissimus* (Engelm.) Ruempler (= 32a)
pectinatus var. *rubispinus* G.R.W. Frank (= 32b)
pectinatus var. **wenigeri** L. Benson (8b)
penicilliformis Linke see under Doubtful Species
pensilis (K. Brandegee) J. Purpus (1)
pentalophus (DC.) Lemaire (12)
pentalophus var. *ehrenbergii* (Pfeiffer) Backeb. (= 16b, see 16a)
pentalophus var. **leonensis** (Mathsson) N.P. Taylor (12a)
pentalophus var. **pentalophus** (12b)
pentalophus var. *procumbens* (Engelm.) P. Fournier (= 12b)
pentlandii (Hook.) Schumann = Echinopsis pentlandii (Hook.) Salm–Dyck ex A. Dietr.
perbellus Britton & Rose (= 36d)
persolutus Foerster see under Doubtful Species
phoeniceus (Engelm.) Lemaire (= 11a)
phoeniceus var. *inermis* Schumann (see 11a)
pleiogonus (Labouret) Ruempler see under Doubtful Species
polyacanthus Engelm. (10, see also 11b)
polyacanthus var. **densus** (Regel) N.P. Taylor (10a)
polyacanthus var. **pacificus** (Engelm.) N.P. Taylor (10c)
polyacanthus var. **polyacanthus** (10b)
poselgeri Lemaire (38)
poselgerianus A. Linke (= 14)
primolanatus F. Schwarz ex N.P. Taylor (35)
princeps Foerster see under Doubtful Species
procumbens (Engelm.) Lemaire (= 12b)
propinquus (Salm-Dyck ex Otto) Hort. F.A. Haage (= 12b, see 16b)
pulchellus (C. Martius) Schumann (43)
pulchellus var. **amoenus** (A. Dietr.) Schumann (43b)
pulchellus var. **pulchellus** (43c)
pulchellus var. **weinbergii** (Weingart) N.P. Taylor (43a)
purpureus Lahman (= 36a)
radians Engelm. (= 41b)
radians hort. (= 41a)
raphicephalus Foerster see under Doubtful Species
rectispinus Peebles (= 7e)

rectispinus var. *robustus* Peebles (= 7a)
reichenbachianus (Terscheck ex Walp.) Hort. F.A. Haage, *sphalm.* (= 36)
reichenbachii (Terscheck ex Walp.) Hort. F.A. Haage (36)
reichenbachii var. *albertii* L. Benson (= 36c)
reichenbachii var. *albispinus* (Lahman) L. Benson (= 36e)
reichenbachii var. **armatus** (Poselger) N.P. Taylor (36b)
reichenbachii var. **baileyi** (Rose) N.P. Taylor (36e)
reichenbachii var. *chisoensis* (W.T. Marsh.) L. Benson (= 34b)
reichenbachii var. **fitchii** (Britton & Rose) L. Benson (36c)
reichenbachii var. **perbellus** (Britton & Rose) L. Benson (36d)
reichenbachii var. **reichenbachii** (36a)
rigidispinus Ruempler see under Doubtful Species
rigidissimus (Engelm.) Hort. F.A. Haage (32)
rigidissimus var. **rigidissimus** (32a)
rigidissimus var. **rubispinus** (G.R.W. Frank) N.P. Taylor (32b)
robustus (Peebles) Peebles (= 7a)
roemeri Hort. F.A. Haage (= 11a)
roemeri (Muehlenpfordt) Rydb. *non* Hort. F.A. Haage (= 11a)
roetteri (Engelm.) Ruempler (see 8 & 11)
roetteri var. *lloydii* (Britton & Rose) Backeb. (see 8 & 11)
rosei Wooton & Standley (= 11b)
rotatus A. Linke (= 36a)
rubescens Dams (= 8c?)
rufispinus Engelm. (= 41b)
rungei Schumann, *nom. inval.* (= 15a)
runyonii Orcutt (= 12b)
russanthus Weniger (= 22a)
salm-dyckianus Scheer (= 9b)
salmianus Ruempler (= 9b)
sanborgianus (J. Coulter) Backeb., *nom. inval.* (= 2)
sandersii Orcutt (= 11h)
sarissophorus Britton & Rose (= 13a)
scheeri (Salm-Dyck) Scheer (9)
scheeri var. **gentryi** (Clover) N.P. Taylor (9a)
scheeri var. **scheeri** (9b)
schmollii (Weingart) N.P. Taylor (39)
schwarzii A. Lau (= 41a)
sciurus (K. Brandegee) Dams (27)
sciurus var. **floresii** (Backeb.) N.P. Taylor (27b)
sciurus var. **sciurus** (27a)
scopulorum Britton & Rose (28, see 27b)
serpentinus (Lagasca & Rodrigues) Lemaire = Nyctocereus serpentinus (Lagasca & Rodrigues) Britton & Rose

spachianus (Lemaire) Ruempler = Echinopsis
spachiana (Lemaire) H. Friedrich & G.
Rowley

spinibarbis Hort. F.A. Haage *sec.* Backeb., *nom.
inval.*? (= 16b)

spinibarbis (Pfeiffer) Schumann = Eulychnia
spinibarbis (Pfeiffer) Britton & Rose

spinigemmatus A. Lau (24)

spinosissimus Walton (= 8c)

splendens (Salm-Dyck ex Lemaire) Lemaire
= Nyctocereus serpentinus (Lagasca &
Rodrigues) Britton & Rose

standleyi Britton & Rose (= 23a)

steereae Clover (= 8c)

stoloniferus W.T. Marsh. (26)

stoloniferus var. **stoloniferus** (26a)

stoloniferus var. **tayopensis** (W.T. Marsh.)
N.P. Taylor (26b)

stramineus (Engelm.) Ruempler (17)

stramineus var. *conglomeratus* (Foerster ex
Schumann) H. Bravo-H. (= 17)

strausianus Hort. F.A. Haage ex Quehl (= 23?)

strigosus (Salm-Dyck) Lemaire = Echinopsis
strigosa (Salm-Dyck) H. Friedrich & G.
Rowley

subinermis Salm-Dyck ex Scheer (25)

subinermis var. *aculeatus* G. Unger (= 25a)

subinermis var. *luteus* (Britton & Rose) Backeb.
(= 25a)

subinermis var. **ochoterenae** (J.G. Ortega)
G. Unger (25b)

subinermis var. **subinermis** (25a)

subterraneus Backeb., *nom. inval.* (see 27)

tamaulipense Fric, *nom. nud.* (= 36a?)

tayopensis W.T. Marsh. (= 26b)

texensis Jacobi (= 36a)

texensis Runge ex Mathsson *non* Jacobi (= 15a)

triglochidiatus Engelm. (11)

triglochidiatus var. *acifer* (Otto ex Salm-Dyck)
H. Bravo-H. (= 10a)

triglochidiatus var. **arizonicus** (Rose ex
Orcutt) L. Benson (11c)

triglochidiatus var. **gonacanthus** (Engelm.
& Bigelow) Boissev. (11g)

triglochidiatus var. **gurneyi** L. Benson (11d)

triglochidiatus var. *inermis* (Schumann) G. Arp
(see 11a)

triglochidiatus var. **melanacanthus**
(Engelm.) L. Benson (11a)

triglochidiatus var. **mojavensis** (Engelm. &
Bigelow) L. Benson (11h)

triglochidiatus var. **neomexicanus**
(Standley) L. Benson (11b)

triglochidiatus var. *pacificus* (Engelm.) H.
Bravo-H. (= 10c)

triglochidiatus var. **paucispinus** (Engelm.)
W.T. Marsh. (11e)

triglochidiatus var. **triglochidiatus** (11f)

tuberosus Ruempler (= 38)

tulensis H. Bravo-H. (see 12b, 13b & 14)

uehrii Hort. A. Blanc see under Doubtful
Species

uspenskii Hort. A. Blanc (= 13a?)

vatteri B. Botzenhart, *nom. nud.* (= 18a)

viereckii Werderm. (18)

viereckii var. **morricalii** (Riha) N.P. Taylor
(18b)

viereckii var. **viereckii** (18a)

viridiflorus Engelm. (23)

viridiflorus var. *chloranthus* (Engelm.) Backeb.
(= 22c)

viridiflorus var. **correllii** L. Benson (23b)

viridiflorus var. *cylindricus* (Engelm.) Ruempler
(= 22b)

viridiflorus var. **davisii** (A.D. Houghton)
W.T. Marsh. (23c)

viridiflorus var. **viridiflorus** (23a)

ebsterianus G. Lindsay (29)

weinbergii Weingart (= 43a)

ECHINOPSIS

amoena A. Dietr. (= 43b)

octacantha Muehlenpfordt see under Doubtful
Species

pectinata (Scheidw.) Fennel var. *reichenbachii*
(Terscheck ex Walpers) Salm-Dyck (= 36a)

valida Monv. ex Salm-Dyck var. *densa* Regel
(= 10a)

MAMMILLARIA

fasciculata Engelm. ex B.D. Jackson (= 7a)

MORANGAYA

pensilis (K. Brandegee) G. Rowley (= 1)

WILCOXIA

albiflora Backeb. (= 37)

australis hort., *nom. nud.* (= 38)

kroenleinii A. Cartier (= 38)

nerispina hort., *nom. nud.* see under Doubtful
Species

poselgeri (Lemaire) Britton & Rose (= 38)

schmollii (Weingart) Backeb. (= 39)

tamaulipensis Werderm. (see 38)

tuberosa Kreuzinger, *nom. illegit.* (= 38)